# TWENTIETH CENTURY VIEWS

The aim of this series is to present the best
in contemporary critical opinion on major
authors, providing a twentieth century perspective on their changing status in an era
of profound revaluation.

Maynard Mack, *Series Editor*
Yale University

# FLAUBERT

# FLAUBERT

## A COLLECTION OF CRITICAL ESSAYS

Edited by

*Raymond Giraud*

A SPECTRUM BOOK

Prentice-Hall, Inc., *Englewood Cliffs, N. J.*

# Table of Contents

# FLAUBERT

# Introduction

## by Raymond Giraud

A fair sign of greatness in a work of art is its inexhaustibility, its capacity to yield fresh insights and richer delights after numerous readings or viewings, to survive changes and even revolutions in critical perspectives, and, of course, to invite successive generations of critics to discover new things to say about it. For a time in the early decades of our century it seemed that there was little left to say about Flaubert's novels, despite and doubtless to some extent because of the great aura of perfection that surrounded some of his work, particularly *Madame Bovary*. If anything remained to be done, it was the debunking of the myth. Flaubert's thought—what there was of it—seemed crystal clear, and most unpleasantly negative and uninspirational at that; his aesthetics were sadly out of date and even the splendidly polished surface of his prose was cracking and demonstrably failing the test of time. It was with something of an air of surprised discovery that André Gide wrote in his *Journal* in 1925, after rereading the *Éducation sentimentale* and finding that it was after all "a great book": "It seems to me that there are still some things to say about Flaubert."

Many Flaubertistes would, I think, agree that despite the number of penetrating studies that have since appeared, criticism of the novels is still far from exhausted. In the years that have passed since that comment of Gide's there has been a radical change in critical attitude toward Flaubert. Now at last one can truly say that Flaubert is in vogue—and perhaps a much more meaningful vogue than at the time of *Madame Bovary*'s short-lived *succès de scandale*. For the first time too it is the young, a generation of gifted new academic critics and even some of the "new" novelists, who are enthusiastic. When the great French critic Albert Thibaudet first published his study of Flaubert in 1922, he felt obliged to admit that "those who place Flaubert's glory highest today do not belong to recent generations."

The years clustered around both world wars, periods that called for intense moral, social, and physical commitment, produced a spirit of impatience, even irritation, with the apparently cold, impassive, Olympian attitude of Flaubert, his disdain for humanity, and his self-imposed imprisonment in style, where he waged his lonely struggle with language. Few critics were disposed to sympathize with the anguish implicit in the grotesque spectacle of Flaubert's striding back and forth in his *gueuloir* at Croisset, shouting out lines of his novels in search of the magic formulas in which sound and sense would coalesce. Already at the turn of the century Paul Bourget, a subtle and intelligent critic, had chosen to stress the pessimism and nihilism of Flaubert's work. Others, like André Suarez, found it empty, in fact a perfect expression of the intellectual vacuum in which Flaubert was presumed to subsist. Others still, like Pierre Gilbert and Léon Daudet, attacked his art, sought to deflate his "false" and "artificial" masterpieces, while university critics found fault with his grammar. He was accused of coldness, sterility, and hopelessness and conceded to be a master only in the creation of a stifling atmosphere that left his readers gasping for fresh air in a prisonlike fictional world.

Some of the greatest writers of this century have had their reservations about Flaubert—among them Valéry, Malraux, and even Proust, despite his sensitivity to Flaubert's stylistic originality and creativity. Gide, whose every utterance was nuanced and who kept volumes of Flaubert's correspondence at his bedside together with the Bible, declared that no one had the right to attack Flaubert who had not loved him first, thereby establishing his own moral justification for saying that Flaubert had blasphemed against life and that he himself considered duty to personal happiness more impelling than Flaubert's unnatural *"devoirs d'artiste."* Even Henry James, a great admirer of Flaubert, wondered why he had chosen to depict "such inferior and . . . abject human specimens" as Emma Bovary and Frédéric Moreau.

It was James who first called Flaubert a "novelist's novelist," a not altogether laudatory comment that probably prompted Edmund Gosse to write a few years later:

Flaubert is a writer who must always appeal more to other authors than to the world at large, because the art of writing, the indefatigable pursuit of perfect expression, were always before him, and because he hated the lax felicities of improvisation as a disloyalty to the most sacred procedures of the literary artist.

Surely it is true that by and large Flaubert has indeed been more likely to attract literati and the adepts of style than have Stendhal, Balzac, or Dostoyevsky, each of whom has a considerable reputation for offering more than polished words to his public, and each of whom can be said in one way or another to have scorned or neglected the artistic beauty of style. But style is no longer deprecated by vigorous minds or relegated to the appreciation of professionals, as might be attested alone by the prodigious success among partisans of "involvement" of Raymond Queneau's *Exercices de style*. (Queneau has himself commented often on *Bouvard et Pécuchet* and can be counted among Flaubert's admirers.)

"Style is man," Buffon had written in the eighteenth century (Flaubert cited him often for remarks he felt anticipated the idea of *l'art pour l'art*). Even the most inscrutable manner of writing can be a revelation of the secret corners of its author's soul. Despite Flaubert's assertion that an author should be in his work as God is in the physical universe, "everywhere present and nowhere visible," perceptive analysis of vocabulary, images, and recurrent kinds of situations in his novels (as in Jean-Pierre Richard's penetrating study, part of which appears in this volume) has made readers increasingly aware that Flaubert is very much visible in everything he wrote. To see in his work only those aspects of style that point to the perfect craftsman and that would be chiefly noted by a fellow professional does not necessarily lead to total misjudgment, but it is a serious underestimation of his accomplishment.

In his letters Flaubert himself anticipated the cruelest things that could be said about him. His own words can be used to support the accusations of escapism, defeat, and retreat from life: "Life is something so hideous . . . that the only way to endure it is to escape it. And one escapes by living in art." There is dogmatic arrogance, but also a confession of bewilderment and sadness, when he writes that "the only truth in this world is in a well-made sentence"— words that approach, but do not quite have the import of Mallarmé's "everything in the world exists to end up in a book." He seems less arrogant and far more human, more vulnerable, and more complex when he makes other confessions that seem for a moment to throw into question the value of all he wrote:

> [Great men] do not have to go in for style; they are strong in spite of their failings and because of them. But we little men find our value only in the perfect execution of our work. . . . Very great men often

write very badly, and so much the better for them. It is not in their work that we must seek the art of form, but among the second-raters.

The literal painfulness of composition and the gnawing sense of inadequacy, of inferiority to geniuses characterized by their seemingly inexhaustible vitality (Shakespeare, Ronsard, Cervantes, and Victor Hugo were among those with whom he did not dare to compare himself), is practically a Flaubertian legacy to the twentieth-century artist. Flaubert complained of his weakness, of fatigue, of the physical effects of his work. *Salammbô* "exhausted" him. "I have pains in my muscles. La Bovary's poisoning made me throw up in my chamber pot and now the assault on Carthage is giving me lumbago. And yet this is what is most pleasant in all that our work offers us." For his writing was as much exaltation as suffering; it was a "sweet torment," and he was as acutely aware of the paradox as a Petrarchan poet writing of love.

Flaubert raised the novel—and that may have been his greatest achievement—to such a level of intense self-commitment that the act of writing became his life. He might well have said of any of his published books, as Baudelaire did of the *Fleurs du Mal:* "I have put my whole heart into this atrocious book." He made the novel an artistic creation to which he sought to give the density, form, and "beauty" that had previously, among literary genres, been associated only with poetry. He did not write "poetic" prose or prose poetry (although these kinds of writing were developed extensively within his own lifetime and certainly have some points of tangency with his work), but his immense concern with the art of the novel, its structure, the orchestration of effects comparable with those produced by music and painting gave his novels a rigor and concentration that the genre had never previously attained. A century earlier Diderot had considered the word "poetry" applicable to all areas of literature and the other arts as well. Both Baudelaire and Edgar Allan Poe gave it the same broad meaning, and it was in this sense that Gautier and Mallarmé spoke of Flaubert's novels as "poems."

Flaubert was openly scornful of the artless spontaneity of sentimental effusions; the period of his artistic maturation coincided with the decline of Lamartine's and Musset's literary fortunes in France. Like the Parnassian poets, with whom he is often compared, he had no tolerance for facility. His concept of a poetry-rivaling prose involved the tautest possible conscious control of diction and form in which every word would be willed, tested, and justified.

His art was painful, exacting, exhausting, not because he was naturally inarticulate but because spontaneity had become suspect to him. In fact, before *Madame Bovary*, before Louis Bouilhet and Maxime Du Camp had judged the manuscript of *La Tentation de Saint Antoine* fit only for burning and compelled him to start on a new tack, he had apparently always written with astonishing ease and without any discernible trace of the specific kind of torture—the word is probably not too strong—that composition became for him afterwards.

Flaubert's suffering, at times demonic, at others perhaps better described as pitiful, was a very personal thing, although there is doubtless significance in the fact that since the mid-nineteenth century an increasing number of artists have been afflicted with psychic disturbances that cannot be disassociated from the problems of artistic creativity. The difficulty he experienced in writing, however, was related to a more general attitude, a feeling that Art is a severe and exigent discipline requiring of its practitioners a priestly devotion. It demanded both sacrifice and total dedication, humility and the *hubris* of a dream of impossible beauty.

The excitement of the peak Romantic years first gave Flaubert a sense of his literary vocation. In words he addressed to his childhood friend Ernest Chevalier when he was only thirteen, he revealed both the moral disillusionment and the cult of the aesthetic that were characteristic of countless schoolboys of his generation, an ephemeral adolescent phase for most, but a lifelong attitude for Flaubert: "Let us devote ourselves ever to Art, which is greater than nations, kings and crowns, and is always there, held aloft by enthusiasm with its divine diadem." He himself described (in his preface to Louis Bouilhet's *Dernières Chansons*) the general fervor of his schoolmates at Rouen for the romantic writers and those whom they claimed as their precursors.

That early attraction to art was passionate and sincere, but Flaubert was very slow to declare himself for a literary career. Indeed, early letters of his express violent repugnance to the idea of any sort of career at all, any commitment, any compromise of his freedom. He rejected contemptuously the idea of earning money with his pen, and years later he would tell Louise Colet that he wrote for himself alone and would feel compromised by publication. That attitude, complex and shifting, though probably never fundamentally altered, was an amalgam of many elements. Flaubert's family finances spared him serious concern with the problem of making a living. Moral rather than economic pressure led him to obey his father and undertake the study of law in Paris. But those studies, never seriously pursued, came to an abrupt end at the time of his "nervous crisis" in January 1844. He had read little law, attended few lectures, failed one important examination, and would, in all probability, never have entered the legal profession in any case. But all was decided for him: the state of his health made a career impossible; the subsequent death of his father removed a possibly reproachful witness. The country house at Croisset had already been bought and occupied, and money was no problem. There was never again any question of career. Flaubert wrote, but *for himself.*

His hesitation to become a professional, to work toward publication, was also due to timidity. Despite Flaubert's arrogance and the savage joy he took in denouncing the stupidity of others, he suffered incessantly from doubts about his own talent and the value of what he was doing. Art itself came into question: "I love art and yet I scarcely believe in it," he wrote in 1847. He frequently spoke of the futility of his labors. In one sad and poetic passage of a letter, he compared himself to a diver fishing for pearls on the ocean's bed and rising at last from his submarine gropings, his face blue, gasping for breath, but with empty hands. Timidity, an overawing sense of the immensity of art and the total inadequacy of his own resources, a foreboding of inevitable failure, a fear of self-commitment, unwillingness to appear presumptuous in his own eyes: all these sentiments restrained him from making the bold entrance into the profession of letters about which others far less gifted than he had no compunctions.

Flaubert was also won over very early to the idea of *l'art pour l'art,* very much in the air in the early 1830's. Gautier had declared the incompatibility of utility and beauty ("the moment something is useful, it ceases to be beautiful"). Flaubert seized upon the idea. It justified the solitude in which he wrote, his refusal to make a career of literature, to serve with it and be served by it. He also readily accepted the idea—already a commonplace—that art is an end in itself and that its true value is independent of the uses to which it is put. And yet, however categorical his proclamations of the total uselessness of art, the idea of his own personal gratuitousness, of the futility of his life, preyed on him and filled him with the sense of his own insufficiency.

> There are animals that live on the earth and plants that can not be plucked and that must remain unknown. There are perhaps spirits created for regions that must be inaccessible. What good are they? None at all! Am I not one of these?

But the tone of his declarations varies according to his mood; it can be confessional, belligerent, or coolly intellectual: "Art is the search for what is useless; it represents in speculation what heroism represents for morality."

No critic with the faintest hope of being taken seriously could possibly revive the argument that *Madame Bovary* is an immoral book because it makes adultery seem attractive. But the idea of the uselessness or gratuitousness of a work of art still provides a moral ground for attack, as does Flaubert's supposed impassiveness and with it the apparent absence of communication between author and reader. Probably the most articulate and most formidable of post-war critics hostile to Flaubert has been Jean-Paul Sartre. His analysis of bourgeois literature of the nineteenth century in "Qu'est-ce que la littérature?" is an indictment of the bad faith of writers like Flaubert who, despite their alienation from a public they despise, recoil before the prospect of the only alternative Sartre thought would have been decent and proper: addressing themselves to a working-class public. And so, concludes Sartre, the bourgeois writer, wanting to judge his class but unwilling to leave it, lives in contradiction and bad faith, even refusing to know for whom he writes.

Sartre recognizes Flaubert's great ability, to be sure, and does not class him with the herd of mediocrities who played the game of literary success. He grants the writer his claim for art's autonomy, asserting that not even in Flaubert's time was this contested, which seems quite an exaggeration. He also rejects the vulgar bourgeois demand for utilitarian art. But he draws the line at uselessness, which is negativity, intensely literary antiliterature. The writer's sense of solitude, his mad pouring out of words or painfulness of expression all fall within the same syndrome and stem from a refusal to admit that the writer is, after all, addressing the bourgeois public he has rejected. Flaubert is by no means alone in this, but is joined by Baudelaire, the Goncourt brothers, Maupassant, Gautier, Mallarmé, Valéry, and Gide, for all of whom failure or error consists in the abstention from communication and the refusal to transmit their experience to the reader.

A variation of this essentially moral argument appears in René Marill-Albérès's recently published *Histoire du roman moderne,* where we find an attack on what one might call the *libido descri-bendi* or the "heresy of description" (needless to say, not Albérès's terms). This argument implies that both writer and reader derive an inhuman aesthetic satisfaction from the beauty of the description of a fictional character's suffering (or from accessory descriptions that obscure that suffering and thus dilute compassion—an offense attributed even to Zola). The "satisfactions of style" are substituted for compassionate identification between the reader and the character of the novel and constitute—not only for Flaubert, but for all the so-called realists who followed him: Maupassant, Zola, Loti, Daudet, and Anatole France, among others—a subtle way of stilling the conscience of the bourgeois reader. "Social misery, dreadful dramas, the monotony of life—the content of the novel matters little; what one appreciates in it is the author's *art.*"

Such objections as these are not lightly swept aside. The writer who deliberately exploits human misery simply in order to excite admiration for his own virtuosity cannot expect unreserved admiration. To paint a miserable slum at twilight with the sole intention of creating picturesque beauty, but with godlike indifference to the unhappiness of those who, unlike both painter and spectator, must inhabit the original slum from which the picture is drawn—this does indeed seem a cruel *utilization* of humanity, the reduction of man to the level of an exotic object. There is no doubt that some artists, both plastic and literary, have been systematically guilty of this sin. There can also be no doubt that with respect to this particular sin no artist's hands are entirely clean. Even Sartre has given poetic beauty to the desolate streets of Bouville. His description is not "prettily" picturesque, but to the extent to which the reader is moved to compliment the writer on his evocative powers and to identify what he has done as art, he runs the risk of being momentarily diverted from purely humanitarian thoughts.

Obviously, Flaubert did not address himself to a proletarian public, and just as obviously he was intent upon the creation of artistic beauty even in the description of the most brutally barbaric scenes of *Salammbô.* He certainly did not practise the kind of literary engagement that Sartre called for at the end of World War II. It can even be justly said that he feared and escaped involvement in his life as well as in art—to the extent to which these can be meaningfully distinguished.

Sartre's analysis in particular is extremely penetrating. It is hard to believe that anyone can read "Qu'est-ce que la littérature?" without having his conception of literature under the Second Empire profoundly and permanently affected by it, though he may be in violent disagreement with most of what Sartre says. But Flaubert has outlived the shock of this attack. Sartre has continued his commentary on him, some of which was already included in *l'Être et le néant,* and his "existential psychoanalysis" of Flaubert deserves serious attention. As in his study of Baudelaire, however, what Sartre has to say seems to derive from psychological and social concerns rather than aesthetic ones. Despite his very sophisticated awareness of literary values, he has primarily utilized Flaubert's work "as a research tool to clarify the biography" (as he himself writes in pages reproduced in this volume).

Not all of Flaubert's various dogmatic assertions about art and the aesthetic of the novel can be applied rigorously to his work, especially his much vaunted impassiveness. It is perfectly clear that Flaubert was emotionally involved in the "story" of his novels. He tells us he vomited in a chamber pot when he composed his description of Emma Bovary's death by poison—a truly "sympathetic" reaction, hardly to be expected of an indifferent god of creation idly paring his fingernails. But was he only responding to a description of medical symptoms or was he also sympathetic to the anguish of his heroine? And, apart from how he felt, what evidence is there of the penetration of his sympathy or involvement into the work itself? Mid-twentieth-century criticism seems very much of the opinion that, as Georg Lukács writes in his analysis of *Salammbô,* "the famous *'impassibilité'* turns out to be an illusion."

As in so many of his critical writings, Baudelaire saw *Madame Bovary* with a vision we are tempted to find much akin to our own. (Flaubert himself said of the review of that novel: "You have entered the secret of the work, as if my brain were your own.") In his discovery of Emma's "virile soul in a charming feminine body" he recognized the complex intimate relationship between Flaubert and his heroine, who, though presented at some moments with irony and even with condescension, is lent time and again her creator's vision and his voice. Jean Rousset has admirably demonstrated the subtle modulation of perspective and point of view in *Madame Bovary.* There are, for that matter, moments in the novel, as indeed in everything that Flaubert wrote, when character and author fuse together; not only tonality of atmosphere but the words and intimately penetrated thought of hero or heroine expose the innermost feelings of Flaubert himself. Characters like Emma and Charles Bovary, Frédéric Moreau, Saint Anthony, even Bouvard and Pécuchet, who at the outset of a novel seem remote, perhaps even grotesque and puppetlike, acquire depth with the passage of time—of the effect of which they themselves are often acutely and tragically aware—and as the pace of the novel quickens, the flickering moments of identification between them and the writer become more frequent and more intense.

Flaubert reveals himself, positively or negatively, directly or indirectly, in the characters he creates. They are, like most fictional characters of any writer, indebted to his past experience, and in them there is often some half-buried hint or even a quite overt expression of his feelings. Their attitudes, gestures and language can all be revelatory. Flaubert's very style, as Sartre maintains and as Jean-Pierre Richard demonstrates in his truly remarkable study, is an objectification of his personality. One might think that the Surrealists' automatic writing, from which conscious control seems totally absent, would be most successful in exposing the secret mechanisms and obsessions of an artist's mind. Yet the taut control that Flaubert imposed upon his style, the trial of the *gueuloir,* and the subordination of thought to rhythm permit the alert critic to penetrate beneath the surface of his prose, to feel the pulse of his breath and the palpitation of his heart. "Through the delicately balanced development of the sentence, existence recovers its harmony," writes Jean-Pierre Richard. The insight is true and deep. For all his strivings in the direction of *artifice* and neutrality, Flaubert reached a language that was in tune with his inner self.

Curiously attracted and even obsessed by stupidity, coarseness, and insensibility, Flaubert seems often to revel in disgust. This probably comes through most clearly in his letters and in reminiscences of his conversation recounted by others. But there are also many scenes in the novels that reveal the strange pleasure it gave him to mouth the trite utterances of the mediocre bourgeois, *"celui qui pense bassement."* We can almost hear his grating laugh, see the flailing gestures of his arms as he read to himself such a scene as Homais's and Bournisien's wake beside poor Emma's funeral bed. But it is clear too that the bitterness and anger we can read between the lines express the horror and sense of desecration that Flaubert feels and throw all the more into relief the poignancy of Emma's life, the absurd tragic disproportion between her suffering and these grotesque chatting clowns who survive her so triumphantly.

The true sadness of the last line of the *Éducation sentimentale* (*"c'est là ce que nous avons eu de meilleur"* ["those were our best times"]) does not derive from cynicism or aloofness, but, as Victor Brombert observes, from the "never-defeated and never-satisfied craving for innocence and beauty." Flaubert has been called an eternal adolescent, and in a way it is true, for he never really made his peace with unpleasant reality, never ceased to miss childhood innocence and resent its destruction. His books might well be considered part of the literature of the absurd, not the absurd of

Pascal and Camus but the dissonant conflict between man's dream of himself and the cruel discovery of what he really is like. He takes a savage delight in exposing mediocrity and trampling illusions brutally under foot, but these are acts of masochism, a kind of scratching at a wound that never healed.

That same sentimental attachment to Frédéric Moreau's innocence is also implicit in his *"Madame Bovary, c'est moi."* Emma is, to be sure, a pitiful creature who dreams futilely of escaping from the life that has become a prison to her. But, like Flaubert himself, she has a romantic thirst for fulfillment of ill-defined urges awakened in her by books, reveries, the ball at Vaubyessard. The inspirations of her flights of fancy may be tawdry and clearly visible as such to both author and reader, but the latter, if he is honest, must admit that he himself has been the victim of similar illusions. Emma is cheated, a victim of her own naïveté and inexperience, but what really matters is not the fraudulent elegance of the ball or the cowardice and baseness of the lovers whom she so sadly misjudges, but the strength of her yearning and her passion.

There are times when Flaubert really seems impassive, when we hesitate between irony and sympathy. Even in the first peaceful days of the honeymoon, marriage is not quite what Emma had expected. Her new condition in life, the disturbing presence of a husband

had been enough to make her believe that she at last possessed that marvelous passion which until then had been hovering like a great bird with rosy wings in the splendor of the skies of poetry—and she could not believe now that the calm in which she was living could be the happiness of which she had dreamed.

Has Flaubert led the reader into the intimacy of Emma's thought only to betray his heroine, to expose her childish dream of a storybook happiness that in some mystifying way has not come true? Certainly not that. But sympathy is held in check by the irony of language which is neither clearly hers nor clearly his.

A sharper discontent, anger, revulsion at the spectacle of her husband's stupidity and clumsiness bring Emma within an emotional range that is more apt to engage Flaubert's sympathy. When she cries out "My God! Why did I marry?" and compares her "cold life" and "boredom, that, like a silent spider, spun its web in the shadow at every corner of her heart" with her gay childhood days, we are already close to the spirit of the conclusion of the *Éducation sentimentale:* "How far off it was, all that! how far away." For

Emma these puzzlingly sad confrontations of memories and reveries with the emptiness of the present occur regularly throughout the novel. Often, some unexpected sensation—hearing the bell of the angelus, seeing a flake of ash float down from a letter, passing the walls of her old convent school—revives anew some memory of past happiness, separated by an abyss of time from the life into which she has somehow allowed herself to drift. And Flaubert lends her his voice, merges with her: "She was not happy, had never been. Whence came then that insufficiency of life, that instantaneous rotting of the things on which she sought support?"

We tend to see—and many of Flaubert's letters encourage us in this—order, control, and repression of emotional involvement in all that Flaubert wrote after 1849. Yet, with the possible exception of the *Trois Contes,* his mature writings are characterized by tension, however delicately equilibrated it is, and by a half-hidden violence, by anger, fury, and even madness. He said of *La Tentation de Saint Antoine* (Albert Thibaudet calls it that "dense, heady, and violent work"): "The subtitle of my book could be: *the height of insanity."* That strange orgiastic work, the one to which he was most faithful, returning to it again and again as Goethe did to *Faust,* may seem, like his others, a book in which illusion after illusion is pricked, in which all knowledge, all beliefs and passions die away or vanish abruptly, but it is in reality a work of frenzied violence and exaltation. From one angle, *Salammbô* is a novel of cold Parnassian perfection; from another, it is a mad riot of barbaric cruelty, but still expressing the yearnings, frustrations and bruised innocence that often seem more apparent in the "modern" novels.

Flaubert's temperament was a passionate one, more likely to explode in anger than in love. Much of the appeal of his work lies not in the triumph of his aesthetic doctrine but in the sympathetic vibrations of the passion, the pathos, that were transmitted to his style and that were, perhaps in spite of his laborious efforts, successful in giving life and truth to his fictions. In those novels, rich and dense, still capable of communicating the thrill of genuinely felt emotion, he did succeed, after all, in transmitting *"à travers le Beau,"* his personal experience of life.

# Flaubert

## *by Jean-Paul Sartre*

Let us suppose that I wish to make a study of Flaubert—
who is presented in histories of literature as the father of realism.
I learn that he said: "I myself am Madame Bovary." I discover that
his more subtle contemporaries—in particular Baudelaire, with his
"feminine" temperament—had surmised this identification. I learn
that the "father of realism" during his trip through the Orient
dreamed of writing the story of a mystic virgin, living in the Nether-
lands, consumed by dreams, a woman who would have been the
symbol of Flaubert's own cult of art. Finally, going back to his
biography, I discover his dependence, his obedience, his "relative
being," in short all the qualities which at that period were commonly called "feminine." At last I find out, a little late, that his
physicians dubbed him a nervous old woman and that he felt
vaguely flattered. Yet it is certain that he was *not to any degree at all*
an invert.[1] Our problem then—without leaving the work itself;
that is, the literary significations—is to ask ourselves why the author
(that is, the pure synthetic activity which creates Madame Bovary)
was able to metamorphose himself into a woman, what signification the metamorphosis possesses *in itself* (which presupposes a
phenomenological study of Emma Bovary in the book), just what
this woman is (of whom Baudelaire said that she possesses at once
the folly and the will of a man), what the artistic transformation
of male into female means in the nineteenth century (we must study
the context of *Mlle de Maupin,* etc.), and finally, just who Gustave
Flaubert *must have been* in order to have within the field of his
possibles the possibility of portraying himself as a woman. The

[1] His letters to Louise Colet show him to be narcissistic and onanist; but he
boasts of amorous exploits, which must be true, since he is addressing the only
person who can be both witness and judge of them.

reply is independent of all biography, since this problem could be posed in Kantian terms: "Under what conditions is the feminization of experience possible?" In order to answer it, we must never forget that the author's style is directly bound up with a conception of the world; the sentence and paragraph structure, the use and position of the substantive, the verb, etc., the arrangement of the paragraphs, and the qualities of the narrative—to refer to only a few specific points—all express hidden presuppositions which can be determined *differentially* without as yet resorting to biography. Nevertheless, we shall never arrive at anything but *problems*. It is true that the statements of Flaubert's contemporaries will help us. Baudelaire asserted that the profound meaning of *The Temptation of St. Anthony*, a furiously "artistic" work which Bouilhet called "a diarrhea of pearls" and which in a completely confused fashion deals with the great metaphysical themes of the period (the destiny of man, life, death, God, religion, nothingness, etc.), is fundamentally identical with that of *Madame Bovary*, a work which is (on the surface) dry and objective. What kind of person, then, can Flaubert be, must he be, to express his own reality in the form of a frenzied idealism and of a realism more spiteful than detached? Who can he, must he, be in order to objectify himself in his work first as a mystic monk and then some years later as a resolute, "slightly masculine" woman?

At this point it is necessary to resort to biography—that is, to the facts *collected* by Flaubert's contemporaries and *verified* by historians. The work poses questions to the life. But we must understand in what sense; the work as the objectification of the person is, in fact, *more complete, more total* than the life. It has its roots in the life, to be sure; it illuminates the life, but it does not find its total explanation in the life alone. But it is too soon as yet for this total explanation to become apparent to us. The life is illuminated by the work as a reality whose total determination is found outside of it—both in the conditions which produce it and in the artistic creation which fulfills it and *completes it by expressing it*. Thus the work—when one has examined it—becomes a hypothesis and a research tool to clarify the biography. It questions and holds on to concrete episodes as replies to its questions.[2] But these answers

---

[2] I do not recall that anyone has been surprised that the Norman giant projected himself in his work as a woman. But I do not recall either that anyone has studied Flaubert's femininity (his truculent, "loud-mouthed" side has misled critics; but this is only a bit of camouflage, Flaubert has confirmed it a hundred times). Yet the order is discernible: the *logical scandal* is Madame Bovary, a masculine woman and feminized man, a lyric and realistic work. It is this

*are not complete.* They are insufficient and limited insofar as the objectification in art is irreducible to the objectification in everyday behavior. There is a hiatus between the work and the life. Nevertheless, the man, with his human relations thus clarified, appears to us in turn as a synthetic collection of questions. The work has revealed Flaubert's narcissism, his onanism, his idealism, his solitude, his dependence, his femininity, his passivity. But these qualities in turn are problems for us. They lead us to suspect at once both social structures (Flaubert is a property owner, he lives on unearned income, etc.) and a *unique* childhood drama. In short, these regressive questions provide us with the means to question his family group as a reality lived and denied by the child Flaubert. Our questions are based on two sorts of information: objective testimonies about the family (class characteristics, family type, individual aspect) and furiously subjective statements by Flaubert about his parents, his brother, his sister, etc. At this level we must be able constantly to refer back to the work and to know whether it contains a biographical truth such as the correspondence itself (falsified by its author) cannot contain. But we must know also that the work *never* reveals the secrets of the biography; the book can at most serve as a schema or conducting thread allowing us to discover the secrets in the life itself.

At this level, we study the early childhood as a way of living general conditions without clearly understanding or reflecting on them; consequently, we may find the meaning of the lived experience in the intellectual petite bourgeoisie, formed under the Empire, and in its way of living the evolution of French society. Here we pass over into the pure objective; that is, into the historical totalization. It is History itself which we must question—the halted advance of family capitalism, the return of the landed proprietors, the contradictions in the government, the misery of a still insufficiently developed Proletariat. But these interrogations are *constituting* in the sense in which the Kantian concepts are called "constitutive"; for they permit us to realize concrete syntheses there where we had as yet only abstract, general conditions. Beginning with an

scandal with its peculiar contradictions which must draw our attention to the life of Flaubert and to his lived femininity. We must detect it in his behavior —and first of all, in his sexual behavior. Now his letters to Louise Colet are sexual behavior; they are each one moments in the diplomacy of Flaubert with regard to this pertinacious poetess. We shall not find an embryonic *Madame Bovary* in the correspondence, but we shall greatly clarify the correspondence by means of Madame Bovary (and, of course, by the other works).

obscurely lived childhood, we can reconstruct the true character of petit bourgeois families. We compare Flaubert's with the family of Baudelaire (at a more "elevated" social level), with that of the Goncourt brothers (a petit bourgeois family which entered into the nobility about the end of the eighteenth century by the simple acquisition of "noble" property), with that of Louis Bouilhet, etc. In this connection we study the real relations between scientists and practitioners (the father Flaubert) and industrialists (the father of his friend, Le Poittevin). In this sense the study of the child Flaubert, as a universality lived in particularity, enriches the general study of the petite bourgeoisie in 1830. By means of the structures presiding over the particular family group, we enrich and make concrete the always too general characteristics of the class considered; in discontinuous "collectives," for example, we apprehend the complex relation between a petite bourgeoisie of civil servants and intellectuals, on the one hand, and the "elite" of industrialists and landed proprietors on the other, or, again, the *roots* of this petite bourgeoisie, its peasant origin, etc., its relations with fallen aristocrats.[3] It is on this level that we are going to discover the major contradiction which the child, Gustave Flaubert, lived in his own way: the opposition between the bourgeois analytic mind and the synthetic myths of religion. Here again a systematic cross-reference is established between the particular anecdotes which clarify these vague contradictions (because the stories gather them together into a single exploding whole) and the general determination of living conditions which allows us to reconstruct *progressively* (because they have already been studied) the material existence of the groups considered.

The sum total of these procedures—regression and cross-reference —has revealed what I shall call the profundity of the lived. Recently an essayist, thinking to refute existentialism, wrote: "It is not man who is profound; it is the world." He was perfectly right, and we agree with him without reservation. Only we should add that the world is human, the profundity of man is the world; therefore profundity comes to the world through man. The exploration of this profundity is a descent from the absolute concrete (*Madame Bovary* in the hands of a reader contemporary with Flaubert— whether it be Baudelaire or the Empress or the Prosecuting Attor-

---

[3] Flaubert's father, the son of a village veterinarian (a royalist), "distinguished" by the imperial administration, marries a girl whose family is connected with the nobility through marriage. He associates with rich industrialists; he buys land.

ney) to its most abstract conditioning (material conditions, the conflict of productive forces and of the relations of production insofar as these conditions appear in their universality and are given as lived by all the members of an undefined group[4]—that is, practically, by *abstract* subjects). Across *Madame Bovary* we can and must catch sight of the movement of landowners and capitalists, the evolution of the rising classes, the slow maturation of the Proletariat: everything is there. But the most concrete significations are radically irreducible to the most abstract significations. The "differential" at each signifying plane reflects the differential of the higher plane by impoverishing it and by contrasting it; it clarifies the differential of the lower plane and serves as a rubric for the synthetic unification of our most abstract knowing. This *cross-reference* contributes to enrich the object with all the profundity of History; it determines, within the historical totalization, the still empty location for the object.

At this point in our research we have still not succeeded in revealing anything more than a hierarchy of heterogeneous significations: *Madame Bovary,* Flaubert's "femininity," his childhood in a hospital building, existing contradictions in the contemporary petite bourgeoisie, the evolution of the family, of property, etc.[5] Each signification clarifies the other, but their irreducibility creates a veritable discontinuity between them. Each serves as an encompassing framework for the preceding, but the included signification is richer than the including signification. In a word, we have only the outline for the dialectical movement, not the movement itself.

It is then and only then that we must employ the progressive method. The problem is to recover the totalizing movement of enrichment which engenders each moment in terms of the prior moment, the impulse which starts from lived obscurities in order to arrive at the final objectification—in short, the *project* by which Flaubert, in order to escape from the petite bourgeoisie, will launch himself across the various fields of possibles toward the alienated

---

[4] In reality the petite bourgeoisie in 1830 is a numerically defined group (although there obviously exist unclassifiable intermediaries who unite it with the peasant, the bourgeois, the landowners). But *methodologically* this concrete universal will always remain indeterminate because the statistics are incomplete.

[5] Flaubert's wealth consisted exclusively of real estate: this hereditary landlord will be ruined by industry; at the end of his life he will sell his lands in order to save his son-in-law, who was involved in foreign trade and had connections with Scandinavian industry. Meanwhile we shall see him often complaining that his rental income is less than what the same investments would bring in if his father had put it into industry.

objectification of himself and will constitute himself inevitably and
indissolubly as the author of *Madame Bovary* and as that petit
bourgeois which he refused to be. This project has *a meaning*, it is
not the simple negativity of flight; by it a man aims at the production of himself in the world as a certain objective totality. It is not
the pure and simple abstract decision to write which makes up the
peculiar quality of Flaubert, but the decision to write in a certain
manner in order to manifest himself in the world in a particular
way; in a word, it is the particular signification—within the framework of the contemporary ideology—which he gives to literature as
the negation of his original condition and as the objective solution
to his contradictions. To rediscover the meaning of this "wrenching
away from toward . . ." we shall be aided by our knowing all the
signifying planes which he has traversed, which we have interpreted as his footprints, and which have brought him to the final
objectification. We have the series: as we move back and forth
between material and social conditioning and the work, the problem
is to find the *tension* extending from objectivity to objectivity, to
discover the law of expansion which surpasses one signification *by
means* of the following one and which maintains the second in the
first. In truth the problem is to invent a movement, to re-create it,
but the hypothesis is immediately verifiable; the only valid one is
that which will realize within a creative movement the transverse
unity of *all* the heterogeneous structures.

Nevertheless, the project is in danger of being deviated, like
Sade's project, by the collective instruments; thus the terminal
objectification perhaps does not correspond exactly to the original
choice. We must take up the regressive analysis again, making a still
closer study of the instrumental field so as to determine the possible
deviations; we must employ all that we have learned about the
contemporary techniques of Knowledge as we look again at the un-
folding life so as to examine the evolution of the choices and
actions, their coherence or their apparent incoherence. *St. Anthony*
expresses the whole Flaubert in his purity and in all the contradictions of his original project, but *St. Anthony* is a failure. Bouilhet
and Maxime Du Camp condemn it completely; they demand that it
"tell a story." *There* is the deviation. Flaubert tells an anecdote, but
he makes it support everything—the sky, hell, himself, St. Anthony,
etc. The monstrous, splendid work which results from it, that in
which he is objectified and alienated, is *Madame Bovary*. Thus the
return to the biography shows us the hiatuses, the fissures, the accidents, at the same time that it confirms the hypothesis (the hypoth-

esis of the original project) by revealing the direction and continuity of the life. We shall define the method of the existentialist approach as a regressive-progressive and analytic-synthetic method. It is at the same time an enriching cross-reference between the object (which contains the whole period as hierarchized significations) and the period (which contains the object in its totalization). In fact, when the object is *rediscovered* in its profundity and in its particularity, then instead of remaining external to the totalization (as it was up until the time when the Marxists undertook to integrate it into history), it enters immediately into contradiction with it. In short, the simple inert juxtaposition of the epoch and the object gives way abruptly to a living conflict.

If one has lazily defined Flaubert as a realist and if one has decided that realism suited the public in the Second Empire (which will permit us to develop a brilliant, completely false theory about the evolution of realism between 1857 and 1957), one will never succeed in comprehending either that strange monster which is *Madame Bovary* or the author or the public. Once more one will be playing with shadows. But if one has taken the trouble, in a study which is going to be long and difficult, to demonstrate within this novel the objectification of the subjective and its alienation— in short, if one grasps it in the concrete sense which it still holds at the moment when it escapes from its author and *at the same time* from the outside as an object which is allowed to develop freely, then the book abruptly comes to oppose the objective reality which it will hold for public opinion, for the magistrates, for contemporary writers. This is the moment to return to the period and to ask ourselves, for example, this very simple question: There was at that time a realist school—Courbet in painting and Duranty in literature were its representatives. Duranty had frequently presented his credo and drafted his manifestos. Flaubert despised realism and said so over and over throughout his life; he loved only the absolute purity of art. *Why* did the public decide at the outset that Flaubert was the realist, and why did it love in him *that particular realism;* that is, that admirable faked confession, that disguised lyricism, that implicit metaphysic? Why did it so value as an admirable character portrayal of a woman (or as a pitiless description of woman) what was at bottom only a poor disguised man? Then we must ask ourselves *what kind of realism* this public demanded or, if you prefer, what kind of literature it demanded under that name and why. This last moment is of primary importance; it is quite simply the moment of alienation. Flaubert sees his work stolen away from him by the very success which the period bestows on it; he no longer recognizes his book, it is foreign to him. Suddenly he loses his own objective existence. But at the same time his work throws a new light upon the period; it enables us to pose a new question to History: Just what must that period have been in order that it should demand *this* book and mendaciously find there its own image. Here we are at the veritable moment of historical action or of what I shall willingly call the misunderstanding. But this is not the place to develop this new point. It is enough to say by way of conclusion that the man and his time will be integrated into the dialectical totalization when we have shown how History surpasses this contradiction.

# Flaubert

## by Georges Poulet

### I

Sometimes (during my grand days in the sun) when I was lit up by an illumination that made my skin tingle from my toes to the roots of my hair, I had an inkling of a state of mind so superior to life that compared to it glory would be nothing, and happiness vain.[1]

Those grand days in the sun, those "happy days when the mind is as open to the sun as the countryside,"[2] form in the life of Flaubert a series of radiant peaks about which works, thought, existence, all cluster. He is, primordially, a romantic: a romantic not so much for his love of the picturesque, as for the consciousness of an exceptional interior experience. But unlike that of the Romantics, the consciousness of this interior experience does not turn Flaubert in upon himself; it opens his mind to the sun; it turns him outward. Like Diderot, like Gautier, from the moment he makes use of his faculties for literary ends, those faculties which he exercises the most and which dominate all the others are precisely those which direct the mind not toward a knowledge of the self but toward a grasp of the non-self and a representation of the world:

I have an extraordinary faculty of *perception**. . .[3]

I have almost voluptuous sensations simply from seeing things, so long as I see them well.[4]

"Flaubert." From *Studies in Human Time* (Baltimore: The Johns Hopkins Press, 1956), by Georges Poulet, pp. 248-261. Copyright © 1956 by The Johns Hopkins Press. Reprinted by permission of Georges Poulet and The Johns Hopkins Press.

* Italics are author's in this and subsequent quotations.
[1] *Correspondance* (*Œuvres*, ed. Conard), II, 395.
[2] *Voyage en Pyrénées et en Corse*, p. 425.
[3] *Correspondance*, III, 270.
[4] *Ibid.*, I, 178.

Only rapports are true, that is to say, the manner in which we *perceive* objects.[5]

The starting point with Flaubert is thus not Flaubert himself; it is the rapport between the perceiving self and the object perceived:

> Often, apropos of no matter what, a drop of water, a shell, a hair, you stopped and stayed motionless, eyes fixed, heart open.
> The object you contemplated seemed to encroach upon you, by as much as you inclined yourself toward it, and bonds were established . . . .[6]

> Sometimes by dint of gazing at a pebble, an animal, a picture, I felt myself enter into them. Communications between human beings are not more intense.[7]

Certainly these are capital passages; they reveal to us the fundamental orientation of Flaubert's mind. Self-awareness is fully experienced by him in the moment when he emerges from himself to become identified—by the simplest but most intense of the acts of the mental life, perception—with the object, whatever it may be, of this perception. Thus objectivity, far from being an acquired discipline with Flaubert, is a natural state, the only truly natural state of his thought. If it is realized fully only in exceptional instances, that is because ". . . man is so made that each day he can savor only a little nourishment, colors, sounds, feelings, ideas";[8] but this nourishment, made up in the first place of colors and sounds and secondarily of feelings and ideas, is the sole possible food. It is to it that one must turn for support and subsistence. Life exists, but only where there are colors, sounds, the outdoors, the sun. One must incline toward it, penetrate into it or be penetrated by it, and become what one feels by the very act of feeling.

An act of identification by which there are abolished not only the interval between subject and object, but their existence as distinct beings:

> Then, by dint of looking, you no longer saw; listening, you heard nothing, and your mind itself ended by losing the notion of that *particularity* which kept it on the alert.[9]

[5] *Ibid.,* VIII, 135.
[6] *Tentation* of 1849, p. 417.
[7] *Correspondance,* III, 210.
[8] *Par les champs et par les grèves,* p. 131.
[9] *Tentation* of 1849, p. 417.

The particularity of the object exists only for him who maintains in his consciousness a gap between the thing perceived and the perceiving mind; it no longer exists for him who, effacing within him any idea of a representing self and a thing represented, limits his present consciousness to the representation itself. In his moments of "contemplative effusion," [10] in his "grand days in the sun," Flaubert arrived at an integral phenomenalism. The mind being what it represents, and the object existing only in its representation in the mind, what remains is simply a unique being that can be called indifferently mind or nature:

> The interval between yourself and the object, like an abyss whose two sides come closer and closer together, was getting increasingly narrower, so much so that this difference disappeared. . . . One degree more and you became nature, or nature became you.[11]

This "one degree more" by which one becomes nature is reached elsewhere:

> By dint of being penetrated by it, of entering into it, we also *became nature,* feeling that it was overpowering us, and taking a measureless joy in that process.[12]

It is a joy that becomes measureless from the moment one is identified with the whole extent of nature and of the activity which animates it:

> Everything in you palpitates with joy and beats its wings with the elements, you are bound to them, breathe with them, the essence of animate nature seems to have passed into you . . . .[13]

At this degree of pantheistic ecstasy, the conception of a mere spatial and logical order proves to be transcended. It would be inexact, therefore, to see in Flaubert only a poetic transcription of Spinozism. What man attains in the Flaubertian experience is less the sense of an *ordo et connexio idearum* than the intuition of life in its cosmic expansion. Life is diffusion, a tireless projection of forms in a space that is the divine immensity:

[10] *Par les champs et par les grèves,* p. 131.
[11] *Tentation* of 1849, p. 417.
[12] *Par les champs et par les grèves,* p. 130.
[13] *Voyage en Pyrénées et en Corse,* p. 425.

There is no nothingness! There is no emptiness! Everywhere there are bodies that move in the immutable depths of Vastness.[14]

To be identified with cosmic life is to be diffused over a divine vastness which can be considered indifferently as holding the variety of things and that of the representations which one makes of them. Thought and the world are an identical extent: "I was, in the variety of my being, like an immense forest of India, where life palpitates in each atom . . . ." [15]

But precisely because it is sheer variety, life cannot be apprehended except through the motion by which it varies. It is not enough to reach some point from which the sentient mind can spread its thoughts over the whole representative field. It is also necessary that, from this point, and without leaving this point—which is the durationless point of the present—the mind should "live within all that life in order to array all its forms, *to endure together with them,* and forever varying, to extend forth its metamorphoses under the sun of eternity." [16] Since life is duration, the moment that absolutely expresses it must be a moment in which the very working of duration is visible. Sometimes this presence of duration in the moment is found by Flaubert in a direct intuition of the genesis of things: "O happy am I! I have seen life born, I have seen motion begin";[17] but more often it seems occasioned in his work by a sensory event. There are the moments when sensation is so perfectly yoked with the general life of things that one becomes, so to speak, the metaphorical expression of the other. Then to feel oneself live is to feel oneself live life, to feel the pulse of duration beat. For instance, we have the scene of carnal love in *Madame Bovary:*

> The silence was everywhere; a sweetness seemed to emanate from the trees; she felt her heart begin beating again, and the blood circulate in her body like a stream of milk. Then she heard afar off, beyond the woods, over the hills, a faint and prolonged cry, a protracted voice, and she listened silently to its mingling, like a strain of music, with the last vibrations of her stirred nerves.

In this passage Flaubert succeeds in giving the moment a spatial and temporal density so particular that one could say (and it is undoubtedly the effect Flaubert wished to produce) that this moment

[14] *Tentation* of 1874, p. 173.
[15] *Novembre*, p. 180.
[16] *Par les champs et par les grèves*, p. 131.
[17] *Tentation* of 1874, p. 200.

belongs to a different duration from that of ordinary days, a duration whose *tempo* of things is made sweeter, slower, and therefore more perceptible; a duration that spreads out. It is as if time, like a passing breeze, could be felt in the renewed beatings of the heart, in the blood that flows like a stream of milk. It is no longer the bitter consciousness of an interval, there is no more interval; there is only a gliding motion which carries away simultaneously the things and the sentient mind with the sense of an absolute homogeneity between the different elements that compose the moment. The mind, the body, nature, and life, all participate in the same moment of the same becoming.

## II

The state of mind glimpsed by Flaubert in his grand days in the sun is thus not different from that experienced by all the great pantheist mystics: a moment of ecstasy when, in the union of the sentient mind and pure sensation, the self is identified with the universe and has for a moment the experience of eternity.

But with Flaubert, even in his grand days in the sun, that state is only *glimpsed*. Thought can neither be established nor isolated within it. The point at which it happens is not a state but a boundary point; a point that is the extremity of a temporal line, a boundary that is that of a movement of thought. Without an antecedent line and movement, it is as inconceivable as a beach without a tide to flow toward it and mark its delimitation.

It is the same with Flaubert when the substance of the lived present is this time constituted not by sense experiences but by memories. There are, for Flaubert, other grand days in the sun when the mind is not open to the present sun, but to the "golden haze" still emanating from suns which have set long ago. There is for him a present that is the terminal place of recollected images as well as a present that is the terminal place of sensorial images.

For the predilection that Flaubert always had for memory, even at the expense of actual sensation, is not due to a particular preference of his for what belongs to the past as such. What does he look for in sensation except a total intimacy with the object of sensation? Now this feeling of total intimacy is rare by reason of the inflexibility of a self that "will not let itself go," the mind naturally here and the object there. But when the sensation is reborn under the form of memory, it reappears not as a thing outside but as some-

thing inside. It is regained within. All distance is now abolished, as
in the rarest and most perfect sensuous union. The reviviscence is,
like pantheistic ecstasy, a pure viviscence. It has the same intensity,
the same richness, it ends in the same synthesis of the object and the
self.

And to begin with, it has the same starting point. Just as with
Flaubert, sensory activity takes its origin from an object encountered ("Often, apropos of no matter what, a drop of water, a sea-
shell . . ."), so it is also through the fortuitous encounter with an
object that the retrospective imagination takes birth: "anything, the
slightest circumstance, a rainy day, a hot sun, a flower, an old piece
of furniture, recalls to me a series of memories . . . ." [18] Sometimes
it happens at the sight of a garment worn in days gone by, of an
engraving hand-colored a long time ago, at the smell of an odor long
ago familiar; it reoccurs oftenest upon revisits to past places. The
object, whatever it may be, lets loose a series of memories. A *series:*
the most striking characteristic indeed of the phenomenon of memory in Flaubert is seriality. One memory calls up another, then still
another, and so on; and each rises into view under the form of an
image which is covered and replaced by the following slide, as in the
projections of a magic lantern:

> . . . He saw again, like ghosts conjured up, the different days of his
> past, some gay, others sad; *and first* those when he played, a child
> laughing at life, without dream or desire; *and the one* on which he
> entered high school, *and that other* on which he left, *the one* when
> he arrived at M. Renaud's, *the one* on which she came into his
> room . . . .[19]

These images are all distinct. Each of them presents a definite picture but brings also with it other images, trains of feelings, the very
emotions of the past surging up from the depths. Now all this awakening of the affective memory takes place, as it were, in the environs
and in the gaps in the series of perceptible images; it connects them,
suffuses them, and ends by mingling them: "My travels, my memories of childhood, all are colored by one another, fall into line,
dance with wonderful gleamings and mount in a spiral." [20] A spiral,
enveloping a thousand diverse images and traversing different zones
of the past—such is the recreative synthesis which crowns the opera-

---

[18] *Mémoires d'un fou*, p. 500.
[19] *Première éducation*, p. 84.
[20] *Correspondance*, II, 371.

tion of memory in Flaubert. It does not consist in drawing upon a repository, in combining elements of different periods, but rather in allowing layers of images to rise in tiers in the mind, each of which keeps the particular form it occupied in time, but, on the other hand, takes color from the reflection of the others. Thus, the consciousness that evokes them appears to itself like a painting in perspective, in the depths of which there appear at unequal intervals with their particular hues—but in a unique ambience (which is the true self)—the phantoms of the past:

> I passed along the Rue des Orties which opens on the court of the college. . . . I saw the chestnut trees under which we played. . . . I saw myself there once more, on the first day, entering, unknown, amongst all of you, and you who first came and spoke to me; *and then all the rest slowly unrolled in my memory,* the cries when we were at play, and the racket of our balls against the wire lattices of the windows, and the hot, humid and stifling air of the classrooms . . . .[21]

In the same manner, Emma, noticing on a letter from her father a little of the ashes with which he had the habit of drying wet ink, sees her father once more, "bending over the hearth to pick up the tongs"; then, this first image leading to others, she recalls "summer afternoons full of sunlight"; and step by step, from memory to memory, she follows the course of her life down to the present moment:

> What happiness then . . . what abundance of illusions . . . . Nothing remained of them now. She had used them up in the surprising experiences of her mind, through all its successive conditions . . . losing them continually in this way *her whole life long,* like a traveler who leaves something of his wealth at every inn along the way . . . .[22]

One feels that the whole force of this passage (leaving aside the feeling of the attrition of experience, of which more later) relates to the *depth of duration* which it suggests—a depth that is glimpsed through a descending perspective, in which the images are spaced out like milestones, along *the whole length of life.* The first memory is like the top of a slope; from that point there is nothing to do but descend again; and to redescend the slope is to retraverse the whole life, to render visible the very pathway of lived time: "Then,

[21] *Première éducation,* p. 36.
[22] *Madame Bovary,* p. 239.

swept along on her memories as if upon a foaming torrent, she soon
came to recall yesterday . . . ." [23]

More rarely (for Flaubert's prospective imagination is poor), the
same phenomenon is discovered with regard to time to come:

> And immediately pictures unrolled endlessly. He saw himself with
> her, at night in a post-chaise, then on the bank of a stream on a
> summer evening, and then under the reflection of a lamp at home
> together.[24]

But the moment when the "contemplative effusion" is most completely realized is the one when the *pictures without end* instead of
seeming to approach or withdraw from the present appear to unroll
within its span: "Then all of his past life appeared to Smarh, swiftly,
in one stroke, like a flash of lightning." [25]

It is as if suddenly the whole field of existence, without losing
anything of its intrinsic multiplicity, were contemplated by the
interior gaze in the interior of the moment. For example, when
Félicité sees the lights of Honfleur:

> A feeling of faintness seized her; and the misery of her childhood,
> the deception of first love, the departure of her nephew, the death
> of Virginie, like the waves of a rising tide, returned all at once, and
> rising in her throat, suffocated her.[26]

In this simultaneity on which all existence is brought to bear, the
retrospective movement attains its perfection and its terminal point:
a revelation of a temporal expanse filled up by the mind just as in
the sensuous ecstasy the mind fills up exterior space.


## III

What is there beyond this *eternal moment?* All the internal
activity is engaged. The mind perceives with an hallucinatory clearness a series of images whose motion is accelerated. They multiply,
they surround it, they besiege it. Exaltation is followed by disquietude, then by anguish. The images that the mind watched

---

[23] *Ibid.*, p. 424.
[24] *L'Éducation sentimentale*, p. 453.
[25] *Smarh*, p. 106.
[26] *Trois contes*, p. 51.

appearing within itself it now sees disappearing outside itself. It is like "a kind of hemorrhage of innervation," [27] as if existence drained away through a bleeding wound:

> My thoughts, which I would like to clasp together . . . slide away one after another and *escape me,* like a sheaf of arrows from the hand of a child who cannot hang on to them, they fall to the ground hurting his knees . . . .[28]

The same thing goes for the moment of union with the past as for the moment of union with the present and with nature. In each case, without any transition, fissure succeeds fusion. The abolished distance is suddenly rediscovered, gaping in the mind:

> One says to oneself: "Ten years ago I was there," and one is there and one thinks the same things and the whole interval is forgotten. *Then it appears to you, that interval,* like an immense precipice in which nothingness whirls round.[29]

It is exactly the inverse motion of that by which the subject had been absorbed in the object of its sensation or of its memory. Then it was a question of an "interval like an abyss whose sides come closer and closer together . . . so much so that the difference disappeared." Now it is a question of the same interval reappearing and affirming the same difference.

A difference which reveals a double change in the nature of space and time. Space is no longer the field of expansion, from the center of which the mind diffuses itself and radiates outward; time is no longer that extent of the past which the mind—starting out from some given memory—fills and overflows with the flux of its reminiscences; on the contrary, extension has become an empty void separating the self from the object, and time another kind of empty extension which no less irremediably separates the present self from its past:

> How far away all that is! Did I not live then? Was that indeed I? Is it myself now? Every minute of my life seems cut off at a stroke from every other by an abyss; between yesterday and today there is an eternity that appals me.[30]

[27] *Correspondance,* III, 270.
[28] *Tentation* of 1849, p. 236.
[29] *Correspondance,* III, 331.
[30] *Novembre,* p. 178.

This eternity is properly called an abyss; it is abysmal because it is the negation of the eternity of plenitude to which it succeeds. It is the infinite absence of things of which one experienced the presence, a sort of atrociously neuter time, since nothing fills or traverses it, whose extent, indifferently comparable to both eternity and a minute, expresses simply an absolute gap. Sometimes this gap is depicted under the aspect of a general petrification of things: "It seems, at certain moments, that the universe is immobilized, that everything has become a statue and that we alone are alive." [31] At other times it takes the form of a perpetual repetition of the same action: "From then on he continually climbed that stairway . . . . He continued to ascend with the strange facility one experiences in dreams." [32] But repetition and immobilization are the unconscious metaphors by which the human mind both expresses and conceals the nakedness of a void, the horror of which he is the only one to perceive. There is no possibility here of that intermediary time which we place mechanically between ourselves and a period of the past which we recall: a consciousness of a duration that is more or less continuous, which joins this moment and that one together. The abysmal time is the time that creates and asserts the abyss, which sees to it that moments do not rejoin each other. The human being is no longer supported from behind by his past. He leans back against nothingness:

> Despite the hubbub in his head, he perceives an enormous silence that separates him from the world. He tries to speak; impossible! It is as if the general bond of his existence were dissolved . . . .[33]

> Something undefined separates you from your own person and rivets you to nonbeing.[34]

In a flash our past self is carried to the other side of an abyss, to a side that is directly opposite to us. We see it from afar, and it appears to us as a stranger:

> Startled by the fidelity of his memories, rendered still vivid by the presence of those places where they occurred in the form of events and feelings, he asked himself if all of them belonged to the same man, if a single life could have sufficed for them, and he tried to con-

[31] *Correspondance*, III, 317.
[32] *Salammbô*, p. 102.
[33] *Tentation* of 1874, p. 15.
[34] *Correspondance*, III, 332.

nect them with some other lost existence, so far away was his past from him! [35]

Existence is divided in two. Actual life now seems only a feeble reflection of another life already lived, one which must have been the only true life: "There are days when one has lived two existences, the second is already a mere memory of the first . . . ." [36] Then one turns toward that past with an ambiguous nostalgia. One half-fancies having already lived in some far-off epoch of history. One experiences what Flaubert calls "the thrill of history." [37] It is an inordinate sadness over the idea that those ages have passed with no possibility of returning. "What would I not give to see a triumph, what would I not sell to enter Suburre one evening at the time when the torches were burning at the doors of the brothels . . . ?" [38] One sets oneself to the endless pursuit of retrospective myths; one ruminates upon past existences lived or dreamed. But the more one's thought is absorbed in them, the more the present appears as an illusion. The past "devours it" and "devours us": "I roam in memories and am lost in them." [39]

It is then that the actual moment reveals all its narrowness and dearth: "I do not experience, as you do, that feeling of a life that is beginning, the wonder of a newly-hatched existence." [40] "The world is not big enough for the mind: it suffocates in the present hour." [41]

To the "interminable series of the passions that have faded away," [42] to the lassitude and to the distaste for the ephemeral, it is vain to try to oppose an activity directed toward the future. The imagination, so intense under its retrospective form, sees nothing ahead of it. Since it is entirely representative and cannot picture perceptible objects in the future, it sees nothing at all there:

And from the past, I go dreaming of the future, and there I see nothing, absolutely nothing. I am without plan, without idea, without project, and what is worse, without ambition.[43]

[35] *Première éducation*, p. 242.
[36] *Novembre*, p. 192.
[37] *Correspondance*, III, 19.
[38] *Ibid.*, II, 6.
[39] *Ibid.*, VI, 377.
[40] *Ibid.*, V, 240.
[41] *Ibid.*, I, 253.
[42] *Ibid.*, III, 308.
[43] *Ibid.*, II, 201.

Deprived of a future, devoured by the past, crushed by the weight of the present, the mind cannot any more experience time except as a motion that slows down, as a *tempo* that is slackening. One feels oneself old from having lived through so many of the "minutes that are as years." [44] The sense of existence becomes that of a continuous addition to this length of duration. Life is reduced to being a repetition: "Must you not awake every morning, eat, drink, go, come, repeat that series of acts which are always the same?" [45]

At this point one would say that the course of duration stops. It is no longer a stream, but still water, "a sleeping fen, so quiet that the slightest event that falls into it makes innumerable circles . . . ." [46] An agitation on the surface, and a general feeling of illusion and of wearing away: with Flaubert it is in these things that the feeling of human time is in grave danger of getting lost.


## IV

There is in the *Première Éducation sentimentale* a passage that is particularly important because it seems to give us the profound reason for the difference, so visible in Flaubert, between the works of his youth and those of his maturity. This passage begins with a long, morose meditation that one of the characters pursues on the formlessness and dejection of his existence. Then gradually, the thought is transformed into images, and once again the past is put to unrolling a series of memory-pictures. But this time the dominating factor in this succession of images is neither the kind of spontaneous homogeneity which is given to the most disparate things by the current of emotions that carries them along nor, on the reverse side, the feeling of radical heterogeneity which reveals itself in them and between them when the current fails to link them together. This time, on the contrary, it is possible to find there a certain coherence. For the first time one can distinguish not only sensory and imaginative events but also events penetrable by the mind:

> Nevertheless from all that there resulted his present state, and this state was the sum of all those antecedents, one which permitted him to review them; each event had of itself produced a second, every

---

[44] *Ibid.*, I, 368.
[45] *Tentation* of 1849, p. 434.
[46] *Correspondance*, III, 289.

feeling had been fused into an idea . . . . Thus there was a sequence and a continuity to this series of diverse perceptions.[47]

It would be hard to imagine a reflection more ordinary or more commonplace. Nevertheless, it is around this reflection that Flaubert tried to reform a life and a work abandoned of themselves to the power of images. The solution he accepts is the middle solution, it is an option in favor of order—an order, moreover, which is perceived and which perhaps exists only when it is discovered as the order of accomplished facts. For it is discovered only in things that are completed and in the postulate that they are completed by reason of other things which have determined their completion: "The thought that comes to you now has been brought to you . . . by successions, gradations, transformations and rebirths." [48] Thus, the order does not depend on the assumption of any transcendence. It is an adequate relationship between what exists in this moment and what existed in all preceding moments. It is an *a posteriori* construction that the mind imposes upon the universe to make it hold together. Thanks to this formula, there are no more *gaps,* no more intervals between things, nor an abyss between the present and the past. We are in the kingdom of immanence, and of so integral an immanence that everything is representable and implied there. Beyond the chain of causes and effects as they are represented in the mind, there is the supposition that the same chain and the same interactivity of causes and effects persist indefinitely; there is nothing else; no mystery; nothing veiled or inexpressible. What the imagination cannot revive the mind can represent to itself.

Representative thought, therefore, chooses a particular moment of life. It perceives this moment and all the sense-data it contains as a relationship between the human being and its immediate environment. Then it proceeds to discern how those sensations are modified by the action of other images coming from the past. From this stage backward, reconstructive thought will begin an ascending movement. It will see how in their turn those images of the past were linked to objects of the past. Behind the environment in which the present self lives, it will discover the milieu in which it has lived and felt; and behind this double past, which is that of being and milieu, it will discover another, and then still another, always making sure of its discoveries and in this way creating a proportionate density of duration in which there is neither hiatus

[47] *Première éducation*, p. 244.
[48] *Tentation* of 1849, p. 418.

nor rupture; a movement which, by its direction as well as by its very nature, is the exact reverse of the "flight of memories," that is to say, the sudden jump by which the mind discovered itself, in the works of Flaubert's youth, thrown away, so to speak, into any moment of the past.

For it is no longer now a question of a sudden plunge into the depths of a former time, from whence one is allowed to descend haphazardly the course of existence. The design of Flaubert is no longer a lyrical but a methodical design. He sketched it in a passage in the *Première Tentation;* there he makes Science speak in the following terms:

> If I could penetrate matter, grasp idea, follow life through its meta-morphoses, understand being in its modes, and thus from one to the other, reascending the ladder of causes like a series of steps, reunite in myself those scattered phenomena and put them back into motion in the synthesis from which my scalpel detached them.[49]

Thus, the first movement of the Flaubertian reconstruction is the ascending movement by which thought climbs, in a series of infer-ences, the stairway of causes, and so progressively withdraws from the domain of sensation or of actual images, in order to pass into that of the order of things, into the domain of law. It is a method strictly opposed to that of Balzac, who, starting with an *a priori* creature, posits at the outset the existence of a law-force, of which there remains simply to express next, in terms more and more con-crete, the descending curve into real life. Balzac, novelist of the *determining;* Flaubert, novelist of the *determined.*

But precisely by reason of the fact that in Flaubert that which is first given is this *determined* actual, indubitable, and resisting ob-ject upon which the representative faculty can rest all its weight, the Flaubertian construction, as high as it may rise, never risks becom-ing abstract. The law is not a non-temporal thing. It does not exist in itself but in the action by which it is exercised. In proportion as one ascends to it, one gathers up, at each step, the perceptible matter with which the human being has remodified itself in each of the antecedent moments of its duration. Thus the human being is some-how found to exist in two ways: by its sensations, whether imme-diate or remembered, which form its variable, contingent reality, though in intimate contact with the reality of things; and on the

[49] *Ibid.,* p. 349.

other hand, by the synthetic order that the concatenating series of causes imposes upon its existence.

A double synthesis, or rather a recapture, in the framework of an objective synthesis, of what had always—but in a subjective, fragmentary, and fugitive fashion—been synthetically expressed in the works of Flaubert's youth.

This is what he himself seems to indicate in a note written in 1859:

> The artist not only carries humanity within him, but he reproduces its history in the creation of his work: first confusion, a general view, aspirations, bedazzlement, everything is mixed up [the barbarous epoch]; then analysis, doubt, method, the disposition of parts [the scientific era]; finally, he comes back to the first synthesis, made wider in the execution.

Having arrived at this peak of synthesis, thought turns itself about to begin its downward movement. If it raised itself up into the regions of causes and antecedents, that was in order to prepare itself to understand and show how, starting out from this region and from the past, the actual is organized. So then the descending movement of Flaubert's thought takes on the aspect of a prospective representation of life which, through a series of states, is brought out of the past up to the present and ends there by giving it the significance of being an effect that is the consequence of all the vast perceptible genetic travail in space and duration—a perspective similar to that which one has when, on the shore, one lifts his eyes slowly to the open sea in order to follow from out there the course of a wave that draws nearer and nearer, and finally perishes at one's feet—an experience that one also has when in writing, say, a periodic sentence (the periodic sentence of Flaubert) one finds that from the protasis to the apodosis the different elements are composed in a rising and falling synthesis which, in coming to its completion, affords the discovery in the written sentence of an indissoluble unity in which everything becomes present. From that point on, the problem of time is simply a problem of style.

# The Creation of Form in Flaubert

*by Jean-Pierre Richard*

"The flesh is weak and my heart, like splashing rain, trembles with the shocks of the earth. . . ." [1] In these words it is hard to recognize the speech of a devouring Moloch. Flaubert had exaggerated his strength. For others the joys of rape, of conquering possession; Hugo, Balzac, Rabelais knead the dough of humanity with a liberal hand; but beside them Flaubert is only a false giant. A massive one, to be sure, and thunderous, too. But within, all is rotten with weakness, and from the outset he knew it:

> It is strange how I was born with little faith in happiness. At the earliest age I had a complete foretaste of life. It was like a nauseous kitchen odor leaking out through the transom. One doesn't have to have eaten any to know that it will make one vomit. [2]

Even before appetite and verve and from the very first moment of consciousness, Flaubert discovered in himself a movement of nausea, of fundamental disgust that he will later seek to forget or to dominate by hurling himself onto things—like a sick traveler who leans toward landscapes to distract himself from his distress—but which he will never really overcome. Far from restraining a true desire, verve serves thus to arouse a flagging appetite. It strives to stir artificially a profound apathy. Through his excitement Flaubert, a traveling salesman creating his own wares for himself, struggles to be gay or have pleasure. In effect, his verve casts him toward the idea or the object to divert him from the realization of his weakness.

"The Creation of Form in Flaubert." From *"Littérature et sensation* (Paris: Éditions du Seuil, 1954), by Jean-Pierre Richard, pp. 125-147. Copyright 1954 by Éditions du Seuil. Reprinted by permission of Jean-Pierre Richard and the Éditions du Seuil. Translated by Raymond Giraud. (The pages reproduced here are only a part of the chapter of the same title.

[1] *Correspondance*, III, p. 307. [Unless otherwise indicated, all references to Flaubert's work are to the Conard edition (see bibliograpby).]

[2] *Corr.*, I, p. 201.

For the natural bent of his sensuality did not lead him to conquer but rather to let himself be won over by things or to slip toward them, to follow that "declivity," of which a philosopher speaks, "which there is from us toward things and which my states of consciousness freely follow, carried along by their own weight and by that mental curiosity which is as instinctive in us as confidence." [3] But can one really call such a limp surrender to nature *curiosity?* Such a relationship with the object suppresses at least all difficulty of assimilation. For this movement goes beneath the surface, penetrates the most intimate substance. Flaubert, said Brunetière, sees only the surface of objects. An astonishing error. He has, on the contrary, the sense of their underlying depth much more than that of their outer skin. And that is why perception never seems like a violation of appearances in his work: for him the surface seems to gape open, like an invitation; when he contemplates it long and closely, it finally disappears, and objects become pure porosity:

> I can see down into the very pores of things, as the near-sighted see, because they put their noses right up against them. [4]

What we call surface or limit is, therefore, in reality for him only the brushing of a certain material texture against a different and immediate neighboring texture. Passing from one object to another, he experiences a change of grain, of consistency, of interior structure, but not of veritable disorientation. There is no leap toward the heterogeneous, as in the engulfing appetite, and that is just why he prefers this mode of penetration, which exacts only suppleness of him. When the world has once appeared to you as fullness, sensuality can distinguish in it from then on only diverse degrees of plenitude and ranges freely from one object to another as in a homogeneous medium. Heterogeneity is, on the contrary, the quality of a long-range vision. Flaubert, said Maupassant, was only capable of judging from afar: he suffered from an ailment of touch; seeing things too close made him dizzy; the interval was blurred; he could no longer distinguish anything. But through this blur it was the penetration of the object, its possession in depth, that was granted him.

That fusion has as its counterpart a diminution, perhaps an annihilation, of personal integrity. In Flaubert material fusion is always accompanied by an interior dissolution. "To be matter!" The famous cry which closes the *Temptation* of 1875 is prepared by a

---

[3] W. Jankelevitch, *La Mauvaise Conscience,* p. 21.
[4] *Corr.,* II, p. 343.

long labor of spiritual disaggregation, in the course of which the parade of divers religious forms in their contradiction finally unsettles all the certainties of the saint and makes him as shapeless within as the protoplasm in which he will finally lose himself. For matter is contacted without tension or prejudices. To succeed in penetrating the substance of a pasty nature one's being must be softened and become liquid. Soon one will feel himself escaping from himself, as in a hemorrhage.

> It is true, often I have felt that something bigger than myself was fusing with my being: *bit by bit I went off*\* into the greenery of the pastures and into the current of the rivers that I watched go by; and I no longer knew where my soul was, it was so diffuse, universal, spread out. . . .⁵

Fusion signifies diffusion, successive dispersion in things. And that loss which appears here as agreeable will be felt as painful when one ceases to stress the attracting object, but stresses rather the lost consciousness: for the suppression of the interval ends simultaneously in the absence of consciousness and in ecstasy.

Even worse. Beyond a certain degree of penetration the object itself will impose by contagion the dissolution of one's being. For it too will be seen to become disassociated, to cease being some particular object as it becomes merely a fragment of matter. That is something that happens when, too intent upon experiencing things from within according only to their differences of texture or density, one neglects the asperities of their surfaces, all that situates and characterizes them—their *particularities*. Sensation then becomes totally absorbing and finally loses all objective content and remains in the consciousness as pure opacity:

> Bit by bit, by dint of gazing, you no longer saw; as you listened, you heard nothing, and your very mind finally lost the feeling of that particularity which kept it awake.⁶

It is then an "immense harmony" which is swallowed up in the soul, an "inexpressible comprehension of the unrevealed whole." But the comprehension of the parts of that whole is thereby also established as impossible. Detail, which fixed upon each object an attention that

---

\* Italics added by author in this and susequent quotations.
⁵ *La Tentation de Saint Antoine,* 1849, p. 418.
⁶ *La Tentation de Saint Antoine,* 1849, p. 417.

was different for each one, now appears only as the superficial grain of a single, homogeneous substance. What stretches out before me, or rather, what submerges me, is no longer the world of objects but the ocean of matter. Individual forms have disappeared. The barriers that once separated kingdoms and species have likewise vanished. The most bizarre animals parade before the gaze of Saint Anthony; but this very gaze, by the mere power of its penetration, suscitates in the object an even more radical disaggregation. Forms no longer burst or combine with one another in strange ways according to the rules of fantasy inspired by Bosch or Breughel. But everything slips from one kingdom to another, melts from appearance to appearance in a series of gradual and supernatural telescopings. All the envelopes—mineral, vegetable, and animal—steadily lose their solidity, and from one disappearance to another the saint finally discovers himself before a totally undifferentiated substance. The unconscious subject is thus lost in amorphous matter: communion in that which is without form.

All feeling is extension.[7]

When I love, my feeling is an inundation that pours out all around me. . . .[8]

In Flaubert, the experience of the *other* appears as fluid as perception. Just like sensation, desire "mollifies." It causes a flowing toward the outside. On both sides there is the same liquefying weakness. It is curious to note to what degree in their movement and almost in their expression these two experiences are alike.

Let us look, for example, at something that Flaubert wrote, still very awkwardly, in an early draft of *Madame Bovary*, where he is seeking to depict the desire Léon feels for Emma:

Now his thought was mingling with her image; he was melting into the object of his gaze [*objectif*] without being aware of it.[9]

A second version makes the following correction:

His very consciousness was being eclipsed as it expanded, carried completely outside of itself.

[7] *Corr.*, III, p. 159.
[8] *Corr.*, I, p. 252.
[9] *Madame Bovary*, ed. Pommier, p. 275.

The third version:

> His very self-consciousness seemed to abandon him, so much did it
> move outward toward this contemplation.[10]

The psychological state, the attitude, the very vocabulary (for example, the word *objectif*), everything evokes the traveler leaning out of
his window or the saint bent toward his spectacle: the same declivity
of the intervening space, the same ensuing ecstasy. Of Emma in love
with Rodolphe, Flaubert writes again that "her soul was becoming
engulfed in this intoxication and drowning in it, shriveled like the
Duke of Clarence in his butt of Malmsey." [11] Drowning, sinking,
intoxication—contact with the object was already effecting all these
forms of alienation.

The alienation of love, however, transports the self into a very different psychological climate, that being so because the loved object is
at the same time a living object, as spongy as—but more insidiously
attractive than—an inert object. Its life is manifested by the emana-
tion of a sort of fluid which envelops, penetrates, and, even before
desire has begun to show itself, succeeds in melting down every inner
barrier in one's being. One "falls in love":

> His tender heart turned soft before the girl's elegance. With eyes shut,
> his new-born desire dwelt lovingly on it. It impregnated his desire
> with deeper emanations like camphor sachets in clothing.[12]

A succession of bold images, which Flaubert will suppress from the
definitive version of *Madame Bovary*, but which help us to understand how the softening provoked by desire differs from the dispers-
ing dissolution caused by the intoxication of perception. One's
being is liquefied just as much, but here it can enjoy its liquefaction,
feel coddled in it before it has flowed out toward the other person.
Under the spell of his beloved's perfume, the hero of *November*
"feels his heart growing softer and mushier than a peach melting on
his tongue." [13] As the tongue delights in the melting pulp, he takes
delight in his own spiritual softening. He savors his own gradual
disappearance. Love is a semiconscious and deliciously progressive
act of drowning.

[10] *Madame Bovary, Ébauches et fragments inédits*, I, p. 374.
[11] *Madame Bovary*, ed. Conard, p. 266.
[12] *Madame Bovary*, ed. Pommier, p. 158.
[13] *Novembre*, p. 199.

Before becoming quite fluid, the lover passes through an intermediate texture in which he retains some vestigial consistency and
just enough lucidity to have a taste of the loss of his own self-con-
sciousness. "I never loved you so much; there were oceans of cream
in my soul," [14] writes Flaubert to Louise. Cream retains a thickness,
an inner cohesion. In the same way pomade—moustache pomade for
the man, make-up or beauty cream for the woman—is the substance
that for Flaubert best incarnates and symbolizes rising desire. It represents a sugary state of being in which liquefaction moves sluggishly, halts in its own enjoyment, while still retaining enough
solidity to radiate outward toward others. Lust, "melting with desire," pours itself unreservedly upon the desired object and "flows
over it like a liquid pomade." [15] On the surface of this half-melted
being, desire forms in beady pearls, like a liquefaction of this very
creamy, pasty substance—a kind of sweat:

> Can my heart contain these softening effusions, which I have only felt
> like sudden sweats? [16]

Even more explicitly:

> Had he then never laid his head on the bosom of a daughter of Eve?
> Had he never felt himself *slowly dissolve* in her love, like a little plant
> that *decomposes under the warm rain* of the storm? Had he not felt in
> his hand *that hand which sweats softness* nor trembled with fear at
> that look which melts enthusiasm and asphyxiates thought? [17]

Love also is a nausea. In it one's being rots slowly, at the same time
that its sweating invites the rotting of the other. The lover loses
his bony structure, he becomes pure plasticity: Léon, waiting for
Emma, "feels a lascivious moistness in his hands," [18] and when those
hands touch those of the desired woman and feel their moistness, we
see both their hands stick together in the same infinitely flexible,
marvelously ductile, gluey substance.

> He felt then, between his fingers, that hand. To Léon it seemed
> *flexible, sweaty, soft, boneless.* A subtle transmission went all the way
> up his arm to his heart, while what was most intimate in him was

[14] *Corr.*, II, p. 430.
[15] *La Tentation de Saint Antoine*, 1849, p. 327.
[16] *Corr.*, II, p. 4.
[17] *La Tentation de Saint Antoine*, 1849, p. 273.
[18] *Madame Bovary*, ed. Pommier, p. 491.

melting in that soft palm, like a sort of dough that was being slowly kneaded in it.[19]

A marvelous phrase in the very form of which we perceive how the double movement of reception and offering that constitutes love—a movement originally as rapid as lightning—bogs down gradually in the flabbiness of contact. Léon and Emma no longer exist separately but constitute a single substance in which they have intimately wedded and lost themselves, but in which they still continue through the instinctive movement of sensual pleasure to feel each other out and to know one another. In an analogous but less complete way Frédéric, clasping Marie Arnoux's hand, feels "something like a penetration into all the atoms of his skin." Love is a carnal interpenetration in which individuals cease to exist as such, but where the throbbing of a common life continues nonetheless. It throws both lovers equally into a carnal anonymity more than into one another.

The other is therefore first of all bearer and offer of flesh. And he seeks very rarely to evade this role or free himself of that anonymity without which he would fall back into particularity, but also into his insignificance. What indeed is Léon, if not the delicacy of his hands, the down on his cheeks, the physical grace of his person? And what is Rodolphe, if not a certain muscular suppleness and boldness, a scent of moustache, and those two thighs that he molds in his saddle breeches, well aware of his fine points? Emma considers both of them as carnal masses in which she can meet her own desire. They never seem to her like distinct persons, nor even like the bearers or symbols of the opposite sex. In them there is no element of the unknown, nothing of that mysterious appearance that can be conferred on people by the idea one constructs of their otherness or by the feeling that they obey the injunctions of a different sexuality. For her they are only a means of attaining herself. "When he saw her continually beset by passions that he did not share," writes Flaubert about Rodolphe, "he began to feel as though he were a source of excitement for her and nothing else." [20] Excitement—desire skims across the other person without being modified by him. Salammbô goes further still. For her, masculinity hovers in the breezes of the air, the vapors of the evening, the caress of the moon, the entire presence of the world, but in no particular being.

[19] *Madame Bovary,* ed. Pommier, p. 316.
[20] *Madame Bovary,* ed. Pommier, p. 416.

For but a brief moment Mathô simply incarnates that diffuse virility. But the profound movement of his sexuality always leaves Flaubert to drown in the indistinct. The kind of vertigo that Hugo feels before the void of the *Bouche d'Ombre* is felt by Flaubert and his heroes before the anonymous plenitude of matter and of flesh.

The first irritation of desire, however, is some troubling detail, something bizarre in body or speech that had first provoked it. It is in the absence or the presence of particularity that, according to the Goncourts, Flaubert distinguished the *beauty* or *excitement:* "Flaubert, his face aflame, proclaims in his loud, gruff voice that beautiful women are not built for physical love, that they are only good as models for statues, that basically love is made from that unknown quality that produces excitement, but very rarely produces beauty." [21] Beauty triumphs in equilibrium, in the absence of character, in its approach to type. But if what one desires is women rather than statues, this is precisely because in them one finds an element of disequilibrium, a particularity which rouses one.

If the absence of character (according to Winckelmann) is what constitutes the sublime, presence of an individual trait or particularity is perhaps the only cause of passion or excitement. A beauty spot on a woman's cheek is something special and intimate, which makes of her a special being in the midst of all the others. This explains the provocation produced by certain attires, certain attitudes, certain qualities of voice, certain raffish eyes: "I had never seen that before." It is a discovery and, as it were, a new sex added to the other.[22]

This "new sex added to the other"—and Flaubert rarely hit upon a more profound expression—breaks open like a fault the smooth equilibrium of beauty. The first movement of desire kindles curiosity for the unknown. He sees in that "something intimate" the sign of a secret, the promise of something's being hidden behind— a soul, perhaps. And thus the supreme opening will be for him the glance, an open cleft in a mask, a window cut into a dark façade:

The ray of light that would escape in the evening through the crack in the shutter of Emma's house produces for him something of that provocation that is silently aroused by a glance, *by a slitting* of a black mask.[23]

[21] Goncourt, *Journal*, II, p. 197.
[22] Carnets, *Notes de voyage*, II, p. 361.
[23] *Madame Bovary*, ed. Pommier, p. 275.

Here sexuality is no longer a blind drive toward interpenetration but the reply to a mysterious provocation, a movement of discovery and of unveiling.

Very rapidly, however, effusion takes the upper hand. In the numbing wait for desire, as in perceptive attention, the mind soon loses the notion of that particularity which had aroused it and first excited it. His eyes fixed on Emma's shoulder, Léon forgets very quickly that he is he and that she is she:

> The young man's thought sweetly dissolved in the flabby softness of memory, sensation and dreams. And Emma at times *seemed almost to disappear* in the radiation that emanated from her.[24]

As she becomes confused with all the other women whom he has desired or dreamed of, Emma becomes *the* woman herself. The beauty spot is drowned here in the impersonality of the flesh.

It was nonetheless important to note at this point that at the very outset of the movement of desire or of perception, there exists an element of restless curiosity on which Flaubert can rely later on when he wants to resist the inclination of nature or the flesh. It will be enough for him to retain this first movement, detaching it from the satisfaction that follows it, to separate himself from the object or the other person, while maintaining the same passion for them. The inaccessible other, cultivated, however, in the provocation of her distance and in a "painful curiosity that had no limits," will become Madame Arnoux of the *Éducation sentimentale*. And the forbidden object, calcified, held at arm's length, studied in all of the richness of its detail, will become the object of art as the author of *Madame Bovary* wants to recreate it. Both sentimental education and artistic education will save Flaubert from being engulfed in the formless. But we must follow him still a bit further into the liquid universe in which he continues to swim.

Flaubert is not naturally a compartmented man. In him everything communicates, and we may even say that one of the most appealing aspects of his genius is the extreme coherence which always joins his inner experience with concrete experience and metaphorical expression. A statistical study of images, like the one undertaken by Mr. Demorest, indeed establishes that love, especially in the most spontaneous works and in the first drafts of the great novels, is translated most often by metaphors of fluidity and liquidity. And Mr.

[24] *Madame Bovary*, ed. Pommier, p. 279.

Demorest[25] rightly concludes that this preference indicates a certain disquiet, a consciousness of the instability caused by passion, almost a condemnation of love. Even more, it seems to us to translate the essential truth that in its nature and its structure love is a dissolution of one's being. A psychoanalytical study would doubtless produce even more probing results.

Better yet. In the daily life of Flaubert, at the root of his most ordinary tastes and in the most familiar scenes of his novels, we can recognize the same obsession with water as a power of absorption and of dissolution. The atmosphere of the *Turkish bath*, for example, of which Du Bos speaks in his marvelous article on Flaubert and which would as much envelop the person and the life of Ingres as that of the author of the *Éducation sentimentale*, should not be considered purely metaphorical. Flaubert loves steam and warm-water baths:

> The other day I took a bath. I was alone at the back of the room. . . . Hot water was flowing everywhere. Stretched out like a cat, I was thinking of a lot of things. All my pores were dilating tranquilly. It is very voluptuous and there is a sweet melancholy in taking a bath that way with no one else around, lost in those dark rooms, where the slightest noise resounds like a cannon while the naked Kellaks call out to each other and knead you and turn you over like embalmers preparing you for the grave.[26]

The body dilates and becomes numb. Consciousness strays off into semidarkness. One's being yields to a happy passivity; half dispossessed of itself, it becomes its own mummy.

Elsewhere joy is more active, and water resembles an eiderdown of flesh in which the self revels and reaches a reciprocal penetration:

> I took a sea bath in the Red Sea. It was one of the most voluptuous pleasures of my life. I rolled in the waves as on a thousand liquid breasts that touched me everywhere all over my body.[27]

If woman attracts as water does, then the sea caresses like a woman. Flaubert experiences in bathing the pleasure of an incomplete fusion, in which he retains consciousness of his own identity and the sense of dominating the liquid by the conquering play of his muscles. The swimmer cleaves this water to which he lends himself

---

[25] *L'Expression figurée et symbolique dans l'œuvre de Gustave Flaubert.*
[26] *Corr.*, II, p. 140.
[27] *Corr.*, II, p. 209.

and on the surface of which he must remain. The bath is only a prelude to love.

Even more detached is the pleasure of a *boat,* where one is separated and protected from liquid absorption by the thickness of the hull. The boat defies and violates the sea. It even permits itself to drift in it. A boat ride—for example, at the end of *Madame Bovary* —is thus more fitting at moments when love is tranquil than at those when it is overflowing. Lost in the happy void of their sensation, the two lovers strive more to live the moment in a common movement than to absorb each other. The flowing of the river gives direction to amorous effusion. It orients their languor. Water makes them live *with* each other. Thanks to it, and in the flux of all things, they know that they are and move together.

The more violently sensual characters surrender to less common reveries. The boat's hull is a hindrance to them, and so too in the bath the obligation of skimming only the surface of the water. They dream of a deeper, submarine fusion; for example, Louise Roche in the *Éducation sentimentale* murmurs that she envies the *existence of fish.*

> It must be so sweet to be rolling so pleasurably in the water, to feel oneself caressed everywhere. And she shivered with little sensual quivers.[28]

The fish inserts itself into the liquid sheet, flows in it; it adheres to it with all its round body. It is flexible. One might imagine it even permeable, a brother of the snake whose body mimics the waves' undulation and symbolizes so often in Flaubert the soft sinuosity of desire. A famous page of *Madame Bovary* thus describes the descent of a moonbeam into the water of a stream. "And that silvery gleam," writes Flaubert, "seemed to twist down to the bottom like a headless serpent covered with scales." [29] The serpent is a stream within the stream. Salammbô's snake recalls even more directly the lunar divinity. In a similar milky climate, reptility, flexibility, and viscosity unite in a promise of total adherence to the liquid caress. In the *Tentation de Saint Antoine* lust slowly rolls and twists.

Flaubert seldom dreams of running waters, which tear apart one's being before absorbing it, and he is primarily sensitive to *permeability,* the slow movement from one element into another. In water, toward water, the coating of the surface is all, as is continuity, and

---

[28] *L'Éducation sentimentale,* p. 361.
[29] *Madame Bovary,* ed. Conard, p. 274.

the most gradual continuity, the most mysterious continuity still remains that which presides over the very birth of water at its appearance on the surface of a hard object. For certain solids sweat it. And it is by no mere chance that *Madame Bovary* (that novel of "lascivious dampness," of "poor, obscure souls, humid with imprisoned melancholy, like those provincial backyards with mossy walls," [30] in which Flaubert, by his own avowal, wished "to render a tone, that damp color of the existence of woodlice" [31]) takes place in a saturated universe, where everything—sensations, feelings, houses, and landscapes—obeys the great law of oozing. Charles Bovary, for example, concretely oozes boredom and greyness. "The long, fine hairs which gave a velvety nap to his cheeks, like a blond mold . . . blurred his quiet face with a colorless down." [32] A marvelous image, making stupidity visible like a mushroom. But most often this mold does not coagulate in moss or in down. We see it on the surface of things, swelling gradually, acquiring weight, and then suddenly detaching itself and splashing on the ground as a liquid *drop*. An obscure operation, rich with inner echoes of which Flaubert has not stopped dreaming.

The drop is indeed mysterious, to begin with by its very origin. It is born from nothing, or rather, it appears in a pearly bead on those elements that are most radically foreign to it. The enigma of the spring might be resolved in the idea of leveling, the notion of an invisible but imaginable liquid continuity. On the other hand, it is hard to imagine the formation of the drop that wells up on the flat surface of a wall or a rock. Everything in that compact façade would seem to discourage its appearance. And yet it is there, alive and come somehow from elsewhere, a sign that we must go beyond the wall or into it to find the diffuse power that allowed it its birth. Guérin, in the depths of the grotto where the Centaur comes to life, had already been violently aware of the gratuitousness of that arrival and had seen in it a sort of sweating out of life, a gift of the gods. In Flaubert the movement is the opposite: the ego transpires toward things, and the drop forms not at the source but at the zenith of life. It is born of an inner relaxation. It takes its beady shape at the surface of the collapse of one's being. It momentarily appeases one's loss of consistency by embodying it and exteriorizing it. It is a confession of weakness or the overfullness of saturation that can no longer be contained. "I have in my heart," said Flaubert, "some-

[30] *Corr.*, II, p. 17.
[31] Goncourt, *Journal*, I, p. 283.
[32] *Madame Bovary*, ed. Pommier, p. 134.

thing akin to the green sweat on the Norman cathedrals." [33] Thus
we see it flowing in all his scenes of desire, boredom, and death, at
all those moments when one's being, half undone, needs to pull
itself together into an ultimate unity, even one that may be liquid
and ephemeral, before abandoning itself to nothingness. Saturation,
swelling, and suspension just before the surrender to desire: the
drop admirably evokes all those states of being, just as it expresses
all the sprawling heaviness of pleasure when it hits the ground.

After falling in love with Emma, Charles sees in this way the
drops of a spring thaw splashing on the girl's parasol:

> Once, during a thaw, the bark of the trees was oozing in the court-
> yard, the snow on the tops of buildings was melting. . . . She was
> standing at the threshold; she went to fetch her parasol. . . . In the
> cozy warmth down below she was smiling; and one could hear the
> drops of water falling one by one on the taut silk.[34]

Elsewhere, in a scene of happy voluptuousness, Emma looks at the
moonlight, like a "monstrous candelabrum from which there
streamed down drops of molten diamond." The streaming flow of
satisfied maturity which echoes her tender feelings and also echoes
the fall in the night of "a ripe peach that dropped by itself from the
espalier." [35] Fruit swollen with ripeness, the dripping of melted snow
—the movement, saturation, and detachment are all the same. During
the ride that precedes Emma's own downfall, the hooves of her and
Rodolphe's horses "struck fallen pine cones in their path." When
Emma runs to Rodolphe toward the end of the novel to borrow
money from him, "a warm wind was blowing in her face; the melting snow was falling drop by drop from buds on the trees." [36] The
rough draught from which we quote goes on: "An enervating odor
exuded from the humid tree trunks, and she felt ill with dizziness,
desire, and apprehension." [37] Let us go one step further: maturation
becomes rottenness. One's being flows out of itself like an overripe
fruit; it trickles away and is lost in other things. When Emma is
dead, she does not disappear entirely. It seemed to Charles "that she
was vaguely spreading, as it were, outside of herself into surrounding
things, in silence, in the night . . . and in the limpid drops trickling

[33] *Corr.*, III, p. 398.
[34] *Madame Bovary,* ed. Conard, p. 22.
[35] *Madame Bovary,* ed. Conard, p. 274.
[36] *Madame Bovary,* ed. Conard, p. 426.
[37] *Madame Bovary,* ed. Pommier, p. 592.

on the walls." [38] In the same oozing trickle life and death reunite. But the symbolism of the drop does not stop there. It can not only represent movement, but also the very consciousness of desire. Imagination sees it then no longer in its formation and its death, but in its renewal and repetition. For the drop flows drop by drop. It is an element in a series and takes its life from that very process of succession. In the numbing of desire, in the continuity of its own watery movement it brings an element of regular interruption that brings to life a sort of semiconsciousness. Flowing drop by drop, one feels satiated: one does not really lose the sense of satisfaction, but the short free space that the formation of each next drop and each next desire gives allows one to catch one's breath and regain consciousness. Emma and Léon, fixed and frozen in their contemplation of each other, hear in just this way the flowing of the water of a fountain:

> The water that was flowing in the courtyard, as it escaped from the nozzle of the pump, and that was falling drop by drop into the trough, *was marking time like a sort of palpitation.*[39]

The regularity of the *drop by drop* brings torpid feeling half to life; it establishes consciousness of an inner palpitation. A sort of obscure duration is thus born, giving a rhythm to the throbbing of desire— swelling, subsiding—and creates in the continuity of the expansion of love those little shocks of consciousness similar to the light trembling impacts that the movement of oars gives a boat on the river:

> The heavy boat moved on slowly in a series of strokes. . . . The flat oars creaked in the iron oarlocks, and with the breathing of the boatman something like an *equal measure* was being kept in the silence.[40]

Effusion has found its profound rhythm, its "measure." Water is not only the medium of gliding and absorption; it also serves to suggest a living equilibrium of one's being. After her surrender to Rodolphe, Emma felt "her heartbeats starting up again and her blood flowing in her flesh like a river of milk." The happy throbbing of the organism coincides at that moment with the circulation of great free and nourishing streams.

Delicious waters, dangerous waters. Every bath presents a risk of

[38] *Madame Bovary*, ed. Pommier, p. 621.
[39] *Madame Bovary*, ed. Pommier, p. 485.
[40] *Madame Bovary*, ed. Pommier, p. 515.

drowning. Water lulls one to sleep like opium. As Mr. Demorest has clearly shown, the whole novel of *Salammbô* is bathed in an aquatic symbolism. In it Tanit, the female goddess, ruler of the seas and humid things, is opposed to Moloch, the male god of blood and war. In the landscape of the novel, governing strategy and thus the plot, the earth meets with the water on every side and assumes the contours of a peninsula. Salvation, with Hamilcar, comes from the sea. The most surprising episode in the novel, however, the one in which Flaubert's "aquatic complex" is portrayed in the richest detail, is still the account of Mathô's and Spendius's way of breaking into the besieged city of Carthage. As the reader knows, they slip into the narrow aqueduct that supplies the city and through which they must swim to the very end. This corridor, filled with a rapid and stifling stream of water—the water "flows just below the upper flagstone"—is an admirable figure for the image of the liquid tomb that Flaubert's anguish dreads. Being stifled, crushed, dragged under, the fall into a black hole—all these torments of death by water are described here one after the other.

> . . . Then the current caught them. An atmosphere heavier than the tomb crushed their chests and, with their heads under their arms, their knees together, as straight as they could make themselves, they darted like arrows into the darkness, stifling, their throats rattling, almost dead. Suddenly, all was black ahead of them and the velocity of the water redoubled. They fell.

From then on it is complete surrender of the body, abandonment to free whirling movement in space. Death is prolonged; it is a suffocation ever begun anew, a frightfully monotonous alternation of upward and downward movements:

> . . . they fell into deep basins and had to rise again, but once more fell back; and they felt a fearful fatigue, *as if their limbs had, while swimming, dissolved in the water. Their eyes closed. They were in the throes of death.*[41]

Until the moment when they feel beneath their feet something solid to permit them to regain possession of themselves. "At last something resistant was under their feet. It was the pavement of the gallery at the edge of the cisterns."

[41] *Salammbô*, p. 87, 88.

This semidrowning in the dark recalls the equally hallucinatory episode of *Les Misérables* in which Jean Valjean feels himself gradually slipping into the mud of a Paris sewer. Georges Poulet has clearly shown[42] how Hugo also knew the fear of being engulfed, the obsessive thought of a support that gives way under you.

> Fulness is like the void.
> Where then is the prop?

But whereas this sort of dizziness occurs in Hugo as a consequence of the overflowing of matter, an overfullness of being that, unable to immobilize itself in a solid equilibrium, sinks heavily into the abyss, it is in Flaubert the expression of a more permanent anguish. Hugo overcomes it by the sheer joy he takes in plenitude and by flight into the void. But for Flaubert from beginning to end plenitude is like a mounting tide. When Emma, abandoned by Rodolphe, thinks of throwing herself out of the attic window, she feels physically attracted by the void and is possessed by a liquid vertigo: "It seemed to her that the ground was rising in oscillations along the walls." She clung "to the edge, almost suspended, surrounded by a vast space. . . . She had only to yield and give herself up." [43] Death is only acquiescence to that liquid tide that has all along sustained and absorbed life.

> What a satisfaction for her to rely at last on something solid—solider than love.

Just like Spendius and Mathô, Emma desperately seeks salvation beneath her in the pavement that will put an end to her drowning. "She struggled naïvely to find support in something, in her little girl's love or her household tasks." [44] But these efforts are in vain and she knows it: how can one hope to find support outside oneself, if one cannot first rely on oneself? Yet in herself Emma perceives only drifting masses and the to-and-fro movement of troubled waters, but nothing solid or pure. She cannot rely on any sure feeling, for feelings do not exist in themselves, substantially; they simply represent the different affective tonalities through which one's being glides. In this gliding movement it is impossible to detach any

---

[42] *La Distance intérieure,* p. 221.
[43] *Madame Bovary,* ed. Conard, p. 285.
[44] *Madame Bovary,* ed. Pommier, p. 399.

single part or perform any analysis. Feelings cannot be separated: they flow in a turbid coherence in which the eye can distinguish nothing.

If, however, one asks Flaubert to explain how a feeling is born, lives, and dies, what is the law of its passage, he will invoke the stirrings of a sort of liquid agitation by virtue of which new psychological configurations come into being.

> Reminiscences from readings, mystical whims, pulverized affections, all was thus confused in the expanse of that passion. A lot of things both petty and grave, common or rare, insipid or savory, were summed up in it, even as they lent it diversity—and it was like those Spanish salads in which we see fruit, vegetables, and slices of citron all floating in the pale oil.[45]

Doubtless because of the crudity of its images, the sentence was suppressed in the definitive edition and must be given its full meaning by indicating an earlier note: "Everything thus was mixed together in this agitation. . . . It overflowed and intoxicated her." It is thus the flow of inner duration that unites elements of the most diverse provenances and assembles them into a heteroclitic mass. Feeling has no power of synthesis here. It results from an accumulation of tendencies that go on living in it, side by side, without being assimilated into each other, and that will resume their detached life whenever the flood of feeling dries up again. Elsewhere, in the absence of an active passion's guiding movement, psychological change takes place through a sort of fermentation due to excessive stagnation of each sentiment in one's being. "Everything mixed together, all those dissatisfactions, all that fermentation turned into acidity." [46] "Love *turned* into melancholy" [47] A chemical turn, a passing to another liquid state, a simple change of consistency in the stream that never ceases to flow within the self.

I live, then, with the stream, adrift. "I go off from one thought to another, like a dry blade of grass on a river, going downstream with the wave." [48] A slow and heavy stream that is hardly more than a slightly roused boredom. One's existence flows down the slope of a powerless imagination, too easily succumbing to the mechanism of the least authentic associations. Emma's imagination leafs through scrapbooks of keepsakes. There is no profound connec-

---

[45] *Madame Bovary*, ed. Pommier, p. 383.
[46] *Madame Bovary*, ed. Pommier, p. 298.
[47] *Madame Bovary*, ed. Pommier, p. 396.
[48] *Corr.*, II, p. 281.

tion from one image to the next, no enrichment of the present derived from the imagination of the future. The future is accepted as unrealizable, and in the very heart of the most joyous dream one gives in to a sort of feebleness of which one is conscious and which even spoils the pleasure of imagination.

At certain moments, however, and especially in retrospect, the agitating force of reverie creates authentic combinations of being. Adrift on the water, in time and in space, I no longer know where, when, or even who I am. The torpor that possesses me gradually attenuates every notion of my concrete situation. I fall into a semi-lethargy in which time and place are obscured. Sometimes it is before falling asleep that this detachment takes place. Emma, for example, dreams half asleep that she is dozing away in another place, in some luxurious house, the presence of which she soon feels about her:

> For by some *double and yet simultaneous perception,* her thoughts fused with her actual surroundings, and the woolen damask curtains turned into silk damask, the tapers on the mantel into silver-gilt candelabra, etc.[49]

The mixture of place and settings turns her illusion into reality for a brief instant. But most often it is an exterior movement that provokes somnolence, such as the swaying of a diligence that is carrying a traveler away. Charles Bovary in the cabriolet taking him in the early morning toward father Roche's farm; Emma in the carriage on the return trip from the Vaubyessard ball or in the Yonville diligence after her long days of lovemaking with Léon; Frédéric in the diligence from Nogent to Paris: all let themselves drift away in the confusion of dozing. "His hopes, his memories, Nogent, la rue de Choiseul, Madame Arnoux, his mother, all seemed to blur together." [50] For Charles Bovary even more precise sensations come together in an inextricable confusion:

> He relapsed into a warm somnolence in which he was still aware of his most recent sensation and saw himself simultaneously a married man and a student, lying in his bed beside his wife as he had just been and also busily striding through a roomful of patients. He felt simultaneously the operating table beneath his elbow and the pillow of his bed. He smelled the odor of poultices and that of his wife's

[49] *Madame Bovary,* ed. Pommier, p. 288.
[50] *L'Éducation sentimentale,* p. 142.

hair. . . . And all this blended, became one, seeking at the bottom
of it all some troubled desire that could not open its leaden wings,
while the confused memory wheeled about down below in him.[51]

From this admirable text, which is itself something of a pathetic
effort to render through awkward and heavy words that "confused
something" that slowly turns beneath them, we can draw two principal indications. The first is concerned with the concrete solidarity
of the present, lived experience and the relived experience remembered from the past. Sensation and memory are experienced simultaneously, merge into a *oneness:* "They oscillate in harmony, one
floats in the other," as one of Flaubert's corrections reads, like two
liquids intimately mixed together. But it is hard to believe that so
perfect a mixture is the result of chance. Between that present sensation and the past memory there must exist a certain essential analogy
that through the intermediary of dozing provokes their juncture.
That odor of the poultice which at the same time *is* the perfume of
hair situates the sensation-memory in a climate in which sensibility
is no longer distinguished from disgust. The same reaction of disgust
envelops the two sensations, each enriched by the special nuance of
nausea, one medical, the other sexual, that the other one brings it.
Let us remember that pomade is like the very dough of desire, and
we shall find easily in a poultice a perfume of bitter pomade. Charles
no longer desires his first wife, who is, after all, also whining and
sick. Elsewhere, in a more wakeful state, that will be the metaphor
that will be loaded with these profound associations. Here we are
in advance of the metaphor at the stage of substantial identity.

Even more important is the final notation of disturbed desire,
the confused memory that "turns about down below." Corrections
in the text make this more precise: "Desire grown dull and merging
with something persistent and obtuse," "which struggled vainly in
the depths of consciousness," "to rise again to the surface, to see
daylight," in an effort similar—and here is the revelatory metaphor
—to that of "lifting heavy eyelids that keep closing of their own
weight." [52] The tragedy of someone half suffocated, wanting to rise
up toward air and light, but whose apathy always drags him down
again. The memory enveloped in uneasiness ("Charles was trying to
recall the fractures he had seen and how to go about treating them")
seeks to penetrate the opacity of the mind. It struggles against the
double tendency toward osmosis and collapse that characterizes every

[51] *Madame Bovary*, ed. Pommier, p. 152.
[52] *Madame Bovary, Ébauches et fragments*, I, pp. 53-54.

liquid life. Consciousness wishes to draw the memory toward it, to bring it to its surface, to expression; but its own weight rejects it into its troubled sleep, into that depth where language cannot penetrate. An effort at self-uprooting a bit like that of a man in quicksand trying to extricate himself or an acrobat whose limbs are coated with lead. "While writing this book, I am like a man playing the piano with balls of lead fastened to every joint of his fingers." [53] It is in just this way that when one leaves the bath one's body seems to weigh three times as much. Everything urged Flaubert toward fluid facility, but for that very reason he chose to write the books "for which he has the least talent." For him writing is an emerging of consciousness, an awaking of the mind.

And it is by describing his own sleep, by taking himself as object and spectacle that he best succeeds in awakening. Most of Flaubert's characters are numbed by a powerful sottishness. They "stagger as though exhausted," [54] possessed by an "invincible torpor like those who in other times took some fatal philtre," [55] "bewitched individuals with a sort of fog in their heads" and whom "neither priest nor doctor can cure." [56] The catoblepas indeed dominates Flaubertian creation, for all these torpid characters finally devour themselves through their own laziness. In their own death one sees them collapse at last. Emma, for example, does not succumb to the mechanical fatality of money, like the victims of a Balzacian novel. She is lost through weakness and negligence and above all by lying—that lying "which is like quicksand; you have barely set your feet in it and it has reached your heart." [57] Her death in fact is very exactly and pathologically such an engulfment in quicksand: "the steps of the staircase [in Rodolphe's house] seemed to give way under her feet"; the furrows of a field appear like "enormous waves spreading about her. The earth under her feet was softer than water, and she was astonished not to sink into it." At the same time—and here we should compare the text with Flaubert's letter to Taine in which he describes the symptoms of his nervous attacks—"her soul abandoned her, everything she possessed by way of reminiscences, images, combinations, escaped all at once, like the thousand fragments of a Roman candle." "She felt her soul escape." [58] Death is that complete dissolution that sleep, sensation, and love had only anticipated. One

[53] *Corr.*, III, p. 3.
[54] *Corr.*, III, p. 49.
[55] *Salammbô*, p. 38.
[56] *Madame Bovary*, ed. Conard, p. 152.
[57] *Madame Bovary*, ed. Pommier, p. 547.
[58] *Madame Bovary*, ed. Pommier, p. 597.

bids farewell to one's self and renounces self-possession. "We disappear into the dew, the breeze, and the stars," speculate Bouvard and Pécuchet. In a sense there is nothing more familiar nor even more reassuring, since from the moment of birth the Flaubertian soul has never ceased dying. It has lived through a succession of faintings. Death is an "uninterrupted swoon." [59]

[59] *Bouvard et Pécuchet,* p. 294.

# Flaubert: Spleen and Ideal

## by Harry Levin

*Alternativement,* the undulant adverb that dangles like a signature at the end of *Hérodias,* subsumes the creative rhythm of Flaubert's career. Alternately is the word; and the alternation starts from, and returns to, *La Tentation de Saint Antoine.* On the rebound from his grandiose and abortive first attempt, he goaded himself into writing *Madame Bovary.* Then, recoiling by way of the second *Tentation,* he plunged into the voluptuous archaeology of *Salammbô.* After that, in the penultimate year of the Second Empire, came *L'Éducation sentimentale:* after the Inexpiable War of Carthage, the anticlimax of Paris in 'forty-eight. The realistic alternative was always for him *malgré lui,* and his kind of realism would be described by Sartre as "the condemnation of reality." On the other hand, at a time when Zola and the Goncourts were already raising the banners of naturalism, Flaubert fell back impenitently on the presumptions of an old-fashioned romanticism. To George Sand he subscribed himself "an old romantic," and to the Princess Mathilde he wrote: "For lack of the *real* one tries to console oneself through *fiction.*" After the Revolution of 1870, his literary reaction was to publish the definitive version of the *Tentation.* Having thereby given his private solace of almost twenty-five years to a world which was far from eager to have it, he might well ask himself again what was now being asked of the century: what next? Was it not, on both personal and public grounds, a time for realism with a vengeance? He considered a culminating project based upon a contemporary theme, such as *Under Napoleon III* or *The Bourgeois in the Nineteenth Century.*

His ultimate commitment, *Bouvard et Pécuchet,* was the belated counterpart of *La Tentation de Saint Antoine,* in that it became a vow and an onus, a wager with himself and a way of life. During his last decade, Flaubert lived it intensely, though distracted from it by ills and losses, and deviating from it toward more colorful and more tractable projects. The most successful of the deviations, indeed his one unqualified success with the immediate consensus of critics and readers, was the *Trois Contes*. Each of these miniatures, which took him no more months than the novels had taken him years to compose, was a pendant to one of the larger works. *Hérodias* was to *Salammbô* what *Un Coeur simple* was to *Madame Bovary*, as Jules Lemaître pointed out; it should be added that the same relationship holds good between *La Légende de Saint Julien l'hospitalier* and *La Tentation de Saint Antoine*. Yet nature makes no sudden jumps; Flaubert's alternations were not clean breaks from book to book, or from historical costume to *complet bourgeois*. It was the essence of his binocular vision to bring the past to bear on the present, and vice versa by turns, superinducing the contrasts implicit throughout his work, which become explicit among the *Trois Contes*. That double perspective, which sets him apart from his fellow prose writers, finds its unique affinity among the poets. It is much more than caprice that so often prompts us to cite Baudelaire when we discuss Flaubert. The novelist, in his quest for themes and values, alternates across a sliding scale which the poet, in the main section of his *Fleurs du mal*, has designated *Spleen et idéal*. Realistic spleen, romantic ideal.

Splenetic by disposition, Flaubert met with more and more to inflame his irritation. In his fifties, he retained no resemblance to the Viking Apollo of student days. Prematurely old and grossly paunched, red-faced and bald-headed, with heavy eyelids and drooping mustachios, he had only to look into a mirror to be reclaimed by the spirit of caricature. Among increasing bodily complaints, he suffered from shingles, more appropriately diagnosed in his case as Saint Anthony's fire. His old friends, wherever they were, seemed to be dropping off. He lost his cherished mother, who—despite his occasional protests against "le culte de la mère"—had centralized his bachelor's existence. His favorite niece, who had grown up under his tutelage, had married a man who proceeded to fail in business; willingly, and without much thanks, the uncle spent his available assets to help them. His income from his books was negligible: 500 francs for the first five years' sales of *Madame Bovary*. Some financial assistance was finally obtained for him, somewhat to his embarrassment, through a nominal post at the Mazarine Library. His half-hearted attempts in the theater merely confirmed his membership in the select group of *auteurs sifflés*, with Zola, Daudet, Goncourt, and Turgenev. But Flaubert was inured to artistic rebuffs, and stoical in facing domestic anxieties. What he blanched before, what he fulminated against, was the national calamity: the defeat of France by Germany, the ensuing fall of Louis Napoleon, and the scarifying interlude of the Commune. For a month and a half of the occupation, Prussian officers were billeted in the ivory tower at Croisset.

It was a crisis which offered the fullest scope to Flaubert's inherent pessimism. His esthetic credo had disavowed the claims of the fatherland upon the artist. Nationality would be regarded as an anachronism in the cosmopolitan future, he had written to Bouilhet from Athens twenty years before. But, with the Franco-Prussian War, he professed himself a French patriot. "Seriously, bestially, brutally," he wanted to fight; he drilled with the militia; he felt within him the warlike pulsation of that Indian blood which, he liked to boast, had been brought into the family by *voyageur* ancestors. As the wave of invasion subsided, and France once more was subdivided against itself, he lapsed into the old feeling of impotent anger. The revolutionary tradition had come full circle; the Commune would revert to the Middle Ages; "the International will triumph in the end, but not as it hopes or as one fears." Nor could he be cheered by the precarious birth of the Third Republic. Impartially, he called down plagues upon the contending parties of both the socialist left and the Catholic right. He made his principal play, *Le Candidat,* an acrid satire on universal suffrage, with its attendant graft and demagoguery. Small wonder that the playwright never achieved the popularity for which he made so inconsistent a bid. Hating all catchwords, he bridled at the prevailing one, democracy, because it exalted grace at the expense of justice, as he put it: social standards were debased by egalitarianism masquerading as Christian charity. "The whole dream of democracy," he argued with George Sand, "is to elevate the proletariat to the level of stupidity of the bourgeoisie."

That argument, for all its disparities, turned out to be his most fruitful meeting of minds. George Sand, surviving her own tempestuous generation, had ripened to a mellow humanity far surpassing her brittle heroines. No one in his succession of male confidants, with the probable exception of Turgenev, could have been rated as Flaubert's peer. None of her actual lovers seems to have touched such responsive chords of womanly insight. For his part, he derived more warmth from her than from any mistress. She was his senior by seventeen years, as Louise Colet had been by thirteen and Elisa Schlésinger by eleven. In the four years between his mother's death and George Sand's, her maternal intervention was the decisive influence upon him. It is she, among his various correspondents, whose letters have proved worthiest of being reprinted with his; and if the *Correspondance* constitutes a writers' bible, as André Gide has said, Flaubert's Old Testament severity has been alleviated by George Sand's evangelical sympathy. She is the *cher maître,* whom he respectfully addresses as *vous;* he is her *vieux troubadour,* with whom she uses the intimate *toi.* To her he confides his self-questionings, along with the terrible doubts that history has been casting up at their feet. How can we any longer believe in science, progress, civilization itself, after the devastating passage of these latterday Huns?

> Ready-made phrases are not lacking: France will rise again! We must not despair! It is a salutary punishment! We were really too immoral! Et cetera. Oh, eternal balderdash! No, there is no recovering from such a blow! I feel affected to the marrow!
> If I were twenty years younger, perhaps I would think otherwise, and if I were twenty years older I should be resigned. . . . All the friends I had are dead or lost. I no longer have any center. Literature seems to me an empty and useless affair. Shall I ever be in a condition to take it up again?
> Oh, if I could only fly to a country where one would see no more uniforms, hear no drums and talk about no massacres, where one was not obliged to be a citizen! But the earth is no longer inhabitable for poor mandarins.

So runs his repeated plaint, which ranges from self-pity to a cynical contempt for the world. When she softens before the spectacle, he assumes a hard-boiled tone, and advises her to cultivate hatred. But the master, unwilling to write off a lifetime of humanitarian idealism as no more than a lost illusion, takes her mandarin disciple firmly to task through a printed *Réponse à un ami.* Why talk so much about classes? The people include you and me.

> No, no, one cannot isolate oneself, or break the ties of blood, or curse or scorn one's kind. Humanity is not an empty word. Our life is composed of love, and to give up loving is to give up living.

And so, betwixt misanthropy and philanthropy, the dialectic alternates. Pressing her charge of self-isolation, the philanthropist makes it a touchstone for their respective attitudes: his desolation as against her consolation. That is a distinction which the misanthrope will not accept. If his theories sound impersonal, if his characters look satirical, it is not because he lacks conviction. On the contrary, he has all too many ideals, and perhaps they are all too exacting. It may be a mere pedantic quip to sign a letter "Bourgeoisophobus," but it is a serious ethical proposition to maintain that "hatred of the bourgeoisie is the beginning of virtue." Such a conception of virtue may seem perverse, and must be difficult to put into practice, especially for one who has been born and bred a thoroughgoing bourgeois. Hence the conflict of the two Gustaves, and the preference of the inner idealist for past epochs and exotic climes. The history of the world, Flaubert had grown fond of saying, comprised three stages: "Paganisme, christianisme, muflisme." His terms for antiquity and for the Middle Ages are decently neutral. His term for modernity is scarcely translatable: *un mufle*, literally an animal's muzzle or snout, is slang for a boor. It is our decadent fate to live in the heyday of boorishness, an epoch which Flaubert elsewhere characterizes as "utilitarian, military, American, and Catholic as well." His pursuit of ideals had led him back to the pagan Salammbô and the Christian saint Antoine. In the same light, Emma Bovary and Frédéric Moreau must be looked upon as protagonists—or, since they are more acted upon than acting, as his agonists—for the age of *muflisme*.

To take up literature again in his final period, under conditions more bleakly antipathetic than ever, was to vent his spleen more fully, to concentrate more directly upon a pair of active *mufles,* to vomit on his contemporaries—in Flaubertian phrase—the disquietude that they inspired in him. "It is indignation alone that sustains me," he explained to George Sand's son, as well as to Edmond de Goncourt, who came closer to sharing his vein. But the indignation itself was hard to sustain indefinitely. In a gentler and more consolatory mood, he set aside *Bouvard et Pécuchet,* and turned out *Trois Contes* within an eighteen-month period between 1875 and 1877. All three of these tales are legends, or saints' lives, in one way or another. *La Légende de Saint Julien l'hospitalier* is the earliest and most conventional. Not an expressionistic dialogue like the *Tentation,* it is a simple narrative whose concluding sentence brings the narrator close to home, with the acknowledgment that he has been animating a stained-glass window devoted to Saint Julian in the Rouen Cathedral. This is a reversal of the direction set by the trysting lovers when they flee from that brooding monument in *Madame Bovary,* evading a moral sanction which Julian seeks. *Hérodias* marks another return to the same ecclesiastical auspices, drawing its iconography from a sculptured tympanum of Salome and

Saint John. Sinners and saints are played off against one another in the ancient tale; in the medieval legend, the sinner becomes a saint. Unlike the self-denying Anthony, Julian acts rashly and brutally. His redemption likewise has its artistic symbolism, if we recollect Flaubert's earlier remark about the current state of literature: "It would take Christs of art to cure that leper."

But the parable, responding to George Sand's benevolence, is primarily social rather than esthetic. At the other extreme from Anthony's withdrawal is Julian's "need to mingle with the existence of others." The surfaces of the story, naïve as a folk-tale, are richly decorated by its large and varied bestiary, like illuminations on vellum. The mute suffering of animals, which preoccupied Flaubert as much as Vigny, is caused by Julian's wanton cruelty. Through a dreamlike sequence of hunting scenes, pursuer and then pursued, he moves toward their fated revenge upon him. His sin is vastly bloodier than the Ancient Mariner's, and accordingly his expiation is more sacrificial. The primitive theme of unwitting parricide has continued to fascinate such moderns as Thomas Mann in *The Holy Sinner*, Albert Camus in *Le Malentendu*, and Robert Penn Warren in *The Ballad of Billie Potts*. For Flaubert it is something more than a ritual drama between generations; it foreshadows the guilty introspection of Proust on his mother's death. The purge of Julian's guilt, through the leper's embrace, is not without its Proustian undertones. In a broader sense, the moral is pointed by the fraternal gesture. Thus the life-denying tendencies are redeemed by the positive aspects of *La Légende de Saint Julien*, just as they are upon the subtler plane of *Hérodias*. The remaining *conte*, which is substantial enough to qualify as a *nouvelle*, is *Un Coeur simple*. Written between *La Légende de Saint Julien* and *Hérodias*, it ushers in the collective volume, which proceeds backward from the modern to the medieval and ancient. Yet *Un Coeur simple* is no less concerned with sainthood than the others. The most affirmative of Flaubert's writings, it is his counterstatement to *Madame Bovary*.

Its simple heart is the very antithesis of Emma's yearning confusion. The dignity of labor, the self-sacrifice, and the good will so fleetingly exemplified in the novel by the old peasant woman, Catherine Leroux, these are the qualities that make servitude a vocation for Madame Aubain's Félicité. Although the Goncourts had prided themselves upon portraying a servant, their Germinie Lacerteux was presented as a sordid sinner. Flaubert's exemplary figure has been remembered from his boyhood, and from the maid-of-all-work who held together his great-aunt's household at Pont l'Eveque. There is such a person in many a well-established bourgeois ménage, upholding its traditions while it disintegrates. There is "nothing heroic" about Flaubert's portrait, not even the moment when the sometime farm-girl rescues her charges from an assaulting bull. Her sympathetic links with the animal kingdom are an intrinsic part of her religion: "she loved the lambs more tenderly through love of the Lamb, and the doves because of the Holy Ghost." Her capacity for love, personally frustrated, lavishes itself on her mistress's children—the boy is a disappointment, the girl dies young—and on a nephew who goes to sea and never comes back. Her sole comfort, as old age and loneliness and deafness close in around her, is the bright and noisy parrot, Loulou. Unwanted by a departing neighbor, the bird for her is "virtually a son, a lover." In its death, preserved by taxidermy, it becomes a fetish, and ultimately a pious offering on a festival altar. As she herself lies dying, it becomes the outlandish incarnation of Félicité's religious devotion; and the apotheosis of the parrot is her vision of the Paraclete.

When she insists on bearing her grotesque burden through the winter night to Honfleur, and is laid prostrate on the Norman road by a flick from a passing coachman's whip, we are reminded not only of the Blind Man struck down behind Emma's coach, but of the crucial seizure that took Flaubert under strikingly similar circumstances. That flash of secret identification may throw some light on what Victor Hugo meant when he declared that Flaubert reveals the soul by combining the ideal with the real. In these succinct annals of forty-odd years, his realism functions at its least eventful and its most meaningful levels. "Monotony of their existence—little facts," he has jotted among his notes. The selected details, the faded souvenirs and damaged relics, are symbols of spent emotion, treasures hoarded in Félicité's room and guarded by her stuffed parrot. Each object, such as the little plush hat of the dead daughter, has its moving association with the family. Dissociation, the disjunction of feelings and ideas, is Flaubert's customary mode of treatment: compare Félicité's death-bed scene with Emma's. For once he has allowed his pity to get the upper hand over his irony; yet the genius of irony had its stroke of revenge; he had sought uniquely to please George Sand, who had not survived to read the tale. *Un Coeur simple,* at all events, has won the widest acceptance as a model of technique for shorter fiction. Ezra Pound testified for his generation, when he averred that it "contains all that anyone knows about writing."

*Three Lives,* the most convincing of Gertrude Stein's efforts to let
the inarticulate speak for itself, was roughly modelled on *Trois
Contes.*

Release from his demons was temporary for Flaubert. With the
opuscula finished, published, and widely admired, he had no excuse
for not turning grimly back to the unfinishable opus magnum, the
child of spleen, *Bouvard et Pécuchet.* From the contemporary night-
mare he could see no means of prolonged escape. When he collab-
orated on a musical fantasy, *Le Château des coeurs,* it was set in
the unmythical land of Pot-au-feu and dominated by the savor of
that homely stew, "emblem of material interests." He had announced
to Turgenev, "1870 has turned a good many people into fools or
imbeciles or angry men. I am in the latter category." As an *enragé,*
he conceived it his duty to put folly and imbecility in their place;
but it was a vicious circle; and he became all the more enraged
while contemplating the targets of his rage. "The work that I am
producing could be subtitled *Encyclopedia of Human Stupidity.*
I am overwhelmed by the undertaking and permeated by my subject," he told a neighbor. The parrot could somehow replace the
dove, in the eyes of saintly simplicity; and yet, to keener observers,
that displacement would carry with it a shocking implication,
scarcely hinted at in *Un Coeur simple* but writ large in *Bouvard et
Pécuchet.* Is the divine afflatus to be identified with the chattering
squawk of repetitious mimicry? Has the Logos of civilization been
addled by its own cult of Loulou: a mindless parroting of words, a
meaningless re-echoing of sounds, a gigantic case of psittacism? No
one can ever have labored more strenuously than Flaubert to validate
the Word. His was a rear-guard action against the devaluation of
language, the *mot juste* against the cliché. Parrots, like monkeys,
engage in the crude imitation of human beings. Such antics have
the additional consequence of reducing the realists to mimetic absurdity.

Ezra Pound recommended *Ulysses* to a French public by recalling
*Bouvard et Pécuchet.* He seems to have had in mind the creation of
a verbal medium out of subliterary materials. James Joyce has since
put forward an even more challenging example of echolalia in *Finnegans Wake.* Flaubert also anticipated Joyce in becoming, as Valéry
impatiently remarked, "haunted by the demon of encyclopedic
knowledge." Documentation in previous undertakings had been
incidental and specific, filling in a historical background or lending
concreteness to some technical matter. Research for *Bouvard et
Pécuchet* was more systematic and comprehensive; everything in

print was grist for the slow-grinding mill; and Flaubert counted some 1500 books which he would have read for no other reason. He was apparently garnering an album of citations, which might well have discouraged an up-to-date Faust from going on in the arts or sciences. Moreover, and we must not confuse the different sorts of documents, he had compiled a dictionary of accepted ideas, *idées reçues,* into which he would dip for turns of phrase we recognize in his fictional conversations. These banalities, in *Madame Bovary* and *L'Education sentimentale,* are highlighted by the sardonic narration; if *Le Candidat* seems painfully flat, it is because the dramatic form does not permit such relief. The *dictionnaire* is an alphabetical listing of clichés and howlers, prejudices and half-truths, hasty generalizations and popular fallacies—a fairly heterogeneous body of statements and misstatements. On the whole, its outlook is consistently philistine: literature is defined as "occupation of the idle." Yet occasionally the encyclopedist resumes his own caustic voice, defining optimist as "synonym for imbecile."

It is hard to imagine any individual who would, seriously and simultaneously, hold both of those contradictory opinions. It would be the bourgeois who confounded art with idleness, and consequently it would be Flaubert who was the implied pessimist. The fact that certain notions are accepted does not make them either false or true; it simply warrants their banality; and Flaubert could still be enough of a romanticist to rank interesting falsehoods above banal truths. As an angry man, his problem was to impersonate the mentality of the fools and imbeciles; and since it was not easy to keep up a dead-pan impersonation, now and then we seem to overhear the author's asides. In any case, as his readers, we are expected to share his suspicion or scorn of what he is exhibiting. This cajoles us into a superior position, which can be a sequestered one. It is quite likely that every country or era, however brilliant it may seem at a distance, has its ideology of platitudes, which the satirist refuses to suffer gladly. Swift's *Polite Conversation* comes to mind for Augustan England, or Mencken and Nathan's *American Credo* for the United States in the nineteen-twenties. These could take the convenient and flexible shape of a manual or a corpus, whereas Flaubert strove to build a work of fiction around his collection of bromides. He may have followed the Balzacian example of *Le Cousin Pons,* where the two old musicians wander into the trammels of legalistic complication. More to his point would have been Musset's *Lettres de Dupuis et Cotonet,* where the partnership of stolid citizens sets up a romantic school of its own, and proceeds to dabble through a sequence of fads and follies. The immediate model seems to have been *Les Deux Greffiers,* a humorous fiction about the bucolic retirement of two clerks of court.

M. Homais would not soon be forgotten; yet, as the mouthpiece of the bourgeoisie, he had played chorus rather than protagonist. Le Garçon, the hypertrophied vulgarian, lingered on as a joke from adolescence; his outrageous twentieth-century embodiment would make a theatrical impact in Alfred Jarry's *Ubu roi.* But Flaubert's heroes had shown, particularly in the two versions of *L'Education sentimentale,* an innate disposition to hunt in couples. The writer whose own personality was split between *deux bonshommes* had a Noah-like addiction to pairs and braces. He had first thought of his testamentary novel as *Les Deux Cloportes,* the two woodlice. Then, needing a couple of appropriate surnames, he had gone through the usual onomastic search. Bouvard was cognate with Bovary, and with the title of the Count de Bouvigny in *Le Candidat.* What a shame that the home-made cordial, "Bouvarine," which might have immortalized François-Denys-Bartholomée Bouvard, was such an unmitigated fiasco! As for Juste-Romain-Cyrille Pécuchet, he might have traced his name to the Latin *pecus,* meaning herd of cattle, and therefore harmonizing with *bos, bovis,* an ox. It was rather embarrassing when an actual M. Pécuchet materialized in connection with Flaubert's depleted finances. But names have their fates, as MM. Bouvard and Pécuchet realize, when they introduce themselves to each other by deciphering their respective hatbands. Characteristically, their initial action is to sit down on the boulevard bench where they meet. There they discover that they are colleagues, not to say predestined soul-mates. Happy coincidence! each is a copying-clerk, one of the white-collared legion of petty employees, on whom the paper-work of business and government depended in Flaubert's day.

Though they will engage in various feats and be discovered in odd postures, they are by occupation as sedentary as heroes could possibly be. The circumstance that henceforth pairs them off, for the reasons that Bergson has analyzed, renders their joint adventures automatically absurd. The threat of suicide, at the nadir of their fortunes, becomes nugatory when both attempt to hang themselves at once, and is capped by anticlimax when, at the last minute, they decide that they must first draw up their wills. If Flaubert could have finished *Bouvard et Pécuchet,* sighed Hérédia, France would have had its *Don Quixote.* This evocation, though it was inevitable, starts to waver just as soon as we wonder which would be the knight and which the squire. Pécuchet would appear to have the advantage, when he pops out of their amateur museum with a pot on his head for a helmet; but it is Bouvard who commonly takes the initiative; and the two are differentiated with a nicety which assists their interplay as a comedy team. Bouvard is more typically bourgeois, corpulent and confident, more the man of the world and the man of property. Pécuchet is the highbrow, angular and diffident, highstrung, liberal, and—until an unfortunate episode—virgin. His intellectual aspirations predispose him to be a victim of physical discomfitures at the lowest comic level; when the right manure is not forthcoming from the local stables, he is not too proud to seek it out at its source upon the highroad. Whereas it is the irrepressible Bouvard who, blandly proposing to the shrewd widow, Madame Bordin, calls her attention to the convenience of having two sets of linen already marked with a B: "Let us unite our initials."

The clerks, released from copying by a windfall, undertake the townsman's classic relocation amid the countryside, and thereupon open up a maximum opportunity for the assorted humors of maladjustment. They pursue their dizzily parallel courses through a series of hobbies, which involve the major branches of practical and polite learning: agriculture, science, archaeology, belles lettres, politics, sex, metaphysics, religion, pedagogy. Bouvard and Pécuchet are autodidacts and self-helpers; all they know is what they have been reading; but they have been reading omnivorously; and they endeavor to carry out their homework methodically and quixotically. In each successive sphere the theories are spun, the experiments are set up, and the explosions logically follow. The experimentalists are slapstick-prone; they are gifted with the preposterous touch that turns gold to dross; things are foreordained to fall apart in their maladroit hands. Inanimate objects seem to display ingenuity, as well as malice, in avenging themselves upon such well-meaning and vulnerable creatures with such a flair for getting in everybody's way. When they fail to cure a hunchback by camphor, we are moved to recall Charles Bovary's failure with the club-footed Hippolyte. That was a specific disillusionment which, in *Madame Bovary,* was diffused into a general consciousness of ineffectuality. The generalization is completed, in *Bouvard et Pécuchet,* by taking a long view of many ridiculous instances. Flaubert ended by humorously accepting what was so bitter and depressing to the naturalists: the losing quarrel of men and women with things. In the early flush of their transplantation, the partners indulge in the national pastime of landscape gardening. Alas! the results are all too symptomatic of man's failures to improve on nature:

> In the twilight it was something frightful. The boulder occupied the lawn like a mountain, the tomb formed a cube in the midst of the spinach, the Venetian bridge a circumflex over the kidney-beans, and the cabin beyond a large black smudge—for they had set fire to its thatched roof so that it would look more poetic. The yews, in the shape of stags or armchairs, lined the way to the lightning-stricken tree, which extended crosswise from the hedge to the arbor, where tomatoes were hanging like stalactites. Here and there a sunflower displayed its yellow disk. The Chinese pagoda, painted red, seemed like a lighthouse on the mound. The peacocks' beaks, struck by the sun, reflected its beams; and behind the lattice, unframed by its slats, the flat fields bounded the horizon.

Naturally, this vista makes an unfavorable impression upon the Norman neighbors who, from chapter to chapter, forgather to pronounce the judgment of common sense. They are recognizable types with predictable responses: the mayor, the squire, the doctor, the priest, the widow—and, weaving in and out somewhat drunkenly, the workman Gorju, who is both a serviceable rogue and an emergent radical. The retired Parisians never manage to sink their roots in the village of Chavignolles. Like Emma at Yonville: "They were generally scorned." When they splash through their self-taught course in hydrotherapy, naked as savages, the villagers peek in and are scandalized. The latter, after all, are the choric spokesmen of public opinion, which Flaubert characterized in a letter to Turgenev as "the eternal and execrable *on*." It is a function not unlike the role of the anonymous "they" in the limericks of Edward Lear, whose cue is to express loud disapproval of the leading character's eccentricities. Bouvard and Pécuchet seem to grow more earnest, as their enthusiasms and innovations persist, and Flaubert seems to grow more expressly critical of their provincial critics. When the Revolution of 1848 reaches Chavignolles, his *bonshommes* sympathize with it—and so, evidently, does he. He goes out of his way to include a mordant episode where the priest brings clerical pressure to bear on the freethinking schoolmaster. He is scathing in his depiction of the venal traffic in religiosity. His political conclusions are summed up symbolically when Bouvard and Pécuchet inspect the attic of the town hall, where plaster busts of Napoleon, Louis XVIII, Charles X, and Louis-Philippe lie discarded and dusty, behind some faded flags and a fire extinguisher.

Judged by the results of the culminating experiment, the book is an anti-educational novel, a *Bildungsroman* in reverse, wherein little is learned and nothing forgotten. In a burst of humanitarianism, Bouvard and Pécuchet adopt two children, and enter the arena of pedagogical controversy. Needless to say, Victor and Victorine prove to be precociously vicious brats, and the methods of their guardians are more inept and ineffectual than ever. Here Flaubert may have been ruefully glancing at his thankless relations with his niece and nephew-in-law. The intolerable situation further deteriorates into an adverse lawsuit, and then the text breaks off. From a detailed synopsis, we learn how Flaubert planned to round out the story. There would have been a scene—of the sort that Ibsen was even then dramatizing—in which the two reformers lectured their fellow citizens. Pécuchet would be pessimistic, Bouvard optimistic; the audience, convinced by neither, would be more hostile than ever; and the upshot would be scandal and stalemate. Yet, out of the depths of the ex-clerks' dejection, will come their simultaneous inspiration: "To copy, as in former days." The handy Gorju will make them a double desk; and, as the novel is scheduled to end, they are getting down to work: sitting down, of course, and resuming the contemplative posture, like two monks in a medieval scriptorium. What will they copy? It has been surmised that the *Dictionnaire des idées reçues* had been collected for that purpose, and was originally intended to appear as a second volume. It has also been conjectured that *Bouvard et Pécuchet* was itself envisaged as a prolegomenon to Flaubert's *sottisier*, the compilation of foolish extracts from famous writers.

But the anthology reads as if it were gathered for private amusement, while the dictionary has been drawn upon for commonplaces scattered through his other works. The ten extant chapters of *Bouvard et Pécuchet* make up a compact tome, which would be amply proportioned if the outline had been carried through. As the book stands, it has been thoroughly seasoned with fatuities quoted from both learned and vulgar sources. It seems possible that, if he had only been able to elaborate the sketchy final pages, Flaubert would have fulfilled his original design, *da capo al fine*. Speculation will never be conclusive; as it happened, the enterprise was literally interminable. When Turgenev and other friends advised him to cut it short, Flaubert replied with weary complaints about the trouble it gave him, yet insisted that it would be his terminal achievement. That it should terminate ambiguously seems altogether fitting. Insofar as it sends its protagonists back to work, to working without philosophizing, it re-enacts the ending of *Candide,* which Flaubert deemed "the greatest moral lesson that exists." Happily for the workers, this does not mean cultivating their garden; nor does it seem to mean a resumption of their former secretarial jobs. Presumably the copying will be done for copying's sake, at their parrot-like leisure, the imitation of imitation with no ulterior aim. Something like a circular movement is indicated, as it is on the last page of *Finnegans Wake;* and, just as Joyce parodies himself in Shem the Penman, so the mute farewell of Flaubert to literature is the scratching of his copyists' pens. His documentary labors had their reward in the historiographic guide of Langlois and Seignobos, where a footnote cites the unfinished monograph on the uninteresting Duke of Angoulême by Bouvard and Pécuchet.

Tiresome fellows! They bored their creator to death. Why then must we recapitulate their wasted motions, their magpie accumulations, their courses in self-improvement which left them worse off than before? Because we are their heirs, willy-nilly, because so much of our cultural heritage seems to have reached us via their copying-desk. It is not for nothing that our printers and publishers refer to manuscript as "copy." Nineteenth-century criticism, deeply immersed in the dense context of Bouvard and Pécuchet's dabblings, could afford to dismiss them as soulless clowns in cotton nightcaps. It is significant that twentieth-century reconsideration seems to be treating them more respectfully and sympathetically. Raymond Queneau has devoted three prefaces to their defense and eulogy. René Dumesnil, the dean of Flaubertistes, would concede that "they have the souls of apostles," while so cogent an intellectual spokesman as Lionel Trilling would enroll them in the company of Flaubert's saints. Without undercutting the hierarchy so freely, we may accept them as the ill-starred champions of culture in its late and mechanized phase. If they begin like Don Quixote, they conclude like Saint Anthony. Slaves to words, they graduate to deeds, are repeatedly overthrown, and return to their clerkly regimen. Yet, in the quixotic process, they have educated themselves; they have been schooled in the incompatibility between their ideal, which extends promiscuously across the whole realm of belief, and the spleen of circumstances, which is to be encountered in all things and in most men and women. "Then"—and the realization significantly coincides with the sight of a dead dog, which plunges them into their most abysmal despair—"a pitiable faculty developed in their minds, that of noticing stupidity and no longer tolerating it."

The Flaubert who wrote that sentence has clearly come out, if but temporarily, on their side; and it is one of the great reversals, like that of Swift, when he joins the horses against mankind. As soon as the issue was formulated between the newcomers' iconoclasm and the natives' routine, Flaubert's sympathies left him no other choice. Bouvard and Pécuchet were as dear—and as repugnant—to him, in their middle-aged foibles, as were Frédéric Moreau and Deslauriers in their youthful illusions. The parting recognition of *L'Éducation sentimentale,* "We were better off then," might no less appropriately have brought his testament to a close. In both cases, the situation is archetypal: a pair of dilettantes surviving their own innocence and weathering the undeceptions of the century. Such a duality seems to have been ingrained within Flaubert's innermost sensibilities. Through his celibate life ran a pattern of intimate friendships, from his adolescent "fraternal love" for Ernest Chevalier to the mature and mutual admiration between him and Turgenev— a pair of "moles burrowing in the same direction." In the line of literary companions, the most devoted was Louis Bouilhet. A minor poet and mediocre playwright, Bouilhet projected a poem on the congenial theme of *Le Boeuf* and dedicated his Lucretian *Fossiles* to Flaubert. They were exactly the same age, looked alike, and—what was most important, given their isolation—Bouilhet visited Croisset every Sunday. The death of this trusted adviser in 1869 was a crushing loss to Flaubert. He reacted, in bourgeois fashion, by campaigning for a commemorative monument at Rouen. When the Municipal Council balked, he poured out the vials of his anti-bourgeois wrath, denouncing them—in a phrase, he borrowed from Heine—as "conservatives who conserve nothing."

But the ideal is never far from the spleen. Turning away from bourgeoisophobe invective, Flaubert paid his personal tribute to Bouilhet in 1870 by prefacing his posthumous *Dernières Poèmes.* The preface says what it can to burnish the dim Parnassianism of the verse, and it puts some Flaubertian critical judgments into Bouilhet's mouth. Its peroration is pure self-revelation, addressing a poignant appeal to younger writers:

> Are there two young men anywhere who spend their Sundays reading the poets together, telling each other what they have been doing, plans for the works they would like to write, comparisons and phrases and words that have come to them—and who, though scornful of

everything else, conceal this passion with a virginal shyness? Let me offer them a word of advice:

Walk through the woods side by side, declaiming your verses, intermingling your souls with the moisture of trees and the timelessness of masterpieces; lose yourselves in the reveries of history, in the bewilderments of the sublime! Enjoy your youth in the arms of the Muse! Her love will console you for others, and replace them.

Afterward, when you have felt the accidents of this world, if they seem transposed into illusions for you to describe, so that everything, including your existence, seems to have no other use, and you are resolute for all affronts, ready for all sacrifices, armed for all ordeals, then venture, publish!

Then, whatever happens, you will view the miseries of your rivals without indignation and their glory without envy; for the less favored will console himself by the success of the more fortunate; he whose nerves are strong will sustain the companion who is discouraged; each will contribute his own accomplishments to the common store; and this mutual record will prevent vanity and put off decline.

Finally, when one of the two is dead—for life was too beautiful— let the other carefully preserve his memory in order to make it a bulwark against meanness, a refuge for weakness, or rather a private chapel where he will go to whisper his worries and relax his heart. How frequently at night, when staring into the darkness beyond that lamp which lit their two foreheads, he will vaguely seek a shade to ask him: "Is it right? What should I do? Tell me!" And if this memory is the eternal food of his despair, it will at least provide company for his solitude.

That lurking shade at the edge of the lamplight could not have been Bouilhet, though he must have played his loyal part in the composite remembrance. Rather, it was the alter ego within Flaubert, who had worn various external faces and had sometimes disappeared altogether. As between the *deux bonshommes,* it was the austere perfectionist, the self-created tutelary colleague, the idealization of the artist. By its very nature, it was a disembodied and depersonalized conception. "I believe that great art is scientific and impersonal," Flaubert disagreed with George Sand. "The first comer is more interesting than Gustave Flaubert," he flatly maintained, to this woman who was so much more interesting than her writings. ". . . The man is nothing. The work is everything." Yet the work was probably not quite so perfect as he desired it to be, and the man was a notable personality in spite of that constraining other self. His flat assertion that he had no biography is contradicted by all the contemporaneous witnesses. True, he seemed warm-hearted to the warm-hearted Zola and calculating to the calculating Goncourts.

But those reflexive testimonials, viewed across a temperament, show the interaction of a stronger temperament. Flaubert's all too human self, the pedestrian *bonhomme,* is his own best witness through the *Correspondance,* where—in contrast to the fastidious standards of taste that he propounds there—the tone is as torrential as Rabelais, and now and then as coarse. Writing *currente calamo,* without revision or reservation, he veers from the savagely indignant to the thumpingly enthusiastic. It is an unwonted pleasure to watch the erstwhile purist register conviction with so inexact and emphatic an adjective as "enormous," spelled *hénaurrrme!!!*

André Gide professed his willingness to trade Flaubert's novels for his letters. When the same revaluation is echoed in Proust's novel, it takes on the overtones of what a horrified Flaubert might have called an *opinion chic.* Paul Valéry restated it more concretely by declaring that he preferred Saint Flaubert to Saint Antoine. However, a writer is never wholly separable from his writing, any more than he is wholly identifiable with it. Granted that there are degrees of proximity, Stendhal is at the opposite pole from Flaubert: a persona rather than an impersonal force, improvising rather than revising, gaining his effects through pace and spontaneity rather than deliberation and plasticity. The more deliberate procedure does not exclude the more casual impulses, as is evident from Flaubert's worksheets. His style is the end-product of an arduous process of refinement, into which he has poured his sensibilities "drop by drop," in the metaphor of Remy de Gourmont, leaving nothing of himself but the lees. The inference is that the best of himself has been absorbed into the writing, which completes the life; the work perfects the man, even as *A la recherche du temps perdu* will resolve the imperfections of Marcel Proust. The resolution is less a depersonalization than, in Sartre's term, an objectivation. So Flaubert's realism obtains the effect of impersonality less by impassively watching than by aggressively resisting his environment. And the cost of such resistance comes high: an austere renunciation of selfhood and a tense estrangement from those assumptions and satisfactions which interlink the lives of most other men. Some of his more orthodox commentators have condemned this propensity as a form of suicide—a condemnation supported by literal rumors, among his fellow townsmen, as to the manner of his death.

But Flaubert, who died a thousand deaths with every book, also lived with each one a thousand lives. The pride that he took in his calling must be measured by its demands for sacrifice and discipline, as he rigorously augmented them. In a world where traditional values had been profaned, an epoch when so little was held sacred, what had survived uncorrupted from the past, if not art? What could durably be handed on to posterity, if not "sacrosanct literature"? This required the ministrations of a special priesthood, whose votaries had more often been the adherents of poetry than of prose. The originality of Flaubert's contribution was that it succeeded in consecrating that upstart genre which had heretofore been assigned to a modest, if popular, rank among the powers and dominions of literature. Others had done much, and others would do more, to broaden the sociological scope of the novel—Balzac, Zola—or to intensify its psychological penetration—Stendhal, Proust. With due regard for both and for other components, Flaubert brought them under the strict control of artistic technique. By establishing the norms that prose fiction could reckon by, insofar as it would be practised by artists, he established himself as "the novelist's novelist." That authoritative epithet was bestowed by Henry James, through whom the cycle revolved to Proust and Joyce, after whom the prospect is still unclear. It seems clear enough by now, however, that the mandarins have all passed. Probably we shall not look at first hand again upon the like of their incisive detachment, their elaborate cultivation, or their dedicated artistry. The retrospect has slightly dimmed already, so that it is becoming equally hard to understand why *Madame Bovary* was prosecuted and how it was ever produced. Some of our novelists, pursuing different aims and feeling pressures Flaubert never felt, wax impatient over his cult of stylistic perfection. He is by no means beyond their criticism. Yet to criticize him, as they should be aware, is to criticize nothing less than the novel itself.

# Art and Hallucination in Flaubert

*by John C. Lapp*

On a cold evening in January 1844, Gustave Flaubert was driving with his brother along a country road near Pont l'Évêque. Suddenly, as a farmer's cart loomed up out of the dark, he dropped the reins and slumped unconscious to the floor. For several hours afterwards he lay as if dead, and when he awoke, weak and sweating, he told of strange visions: a thousand images and the bursting of dazzling lights, "like a fireworks display." This was the first of a series of attacks, resembling in several details the lesser form of epilepsy known as *petit mal*, that were to recur with some frequency for about ten years, while he was completing the first *Éducation sentimentale*, *La Tentation de Saint Antoine*, and *Madame Bovary*.

Although it is well known that Flaubert suffered from these convulsive seizures, no complete or detailed attempt has been made, as far as I know, to demonstrate the extent to which he exploited them and the phenomena which characterized them. René Dumesnil has declared, without elaboration, that Flaubert very clearly used his nervous malady, "through a phenomenon of auto-observation," to create images. D. L. Demorest, in his work on Flaubert's imagery, refers frequently to the hallucinations, but makes no detailed examination of their use.[1] It has occurred to me, although I am aware that this is dangerous ground for the literary critic, that it might be of value to try to determine with some exactness just how the hallucinatory experience affected Flaubert's art. Fortunately for our purpose, he carefully described the sensations accompanying them in several letters, in particular those he wrote to Taine when the latter was gathering data concerning the artistic imagination for

[1] René Dumesnil, *Gustave Flaubert, l'homme et l'œuvre*, Paris, Desclée et Brouwer, 1947, pp. 450-2; D. L. Demorest, *L'Expression figurée et symbolique dans l'œuvre de Gustave Flaubert*, Paris. Conard, 1931, p. 472.

*De l'Intelligence.* . . . The best known of these, and the most
frequently quoted, will forever serve as an example of the novelist's
identification with his characters: "When I was describing the poisoning of Madame Bovary," wrote Flaubert, "I had so strong a taste
of arsenic in my mouth, I was so truly a victim of the poison myself,
that I had two attacks of indigestion; real indigestion, too, for I
vomited my dinner."

Taine received a number of other letters from his friend concerning hallucination and artistic creation from which he did not quote,
and which have come to light only in recent years.[2] These contain
careful descriptions of Flaubert's own hallucinations and their accompanying sensations, and are thus directly relevant to any attempt
to discover the relationship between his attacks and his imagery.

If I had been asked, before reading these letters, which of Flaubert's works would best lend itself to a study of this kind, I would
have been tempted to answer *Madame Bovary.* First of all, for its
richness of imagery; it is, as Thibaudet has said, "of all his novels,
the only one to provide a cluster of images." And secondly, I feel
that what Lionel Trilling has remarked of the neurotic artist in
general is applicable to Flaubert and *Madame Bovary:* "the more
a writer takes pains with his work and the further he removes it
from the personal and the subjective, the more—and not the less—
he is expressing his unconscious." [3]

This feeling was confirmed when I first read the letter to Taine in
which Flaubert most vividly recalls his hallucinations. After describing, without knowing it, what modern psychiatrists would call his
"aura"—"there's always terror, you feel your personality is escaping,
that you're about to die"—he writes:

> Suddenly, like a thunderclap, there is the invasion, or rather the
> instantaneous irruption of memory, for hallucination, properly speak-
> ing, is nothing else but that, to me, at any rate. It is a sickness of the
> memory, a letting loose of what it hides. It seems as if everything in
> one's head bursts at once, like a thousand rockets in a fireworks dis-
> play, and one hasn't the time to watch these inner images rushing
> furiously past. On other occasions, it begins by a single image which
> increases in size until it finally covers objective reality, as for example,
> a spark which flies about and becomes a great flaming fire. In this last
> case, one may quite easily be thinking of something else at the same

[2] G. Flaubert, *Correspondance. Supplément,* ed. R. Dumesnil, J. Pommier et
C. Digeon (Conard, 1954, 4 vols.), III, 90-6.
[3] "A Note on Art and Neurosis," *Partisan Review,* XII (1945), 45.

time, and this may be almost identical with what we call "seeing black butterflies"—that is, those round bits of satin that some people see floating in the air when the sky is gray and their eyes are tired.

The reader will have seen at once how very similar this is to Emma's fearful experience just before her fatal visit to Homais's capharnaüm with its waiting jar of arsenic:

> All the thoughts and memories in her mind came rushing out to-gether, like a thousand rockets in a fireworks display. She saw her father, Lheureux' office, their room, another landscape. Madness was taking hold of her. Terrified, she managed to pull herself together, though in some bewilderment, for the very thing that had brought her to this frightful condition, her need of money, she could not recall. Only in her love did she suffer; through the thought of that she felt her soul escaping from her just as the wounded in their last agony feel life flowing out through their bleeding wounds.
> Night was falling. Rooks flew overhead.
> All at once it seemed as if the air were bursting with little globes of fire, like bullets, flattening out as they exploded. Round and round they went and finally melted in the snow amid the branches of the trees. In the centre of each the face of Rodolphe appeared. They multiplied, bore down upon her, penetrated her. Then everything vanished, and she saw the lights of the houses glimmering far off through the fog.

The one striking image in this passage that is not found in the letters to Taine (although he speaks there of his "personality escaping," and compares the rapidity of the images to the flow of blood) Flaubert had already used in writing of his seizures to Louise Colet (December 27th, 1852): "I have often distinctly felt my soul escaping, as one feels the blood flow out through a bleeding gash."

Another character, earlier in the novel, has an hallucination, but of a non-violent type, the kind Taine called "benevolent." In the last of the four questions he addressed to Flaubert, he wrote:

> No doubt you are familiar with the intense but tranquil images, and the benevolent hallucinations that precede sleep. As one dozes off after dinner, or while poking the fire, one can quite easily notice them, one is still conscious enough. Does the artistic and poetic intuition or image, as you know it, differ greatly in intensity from these? Or is it only that these hallucinations or images on the threshold of sleep lack order, are unsummoned by the will?

Here is Charles Bovary on his way to Les Bertaux farm in the grey light of early morning:

> . . . On the leafless branches of the apple-trees birds sat motionless, ruffling their little feathers in the cold morning wind. The flat countryside stretched as far as the eye could see; clumps of trees round the farmhouses made patches of dark violet at distant intervals on that vast grey surface which merged at the horizon into the sombre tones of the sky. From time to time Charles opened his eyes. But then, his senses growing weary and sleepiness automatically returning, he soon went off into a kind of doze, wherein recent sensations were confused with memories, and he saw himself as two selves [*se percevait double*], student and husband at once—lying in bed as he had been an hour ago, and going through a wardful of patients as in the old days. A warm smell of poultices mingled in his consciousness with the green odor of the dew, the sound of the iron curtain rings on hospital beds with his wife sleeping.

The dozing Charles's "benevolent" hallucination does not, of course, include fiery visions. But what features do these experiences of Charles and Emma have in common? In both, what strikes one immediately is a characteristic simultaneity evident first of all in the use of background. It is against a dim screen of dawn or twilight sky that in Emma's case, fiery visions explode, or in Charles's, birds with ruffled feathers perch on deeply etched bare branches. Without relating them to the seizures, Faguet aptly called Flaubert's landscapes "precise," possessing "the relief, the sharp angles and contours of objects in a dream, seen suddenly against the dark curtain of sleep." This sharpness of contour depends on the use of background, and Flaubert's characteristic use of the tiny detail against a dull surface has manifold effects, since it occurs in the most disparate passages. If he wants to suggest the calmness and immobility of a summer afternoon he sketches the thin legs of insects on lily pads; if he would show ironically how far the indolent nobility have retrogressed from their glorious ancestors, he describes not the paintings in the busy billiard-room at La Vaubyessard, but only the fine cracks in the canvases.

The landscape itself exists simultaneously with and independently of the inner visions, which are themselves simultaneous. Charles sees himself as two selves, *at the same time* a student and a married man. The pictures from Emma's past burst *all at once* upon her consciousness like a thousand fireworks going off. And in both passages the subject retains a sensorial anchor to the real world; as Flaubert told Taine: "In a hallucination pure and simple, you can easily see an unreal image with one eye, and real objects with the other," and again: "you can easily be thinking of something else, *at the same time.*"

Besides this characteristic simultaneity, this co-existence of the real and the visionary worlds in which mental visions are superimposed upon reality, we may list as typical of the hallucinations: (1) Visual, aural, or olfactory memories, lacking chronological order, and (2) Unreal visual phenomena, especially lights having a whirling or hovering movement.

We may now consider how *Madame Bovary* reflects these characteristics. The hallucinations involve questions of time; not only do they have simultaneity, they consist, in Flaubert's own words, of a "sickness of the memory"—a brutal invasion of the past. The time scheme of the novel itself seems to reflect certain of these temporal characteristics. For one thing, there is a recurring pattern of simultaneity, and it is this pattern more than any other single factor that effectively prevents the novel from having any real forward movement. A famous example of Flaubert's simultaneous technique, in which the see-saw from one level of action to another dissolves the narrative sequence, is the "symphony" of the *comices agricoles* [agricultural fair], which has already been discussed by Joseph Frank in his pioneer article on spatial form.[4] But despite Frank's conclusion that "with this one exception, the novel maintains a clear-cut narrative line," the technique reaches far beyond the single instance he cites. Besides Binet's lathe, famous as a symbol of monotony, but even more an ironic accompaniment to the crises in Emma's life, we have the many occasions on which Flaubert juxtaposes sounds and actions, like the clinking of cutlery from Homais's dining-room as Emma is finding and devouring the arsenic. The technique may even be extended to dialogue, as in the long scene when Emma first meets Léon at the inn, and two conversations (Charles and Homais, Léon and Emma) go on at the same time. In general, Flaubert thus evokes the inevitable presence of indifferent society, so that Emma's actions, which taken singly might seem dynamic and forward-moving, are muffled by the contrasting habitual actions of the Binets and the Homais.

A similar ironic counterpointing, on a vaster scale, is achieved by his use of the present tense in the description of Yonville at the

[4] J. Frank, "Spatial Form in Modern Literature," in *Criticism: The Foundations of Modern Literary Judgment*, ed. M. Schorer, J. Miles and G. McKenzie (New York, Harcourt Brace, 1948), pp. 379-92.

beginning of Part II. The town as described is not contemporaneous
with the heroine, but with the author and the reader; its permanence overwhelms Emma's subsequent actions: "Since the events
that we are about to relate, nothing, in fact, has changed in Yonville," etc. Thus Flaubert establishes the pastness of all the actions
to follow. The future towards which Emma looks with such antici-
pation is really a past, and the progression Tôtes—Yonville is
robbed of its dynamism.

If the novel's vertical rather than horizontal time-scheme can be
related to the simultaneity of the hallucinations, the action itself can
be described in terms of Emma's futile struggle against the "sickness
of the memory," ending in a final triumph of past over present. At
carefully selected moments, beginning with the ball at La Vaubyessard, external stimuli confront her with images out of her past. The
very first instance reminds one unmistakably of the hallucinations,
with its suggestion of an inability to distinguish past and present:

> Then the recollection of Les Bertaux came to her. She saw the farm,
> the muddy pond, her father in his smock beneath the apple-trees, and
> she saw herself, as before, skimming cream off the milk in the dairy.

It is true that a moment later the splendour of the ball blots out
these memories, and the present, overshadowing the past, implies
future triumphs:

> . . . in the dazzling splendour [*fulgurations*] of the present moment,
> her past life, until now so clear in her mind, began to slip right away
> from her, and she could not quite be sure it had ever happened.

but this supremacy is short-lived. As the novel continues, Emma's
look is increasingly backward. Neatly balancing and seemingly intended to recall the earlier passage are the homely images of the farm
that crowd in upon her consciousness as she reads a letter from her
father long after her marriage and first unhappy love-affair:

> . . . she could almost see her father bending down over the hearth
> to pick up the tongs. How long it was since she had sat at his side, on
> the settee by the fire, holding a stick in the great crackling furze
> flames. She remembered summer evenings filled with sunshine. The
> foals whinnied as you passed, and went galloping, galloping away.
> . . . Under her window was a beehive, and sometimes the bees, cir-
> cling in the light, would bounce against the glass like golden balls.

What happy days! What freedom! What hope! How full of illusions she had been!

If we contrast two other passages, similarly balanced one against the other, we shall see how Flaubert depicts the gradual disintegration of her personality through different degrees of obtrusiveness of the past. Just before her visit to the village priest Bournisien, she hears the Angelus and at once she is lost in memories of convent life. Certain verbs (*elle se rappela, elle aurait voulu*) show that she still retains control, that her summoning up of the convent scenes is at least partially willed, but in the last lines there is already a hint that the anchor is dragging:

> The repeated sound of the chimes sent the young woman's thoughts roaming among old memories of her childhood and school days. She remembered the altar at the convent, the tall candlesticks that dwarfed the flower vases and the tabernacle with the little columns. She wished she could vanish once more into that long line of white veils broken here and there by the stiff black hoods of the nuns bowed over their prie-Dieux. At mass on Sundays, whenever she raised her eyes, she had seen, through the blue-grey swirls of incense rising, the gentle face of the Virgin. Moved by the memory, she felt soft and limp as a feather whirling in the storm, and it was quite unconsciously that she was drawn in the direction of the church, prepared for any act of worship, if only it would absorb her soul and swallow up her entire being.

Much later, as the liaison with Léon is drawing to a close, when she sits down for a moment beside the convent of her youth, she slips quite effortlessly into a swirl of memory images:

> What calm in those days! How she envied the ineffable feelings of love that she used to try, according to her books, to imagine! The first months of her marriage, her rides through the forest, the viscount waltzing, and Lagardy singing, all passed before her eyes. . . . And Léon seemed as far away as the others.

After all her possessions have been seized, and she has taken refuge with the nurse, Mme Rolet, she must actually ride the wave of images to reach the immediate past:

> One day, with Léon. . . . Oh! how far away it all was . . . the sun was shining on the river and the clematis gave off its perfume.

. . . Then, carried off by her memories as by a boiling torrent, she soon succeeded in recalling the day before.

In these instances the automatic influx of memories appears as a sign of Emma's disintegration, as a preparation for her death, and they produce a dream-like, supra-temporal quality. But Flaubert imparts a hallucinatory tinge to Emma's triumphs as well as her defeats. These triumphs are, of course, sexual, and it is significant that Flaubert frequently described his sensations during an attack in sexual terms. In this connection there is the very explicit and revealing comparison in a letter to Taine between his aura and the sexual act, as well as a similar, though more veiled statement to Louise Colet;[5] and a phrase he wrote to her, describing, not his feelings during a hallucination, but his contentment after a rendezvous with her—"In my soul I had oceans of cream"—should also be borne in mind when we consider the following passage, quoted by G. Poulet as an example of "duration that spreads out," [6] one which seems to occur independently of the flow of time:

The shades of evening were falling. The setting sun shining through the branches, dazzled her. Here and there around her, in the foliage or on the ground, hovered spots of brightness, as if humming-birds had shed their wings in flight. Silence was everywhere; a softness seemed to breathe from the trees, and she could feel her heart beginning to beat again, and the blood flowing inside her flesh like a river of milk.

There is scarcely need to point out the elements typical of the hallucination: the dark background, the hovering spots of light. The odd final simile becomes clarified in the context of the phrase to Louise Colet and Flaubert's frequent comparison of his sensations to the blood flowing from a wound.

Emma's first awareness of sexual power had been accompanied by a hallucinatory experience; as she sat with Rodolphe in an upper room of the Town Hall she caught sight of L'Hirondelle, the stage coach that had borne Léon away to Paris:

She had a vision of him at his window across the way. Then everything blurred, clouds passed; and it seemed to her that she was still

---

[5] *Corr. supplément,* II, 94, and *Corr.* (ed. Conard), 3ᵉ série, IV, 77.
[6] G. Poulet, *Studies in Human Time,* tr. E. Coleman, Baltimore, Johns Hopkins Press, 1956, p. 248.

circling in the waltz, in the glare of the chandeliers, on the Viscount's arm, and Léon was not far away, he was just coming.

At the same moment, Rodolphe's pomade, of an odor similar to the Viscount's, excites in her vague sexual desires:

> Her old desires became imbued with the sweetness of the present sensation, and on this subtle breath of perfume that was being shed upon her soul, they were whirled about like grains of sand in a gust of wind.

In the first of these quotations we note the deliberate confusion of real and visionary in the phrase "everything blurred; clouds passed," and of course once again the verbs of whirling.

The imprint of the hallucinations is frequently found where the author is not immediately concerned with unusual affective states in his characters. What may seem purely expositional passages, such as the chapter describing Emma's identification with the Romantic heroines of history and fiction, suddenly fall into the pattern when we read that these women "stood out like comets in the shadowy vastness of history." Leo Spitzer may have spoken truer than he knew when he called this simile "an impressionistic, almost schizoid picture of world history." [7] In the same chapter swans on a lake in one of Emma's illustrated books "stand out in relief like white excoriations on a steel-gray background." Of his whirling lights Flaubert told Taine, we remember, that they may occasionally be confused with what people call *les papillons noirs*—[black butterflies] —"those round bits of satin that some people see floating in the air when the sky is grey and their eyes are tired." From this derives one of the most startling images in the novel, startling not merely for its evocation of the physical scene, but because it conveys Emma's mood of detachment, her hypnotized upward gaze as she watches, against the background of the fire-back, the floating ashes of her discarded wedding-bouquet:

> She watched it burn. The little cardboard berries popped, the wires twisted, the braid melted away and the shrivelled paper petals hovered like black butterflies against the back of the fireplace.

Of significantly similar texture and movement are the passages describing the scattered pieces of Emma's note, falling upon a field of

[7] *Modern Language Notes*, LXVIII (1953), 583-90.

red clover "like white butterflies," and the cloud of flies whirling in the bright air of afternoon just in front of Emma and Léon as they walk along the river.

The reader will have noticed in the passages already quoted that the turning movement is frequently expressed by verbs like *tourbillonner* [whirl], which evoke related images of wind and water. Very early in the novel Emma feels "an intangible unease that changes like the clouds, whirls like the wind." The incense upon the convent altar rises in bluish whorls, and in the same passage she feels lax and abandoned "like a bird's downy feather whirling in the storm." Past desires whirl through her mind "like grains of sand in a tempest"; when she is on the verge of leaping from the attic window, "The blue of the sky filled her; the air whirled through her vacant head"; she is carried off by her memories "as by a boiling torrent." Or again the swirling movement combines with Baudelairean metaphors in which the heart or the soul is an empty building or an abyss: the blind beggar's cry, "penetrated to the depths of her soul like a whirlwind in an abyss."

In describing his hallucinations, Flaubert linked the whirling motion to sensations like Emma's sinking feeling ("the ground beneath her feet was softer than a wave"): "Such a whirlwind of ideas and images rushed through my brain, it seemed my consciousness, my very being was sinking, like a vessel in a storm." [8] (Poulet is surely right to call the circle image "the essential image through which the Flaubertian imagination expresses the relationship between the world and the being.") In his letters describing his seizures, Flaubert never referred to sensations like Emma's sinking feeling, or to her abnormally acute sense of hearing. In moments of stress she hears the pulsing of her own arteries, and Rodolphe's letter crumpling in her hand crackles like sheet metal. Perhaps in the latter case, recalling the auditory phenomenon that accompanied his seizures (the sound of cart wheels), he hit on this method of conveying his character's tension. And to intensify the characteristic sensation of the blood flowing through his veins by making it audible (in an interesting reminiscence of Poe)[9] would have been a relatively simple step.

In a less specific way, the strangeness of certain metaphorical passages becomes explicable in the light of our knowledge of the hallucinations. The two-page description of Emma's melancholy fol-

[8] *Corr.* 4ème série, V, 180.
[9] Cf. *Corr.*, 4ème série, V, 169: "I have felt and *seen* everything in Saint Theresa, Hoffmann and Edgar Poe; I fully understand hallucinated people."

lowing Léon's departure for Paris reveals many typical ingredients. In the beginning, "everything seemed wrapped in a dark haze which hovered vaguely over the surface of things," and her sorrow is compared to the winter wind howling in abandoned castles. She recalls La Vaubyessard "when the quadrilles whirled through her head," and her visions of Léon, though still controlled and orderly visual and auditive associations, have the quality of hallucination. There follows that strange metaphor, extending through two long paragraphs, in which Emma's love is a traveller's fire on the Russian steppe, the metaphor Thibaudet despairingly called "the longest and the most laborious in the French language." Yet this fantastic structure becomes at least understandable when we recall the content of Flaubert's visions. Its very involutions remind us of the chaotic images he described; here, as in the hallucinations, a flame glows against a large expanse; ennui is spatialized. The search for the dry wood of memories past and present ("the remotest reminiscences as well as the most recent occasions") to feed the fire of love prefigures the "sickness of memory," and the fading of her emotion, like the aftermath of the visions of whirling lights, is a shivering darkness and cold.

At this juncture I should like to say that, although I have restricted the scope of this essay, I do not mean that any discussion of the particular images considered here should henceforth be confined to the context of the hallucinations, although I think a case can be made for calling Flaubert's style "hallucinatory" rather than "apoplectic," as Kenneth Burke has proposed. It is quite likely, for example, that the "river of milk" image discussed above could be related to various images involving rivers or streams. And as I have tried to suggest by linking the "simultaneity" of the hallucinations with the novel's time-scheme, their impact undoubtedly goes far beyond the close verbal relationship between Flaubert's description of his visions and his metaphorical language in the novel. It would not, I believe, be far-fetched to see in the structure itself, consisting as it does of a series of crescendi and decrescendi—big moments followed by let-downs—a reflection of Flaubert's successive periods of relative good health, sudden attacks and *détentes*. Flaubert may have had this in mind when he described his heroine's sufferings, after Léon leaves for Paris, as "the pain that is caused by the interruption of any habitual movement, the abrupt cessation of a long vibration."

It should also be emphasized that the question of realism is not pertinent here. Had Flaubert been creating a character who suffered from some sort of nervous malady of which hallucinations would be symptoms, he could have been presumed to have been aiming at scientific realism in the manner of Zola. But Emma's hallucinations are not intended to suggest physical ills; of her final traumatic experience Flaubert says, simply: "she suffered only from her love." Thus, apart from the multiple instances where his own visions coloured his descriptive language, even the abnormal visions of his character remain in the realm of metaphor: they are remarkably effective metaphorical representations of states of mind.[10]

Perhaps the most obvious reason why, of all Flaubert's works, *Madame Bovary* reflects the hallucinations most prominently[11] was that of all the characters this "grand féminin" created, Emma was closest to his own nature; "Madame Bovary, c'est moi" was no *boutade*. The Correspondence suggests another reason. We are frequently told that the writing of *Madame Bovary* had cathartic properties for its author; it was to purge him of Romanticism, and so forth. But it may well have had a therapeutic value of another sort. Despite periods of despondency, Flaubert never lost confidence in his own power of reason. In the series of letters we have discussed, he told Taine that he had frequently rid himself of his seizures "by force of will." Elsewhere he actually asserted that he was responsible for his own recovery. While it is impossible to tell accurately what the span of the illness was, he seems to have stopped having attacks some time between 1852 and 1857.[12] In a letter dated May 18th,

[10] There are, to be sure, dangers in this method. Emma's final hallucination is prepared for by the many hallucinatory moments we have noted, by her frequent alternations between calm and distress, suggestive of the *aura*. But Flaubert lends certain of his symptoms to Farmer Rouault as well. Nothing whatever has led us to suspect that this "stout little fifty year old man" would twice fall down in a faint, first at the news of Emma's poisoning, and then at the sight of the funeral cloth, or that en route to her bedside he should suddenly see a vision of her lying dead in the middle of the road!

[11] Perhaps because *La Tentation de Saint Antoine* is so overtly *about* hallucinations the Saint's visions are elaborate structures having little in common with Flaubert's. A final image in the work does recall Emma's vision of Rodolphe's face in the fiery globes: "In the very disk of the sun there shines the face of Jesus Christ." Cf. J. Seznec, *Nouvelles Études sur la Tentation de Saint Antoine*, London, Warburg Inst., 1949, p. 89, for a discussion of this vision. In the first *Éducation sentimentale* there occurs a hallucinatory passage when the hero, wandering by moonlight, meets a strange dog whose eyes dart fire, then grow and take on human form (Paris, Conard, 1910), pp. 251-2. Curiously the fire-darting eyes are not only present in *La Tentation*: "Two red arrows seemed to dart from Hilarion's eyes"; but in *Madame Bovary*: "She fixed upon Charles the flaming barbs of her eyes, like two red arrows about to be shot."

[12] Probably in 1854. He wrote to Mlle Leroyer de Chantepie, March 30th, 1857: ". . . at twenty one I nearly died of a nervous illness . . . it lasted ten years." (*Corr.*, 4 ᵐᵉ série, V, 169).

1857, he confided to Mlle Leroyer de Chantepie how he had brought about his own cure:

> You have asked me . . . how I cured myself of the nervous hallucinations I suffered from. By two methods, (1) by studying them scientifically, that is, by trying to understand them fully, and (2) by strength of will. I have often felt madness approaching. In my poor brain there was a whirlwind of ideas and images in which it seemed my consciousness, my self, was sinking like a vessel in a tempest. But I clung to my reason. It dominated, although beaten and besieged. . . . I conquered the malady by coming to grips with it.

Might we not be permitted to interpret this "scientific study," this triumphant "coming to grips" with his malady as the artist's successful attempt to transform his experience, to exorcize its spell by endowing the world of his novel with its sensations and visions? Without this struggle, of course, the hallucinations would have little importance. They were an occasion, an impersonal factor like the condensations of moisture on the horizon which produce sunsets. As William James once said, to the majority these illuminated bits of cloud will suggest supper-time, to a few, heroes' deaths. That Flaubert happened to combine artistic genius and a nervous malady is far from unusual; that he strove, with a large measure of success, to sublimate his abnormal experiences in his novel's characterization, structure and imagery, offers yet another reason why he is unique among novelists.

# Madame Bovary

## by Charles Baudelaire

### I

In the realm of criticism, the situation of the writer who comes after everyone else, the writer in arrears, holds some advantages not enjoyed by the prophetic writer, who heralds success and produces it, so to speak, by the authority of his boldness and devotion.

Mr. Gustave Flaubert no longer needs devotion, if indeed he ever did. Many artists, among them some of the most perceptive and most highly accredited, have praised and honored his excellent book. Criticism now need only suggest some forgotten points of view and stress a bit more forcefully than has been done some elements and insights that have not yet in my opinion been sufficiently praised and commented on. Besides, there is a paradoxical charm, as I was trying to hint, in this position of a writer behind others, coming at some distance after. Freer because he is isolated like a laggard, he has the appearance of recapitulating debates, and because he is obliged to avoid the vehemence of accusation and defense, he is under orders to blaze a new path without any other stimulus than that of justice and love for the beautiful.

### II

Since I have pronounced that splendid and terrible word, Justice, let me be allowed—also because I find this very agreeable—to thank the French magistracy for the shining example of impartiality and good taste that it has set in this circumstance. Called upon by a blind zeal, too vehement to be called morality, by a spirit which had mistaken its ground, faced with a novel, the work of a writer hitherto unknown—and what a novel! the most impartial, the most honest—a

"*Madame Bovary*," by Charles Baudelaire. From *L'Artiste* (October 18, 1857). Included in *L'Art romantique*, 1868. Translated by Raymond Giraud.

field, banal like all fields, whipped and soaked like nature herself by all winds and all storms—the magistracy, I say, has shown itself to be as honest and impartial as the book that was brought before it in a holocaust. And better yet let us say, if it is permissible to conjecture on the considerations that accompanied the judgment, that if the magistrates had discovered something truly reproachable in the book, they would nevertheless have amnestied it in favor and in gratitude for that BEAUTY in which it is clothed. This remarkable concern for Beauty, in men whose faculties are only called upon for the Just and True, is an extremely touching symptom, compared with the burning concupiscence of a society which has definitely abjured all spiritual love and which, neglecting *its ancient entrails,* no longer cares for anything but its viscera. In short, we can say that this decision, through its high poetic tendency, was definitive, and that victory was accorded to the Muse, and that all writers, at least all those worthy of the name, have been acquitted in the person of Mr. Gustave Flaubert.

Let us therefore not say, as so many others are affirming with some slight and unconscious ill temper, that the book has owed its immense success to the trial and the acquittal. Without having been harassed, the book would have obtained the same curiosity, created the same astonishment and agitation. Besides, it had won the approval of all literate people a good deal earlier. Already in its first form, in the *Revue de Paris,* in which imprudent cuts had destroyed its harmony, it had excited an ardent interest. The situation of Gustave Flaubert, suddenly illustrious, was simultaneously excellent and bad, and I shall give as well as I can the diverse reasons for this equivocal situation over which his true and marvellous talent was able to triumph.

## III

Excellent, for ever since the disappearance of Balzac, that prodigious meteor that will cover our country with a cloud of glory like a bizarre and exceptional dawn, like a polar aurora inundating the frozen desert with its fairy lights—all curiosity relative to the novel had abated and had become dormant. Some astonishing attempts had been made, we must admit. Already a good while back, Monsieur de Custine, famous in an increasingly rarified circle through his *Aloys, le monde comme il est* and *Ethel* and the creator of the ugly ingenue, that type so envied by Balzac (see the true *Mercadet*), had given to the public *Romuald ou la vocation,* a work of sublime awkwardness in which inimitable pages both condemn and absolve its lengthiness and clumsiness. But Monsieur de Custine is a sub-genre of genius, a genius whose dandyism rises to the ideal of negligence. This genteel good faith, this romantic ardor, this sincere banter, this absolute and nonchalant personality are not accessible to the senses of the great herd, and this precious writer drew upon himself all the bad luck that his talent deserved.

Monsieur d'Aurevilly had violently attracted attention with *Une Vieille Maîtresse* and *L'Ensorcelée.* This cult of truth, expressed with a shocking ardor, could only displease the crowd. D'Aurevilly, a true Catholic, evoking passion in order to conquer it, singing, weeping, and shrieking in the midst of the storm, planted, like Ajax, on a rock of desolation, and always seeming to say to his rival—man, lightning, God, or matter—"destroy me or I shall destroy you!" He too could not stir up a drowsy species whose eyes are closed to the miracles of the exception.

Champfleury, in a childlike and charming spirit, had very felicitously dabbled in the picturesque and had pointed poetic binoculars (more poetic than he himself thinks) on the burlesque or touching accidents and chances in the family or on the street; but through originality or through lack of vision, voluntarily or fatally, he neglected the commonplace, the crowd's meeting place, the market place of eloquence.

Still more recently Monsieur Charles Barbara, a rigorous and logical soul eager for intellectual gain, has made some incontestably distinguished efforts. He has sought (an always irresistible temptation) to describe and elucidate exceptional situations of the soul and to deduce the direct consequences of false positions. If I do not express here all the sympathy with which the author of *Héloïse* and the *Assassinat du Pont-Rouge* inspires me, it is because he only occasionally enters my theme as an historical note.

Paul Feval, on the other side of the sphere, enamored of adventures, admirably endowed for the grotesque and the terrible, closely followed behind Frédéric Soulié and Eugène Sue like a tardy hero. But the rich talent of the author of the *Mystère de Londres* and the *Bossu* could not, any more than those of so many exceptional intellects, accomplish the sudden, airy miracle of that poor little adulterous provincial woman whose whole story, without intricacy, is composed of sadness, disgust, sighs, and a few feverish swoonings, wrenched from a life terminated by suicide.

That these writers—some Dickensian, the others in the mold of

Byron or Bulwer, too talented perhaps, too scornful—should not have been able, like a simple Paul de Kock, to force open the frail door of Popularity, which alone among immodest ladies begs for rape, is a sin I shall not be the one to accuse them of, nor shall I praise them for it either. Likewise, I cannot be grateful to Monsieur Gustave Flaubert for having at the first try obtained what others seek throughout their lifetimes. At the most I see in it a superrogatory symptom of power and shall seek to define the reasons which caused the author's mind to move in one direction rather than in another.

But I have also said that this situation of the newcomer was bad, alas, for a lugubriously simple reason. For several years the share of its interest that the public grants to spiritual things had been singularly diminished; its budget of enthusiasm had been constantly shrinking. The last years of Louis-Philippe had seen the last explosions of a spirit still capable of being excited by the play of the imagination; but the new novelist found himself confronting an absolutely worn-out society—worse than worn out—stupefied and gluttonous, horrified only by fiction and loving only possession.

Under such conditions a highly cultivated mind, full of enthusiasm for the beautiful but brought up in a hard school, judging both the good and the bad of these circumstances, must have thought: "What is the surest means of stirring all these tired souls? They are really unaware of what they might love; they have a positive disgust only for what is great; naïve, ardent passion and poetic abandon make them blush and wound them. Let us therefore be vulgar in our choice of subjects, since the choice of too lofty a subject is an impertinence for the nineteenth-century reader. And also, let us beware of letting ourselves go and speaking our own minds. We shall be icy in relating passions and adventures that warm the blood of the common herd; as the school says, we shall be objective and impersonal.

"And also, since our ears have been buffeted in these recent times by childish school babblings, as we have heard of a certain literary process called *realism*—a disgusting insult hurled in the face of all analysts, a vague and elastic word signifying for the common man not a new method of creation but a minute description of accessories —we shall profit from the public confusion and universal ignorance. We shall apply a sinewy, picturesque, subtle, and exact style upon a banal canvas. We shall put the hottest and most passionate feelings into the most trivial adventure. The most solemn and decisive words will escape from the stupidest mouths.

"What is stupidity's stamping ground, the setting that is stupidest, most productive of absurdities, most abundant in intolerant imbeciles?

"The provinces.

"Who there are the most intolerable actors?

"The humble people, occupied with minor functions, the exercise of which falsifies their thinking.

"What is the most overdone and prostituted theme, the most hackneyed sob story?

"Adultery.

"I do not require," said the poet to himself, "that my *heroine* be a heroine. Provided that she is sufficiently pretty, that she has fortitude, ambition, and an uncheckable aspiration toward a higher world, she will be interesting. The feat, moreover, will be nobler, and our sinful lady will at least have this merit—comparatively very rare—of being distinguished from the ostentatious chatterers of the era preceding our own.

"I need not worry about style, picturesque arrangement, the description of my settings; I possess all of these qualities more than amply. I shall proceed supported by analysis and logic, and I shall thus prove that all subjects are indiscriminately good or bad according to the manner in which they are treated, and that the most vulgar ones can become the best."

From that moment on, *Madame Bovary*—a wager, a true wager, a bet, like all works of art—was created.

It remained only for the author to accomplish this feat all the way, to strip himself (as much as possible) of his sex and to become a woman. A wondrous thing resulted from this: in spite of all his thespian zeal, he could not keep from infusing virile blood into the veins of his creature, and because of her energy and ambition and capacity for revery, Madame Bovary remained a man. Like the armored Pallas sprung from the forehead of Zeus, this bizarre androgyne has kept all of the seductive quality of a virile spirit in a charming feminine body.

Several critics have said: this work, truly lovely in the detail and lifelikeness of its descriptions, does not contain a single character representing morality or expressing the conscience of the author. Where is the proverbial and legendary character charged with explaining the fable and directing the intelligence of the reader? In other words, where is the indictment?

Absurdity! Eternal and incorrigible confusion of functions and genres! A true work of art needs no indictment. The logic of the work suffices for all postulations of morality, and it is up to the reader to draw conclusions from the conclusion.

As for the intimate, profound character in the fable, she is incontestably the adulterous woman. She alone, the dishonored victim, possesses all the graces of the hero. I was saying a moment ago that she was almost masculine and that the author had adorned her (unconsciously, perhaps) with all the virile qualities.

Let us examine attentively:

(1) Imagination, that supreme and tyrannical faculty, substituted for the heart, or what is called the heart, from which reasoning is ordinarily excluded and which generally dominates in woman as in the animal;

(2) Sudden energy of action, rapidity of decision, mystical fusion of reasoning and passion, which characterize men created for action;

(3) Immoderate taste for seduction, domination, and even all the vulgar means of seduction, going down to charlatanism in costume, perfumes, and pomade—all summed up in two words: dandyism, exclusive love of domination.

And yet Madame Bovary gives herself; carried away by the sophistries of her imagination, she gives herself magnificently, generously, in a completely masculine way, to wretches who are not her equals, exactly as poets give themselves to despicable women.

A new proof of the totally virile quality that nourishes her arterial blood is that in the final analysis this unfortunate woman suffers less from visible, exterior shortcomings, the blinding provincialisms of her husband, than from that total absence of genius, that spiritual inferiority demonstrated by the stupid operation on the clubfoot.

And in this connection, reread the pages which contain that episode, so unjustly treated as parasitical, whereas it serves to throw a vivid light on the whole character of the person. A dark rage that had long been building up bursts out of all the wifely pores of Madame Bovary. Doors slam; the stupefied husband, who has been unable to give any spiritual satisfaction to his romantic wife, is relegated to his bedroom. He is in penitence, ignorant culprit! And Madame Bovary, hopeless, cries out like a little Lady Macbeth yoked to some inadequate captain: "Ah! If I were *at least* married to one of those old bald and bent scholars whose eyes, shielded by green glasses, are always focused on the archives of science! I could proudly take my place by his side; I should at least be the consort of a spiritual king; but to have as a partner in fetters this imbecile who cannot straighten a cripple's foot! Oh!"

This woman in reality is sublime, considering her class, her petty background, and her limited horizon.

(4) Even in her convent education, I find proof of the equivocal temperament of Madame Bovary.

The good sisters noticed in this girl an astonishing aptitude for life, for deriving pleasure and satisfaction from life—there is your man of action!

The girl, however, was deliciously intoxicated by the color of the stained-glass windows, by the oriental hues that the long, ornate windows cast upon her schoolgirl's prayer book; she gorged herself on the solemn music of vespers and, in a paradox, the credit for which must all go to her nervous hysteria, she substitutes in her soul for the true God the God of her fantasy, the God of the future and of chance, a picture-book God with spurs and moustache—there is the hysterical poet!

Hysteria! Why would this physiological mystery not make the basis and substance of a literary work, that mystery that the Academy of Medicine has not yet resolved and which, manifesting itself in women by the sensation of a rising and asphyxiating lump in the throat (I am speaking only of the principal symptom), reveals itself in nervous men by all manner of impotence and also by an aptitude for every excess.

In short, this woman is truly great. She is, above all, deserving of pity, and in spite of the systematic hard-heartedness of the author, who has tried his best to be absent from his work and to play the role of a manipulator of marionettes, all *intellectual* women will be grateful to him for having raised the female to so high a power, so far from the pure animal, and so close to the ideal man, and for having caused her to participate in that double character of calculation and reverie that constitutes the perfect being.

It is said that Madame Bovary is ridiculous. Indeed, here she is, at one moment taking for a hero out of Walter Scott a sort of gentleman—shall I even say, a country squire?—wearing hunting vests and unmatched suits! And now we see her in love with a little notary's clerk (incapable even of committing a dangerous act for his mistress), and finally the poor woman, exhausted, a bizarre Pasiphae relegated to the narrow confines of a village, pursues the ideal in the dance halls and bars of Rouen. What does it matter? Let us say it, let us confess it: she is a Caesar at Carpentras, she is pursuing the Ideal!

I shall certainly not say, like Pétrus Borel, the Lycanthrope of insurrectional memory, that abdicated rebel: "Confronted with all the platitudes and stupidities of the present, are we not left with cigarette paper and adultery?" But I shall affirm that, after all, when all is said and done, when all has been weighed on the most precise scales, our world is a harsh one indeed for having been engendered by Christ, and that it is hardly entitled to cast a stone at adultery, and a few grotesque couplings more or less will not accelerate the rotation of the spheres and will not advance by one second the final destruction of the universe. It is time to put an end to increasingly contagious hypocrisy and for us to recognize how ridiculous it is for men and women who are perverted even in their most trivial doings to cry shame upon a poor author who has deigned with his poet's chastity to cast a veil of glory on bedroom adventures, always repugnant and grotesque when Poetry does not caress them with its opaline, lamplike glow.

If I gave in to this analytic bent I should never finish with *Madame Bovary*. This essentially suggestive book could fill a whole volume of observations. For the moment I shall limit myself to observing that several of the most important episodes were at first either neglected or vituperatively attacked by the critics. Some examples: the episode of the unfortunate operation on the clubfoot, and the one so remarkable, so full of desolation, so truly *modern,* in which the future adulteress—for she is still only at the beginning of her descent, poor woman!—goes to seek aid of the Church, of the divine Mother, of her who has no excuse for not being ever ready, of that Pharmacy where no one has the right to slumber! The good priest, Bournisien, concerned only with the little rascals in his catechism class playing games amid the pews and chairs in the church, replies ingenuously: "Since you are ill, Madame, and since Monsieur Bovary is a doctor, *why don't you consult your husband?*"

What woman, confronted with this curé's inadequacy, in the madness produced by such amnesty would not rush to plunge her head into the swirling waters of adultery? And who among us, in a more naïve age and in troubled circumstances, has not inevitably encountered the incompetent priest?

## VI

I had originally intended, with two books by the same author at hand (*Madame Bovary* and *La Tentation de Saint Antoine,* the fragments of which have not yet been assembled in a volume), to suggest a sort of parallel between the two. I wished to establish equations and correspondences. It would have been easy for me to discover beneath the minute web of *Madame Bovary* the high qualities of *irony* and *lyricism* that intensely illuminate *La Tentation de Saint Antoine*. Here the poet had not disguised himself, and his *Bovary*, tempted by all the demons of illusion and heresy, by all the carnal temptations of surrounding matter—his *saint Antoine,* in short, harassed by all the kinds of madness that circumvent us, would have made a stronger apologetic than his little bourgeois novel. In this work, of which the author has unfortunately only given us fragments, there are some dazzling passages. I do not speak only of the prodigious feast of Nebuchadnezzar; of the marvelous appearance of that little goose, the Queen of Sheba, a miniature dancing on the retina of an ascetic; of the charlatanic and bombastic staging of the entrance of Apollonius of Tyana, followed by his elephant-driver, or rather by his keeper, the imbecilic millionaire whom he leads through the world. I should like especially to draw the reader's attention to that quality of pain, subterranean and rebellious, which runs through the whole work, that dark vein which illuminates—what the English call *the subcurrent*—and which serves to guide us through this pandemoniacal bedlam of solitude.

It would have been easy for me to show, as I have already said, that Monsieur Gustave Flaubert voluntarily veiled in *Madame Bovary* the lofty lyrical and ironical qualities displayed without reservation in *La Tentation*, and that this latest work, a secret chamber of his spirit, is obviously the more interesting one for poets and philosophers.

Perhaps some day I shall have the pleasure of accomplishing this task.

# Madame Bovary

## by Martin Turnell

Virginia Woolf once spoke of "the fear which attacks the recorder of centenaries lest he should find himself measuring a diminishing spectre and forced to foretell its approaching dissolution." A centenary should not be a mere formality, an excuse for unrolling the red carpet and paying a few perfunctory compliments to an established classic. It should be an opportunity for re-assessment, for deciding whether a writer still deserves his classic status or whether he should be quietly dropped from the syllabus and the reading list. A classic cannot be lightly discarded, but he should not be retained simply to fill a gap in the syllabus. He should only be retained provided that he still has something to offer the contemporary reader. In the case of Flaubert the task of re-assessment is by no means an easy one. He was a writer with serious weaknesses who has always divided the critics. His work also arouses strong partisan feelings. We remember Sartre's unfortunate observations on his "political unreliability," while in England the centenary started badly with a broadcast attack by a Frenchman under the disparaging title of "No Orchids for Madame Bovary." If a good deal of the criticism of his novels has been off the target, or has concentrated on their *content* instead of their *method,* Flaubert himself is not free from blame. His letters are not invariably a source of illumination for the critic; they have too often directed the discussion into unprofitable channels. There were times, however, when he proved more discerning than some of his commentators. In a letter written to Louise Colet in May 1853, two years after the beginning of his five year stint, he said of *Madame Bovary:*

This book, all cunning and stylistic ruse, does not have my blood in it. I am not carrying it in my bowels. I feel it is a calculated artificial

*"Madame Bovary,"* by Martin Turnell. From *The Sewanee Review,* LXV, 4 (October-December 1957), 531-550. Copyright © 1957 by The University of the South. Reprinted by permission of Martin Turnell and The University of the South.

thing. Perhaps it will be a *tour de force* that some people will admire. . . .

What really needs saying in this, the centenary year, is that Flaubert was the greatest virtuoso who ever practised prose fiction, that he was the creator of the contemporary novel, and the source of nearly every important technical advance made since the middle of the last century. For there is a gulf between the novels written before and after *Madame Bovary*. The core of the pre-Flaubertian novel was narrative. However subtle their psychology, Flaubert's predecessors were concerned with a succession of events in time which constituted the relation between the novel and what is loosely called "reality." It might be replied that *Madame Bovary* is the story of a young woman with Romantic ideas, that it begins with her schooldays, goes on to her marriage to a dull country doctor, and ends with her death. This is not the correct answer, and it was not Flaubert's answer. "A novel's story or adventure doesn't matter to me in the least," he told the Goncourts. "When I am working on a novel,[1] my thought is that I am rendering a coloration, a nuance." The meaning of the novel lies in an elaborate—an immensely elaborate—network of interrelated images which all reflect the "coloration" or the "nuance" at which the writer was aiming. The "stylistic ruses" are so much in evidence that there is scarcely an incident or an image, scarcely even a sentence which does not look back to something which has gone before or forward to something which comes after it, turning the whole book into a "forest of symbols."

"Symbolism" is a term that needs to be carefully defined. When used of Flaubert it means the practice of substituting an image—usually a visual image—for direct description or for statements about feelings. Symbolism in this sense has probably existed to some extent in all literatures at all times, but it was left to the nineteenth-century writers in general, and to Flaubert in particular, to exploit its possibilities consciously and systematically. Baudelaire's use of symbols was based like Flaubert's on musical notation, but it was much less systematic and much less influential. I felt inclined to describe Flaubert's influence as "decisive," but the right word is "seminal." It was essentially creative because it enabled writers whose natural endowment was superior to Flaubert's to realize their potentialities to the full. Without Flaubert's example it would have been impossible for Proust, Henry James, and Conrad, or lesser writers like Zola, James Joyce, and Virginia Woolf to achieve all they did. Flaubert's influ-

[1] *Journal*, I, 366-7.

ence was not confined to the novel: it extended to poetry. Laforgue's free verse would not have been nearly as effective as it was without the Flaubertian use of the recurring image which in the *Derniers vers* became a form of poetic shorthand. Without Laforgue we should scarcely have had *The Waste Land*. Proust and Thibaudet both criticized Flaubert's imagery severely, but the intrinsic quality of his images is less important than the relations between them. What matters is not the image in isolation, but the image in perspective. And the perspective is constantly shifting as the themes weave in and out of one another, sometimes blending and sometimes clashing, to form the pattern which is the novel.

I think we must add that Flaubert's method has been so completely absorbed, has become so much a part of the contemporary literary heritage, that we are inclined to forget where it came from. This explains why later writers, who without Flaubert could scarcely have existed, have been so reluctant to spare an orchid for *Madame Bovary*.

The nineteenth-century novelists were splendid starters. Not for them the eighteenth-century device of the manuscript found in a bottle or a drawer. In *Madame Bovary* we are plunged straight into the midst of things: "We were in Big School when the Head came in, followed by a new boy in ordinary day-clothes, and by one of the juniors carrying a large desk."

The arrival of Charles Bovary as a new boy at school, the uproar caused by his hat and his accent, the furious master dealing out *pensums* are related by an anonymous eyewitness who makes a solitary appearance and then vanishes for good. On the second page we come across the description of Charles's extraordinary hat:

> It was one of those composite headdresses combining a number of different features—part busby, part lancer's cap, part pillbox, part otterskin cap, part cotton nightcap, one of those shoddy objects in short whose dumb ugliness has depths of expression like the face of an idiot. Its general shape was that of an egg and the upper part, stiffened with whalebone, rose from a base consisting of three bulging, circular protuberances. Above them was a pattern consisting of alternating lozenges of rabbit fur and velvet separated from one another by strips of some scarlet material. Higher still was a species of bag ending in a polygon of cardboard covered with a complicated design in braid, and finished off with a long and excessively thin cord from which hung a small cross of gold thread in place of a tassel. The whole contraption was new; the peak glistened.

It is no exaggeration to say that the whole novel grows out of this one image as surely as the twenty volumes of the Rougon-Macquart cycle grow out of the image of the disused cemetery of Saint-Mittre on the first page of *La Fortune des Rougon*. Flaubert's novel is not, as it is sometimes said to be, a study of the twin themes of stupidity and Romantic illusion. Stupidity is the major theme and Romantic illusion simply one of its forms. For the essence of stupidity is an inability to make a correct appreciation of reality and to adapt oneself to it. The image of the hat is therefore a compelling statement of the major theme. It is primarily a dunce's cap—this explains the spontaneous roar of laughter when Charles arrives at school—and a symbol of the society to which the wearer belongs.

The words "composite" and "circular," the construction of the hat in "layers" or "tiers" are an important part of Flaubert's symbolism. Charles Bovary stands for "la bêtise à l'état pur," for stupidity in its pure state. He is the centre of a circle, the source from which stupidity seems to emanate, the prototype of all the other examples of stupidity and professional incompetence which surround him. Stupidity is not the monopoly of any one class; it runs all through society from top to bottom. The layers of the hat, with their mixture of aristocratic, middle-class and proletarian trappings, emphasize that stupidity has no frontiers, social or otherwise.

Confusion of styles is a recurrent theme. It can be said of Flaubert's characters: By their dress ye shall know them. Charles's hat is not simply the model of all the other strange hats worn in the book from Homais' pretentious "bonnet grec" to Rodolphe's rakish "boater"; there is a connection between the hat and the medley of clothes worn by the country bumpkins, the vehicles they drive and the geography of the country. At the beginning of Part II we read:

> Here we are on the borders of Normandy, Picardy and the Ile-de-France, a bastard land, whose language is without accent as its landscape is without character.

The "bastard" of this passage matches the "composite" of the earlier one. It is a nondescript, characterless country, a waste land lying on the borders of three different provinces and belonging to none of them.

"What you describe as repetitions," said Zola in a letter written in October 1894 to a certain Monsieur Bonnet, "are to be found in

all my books. They are in fact a literary device that I used sparingly
to begin with, and was later perhaps inclined to overdo. In my opinion they give the work more body, a closer unity. In a way they are
like the *leit-motifs* in Wagner, and if you happen to have a musician
among your friends who can explain their use to you, it will give
you a good idea of my particular literary device."

Zola was heavily indebted to Flaubert and knew what he was
talking about. His observations on structure are of considerable interest. The relations between Flaubert's images are seldom simple.
Repetition gives them a cumulative, sometimes a tragic force. They
grow like snowballs, collecting more and wider associations as more
and more of the final pattern emerges in the succeeding images. In
this way they give the novel its solidity of structure, which is one of
its principal merits, and weld the three parts into a whole.

The three parts are curiously symmetrical. They are all organized
around a central incident and a central image. The incidents are
the marriage in Part I and the seductions in Parts II and III. The
images are the visit to La Vaubyessard, the Comices Agricoles and
the meeting between Emma and Léon in Rouen Cathedral. The
images are not merely related; each leads almost inevitably to the
next. They are reinforced by a series of supporting images which
emphasize and prolong their psychological repercussions. It is characteristic of both the main and the supporting images that they are
images of destruction. They are directed against the marriage which
begins to founder in Part I, and is finally ruined by the seductions in
the second and third parts which are themselves the source of additional suffering.

The tightness of the book's construction is illustrated by the
events leading to the marriage. Charles first meets Emma when he
goes to the Bertaux to set her father's leg. At that time he is married
to a woman older than himself who is comfortably off. Soon afterwards her lawyer decamps with her savings—it is the first mention
of financial disaster which plays such a large part in the book—and
she dies of chagrin. Charles begins to court Emma. When his horse
shies violently as he arrives at the farm on his first visit, the "grand
écart" is a form of oracle, a premonition of what is to come, a warning against a disastrous marriage. The crash of the shutters against
a wall as Charles stands, on another occasion, beside his tethered
horse waiting for the result of his marriage proposal, is a sign that
the warning has gone unheeded and that his doom is sealed.

In the account of the return of the wedding procession we read:

Emma's dress was too long and just touched the ground. Now and again she stopped to raise it, and daintily, with her gloved hands, to pick off the wild grasses and prickly thistles, while Charles, empty-handed, waited for her to finish.

This clearly looks forward to her first ride with Rodolphe, which ends with the seduction in the wood:

The high bracken on the edge of the path kept getting entangled in Emma's stirrup. Rodolphe, without slowing down, leaned across whenever it happened, and pulled it loose. . . . They dismounted, and Rodolphe tethered the horses. She walked ahead of him on the mossy turf between the ruts. But her long dress got in her way, though she was holding up the train, and Rodolphe, following behind, kept his eyes fixed on the strip of thin white stocking which showed between the stuff of her riding habit and her black boots. It had for him something of the quality of her bare flesh.

It is no accident that we are told on both these momentous occasions that Emma's dress was too long and got in her way. The dress stands for the obstacles which she repeatedly encounters in her married life and which come between her and happiness. There is a contrast between her husband standing on one side "empty-handed" and incapable of helping her as he will always be incapable of helping her, and the more practical Rodolphe who "without slowing down, leaned across . . . and pulled it loose." The husband fails her by doing nothing; the lover helps to destroy her by being too enterprising.

We are told of the visit to La Vaubyessard: "Her journey to La Vaubyessard had made a hole in her life in the manner of those great crevasses that a storm sometimes causes in a single night in the mountains." It is not a happy way of putting it, but the implications are plain. The visit, which has provided Emma with a glimpse of a world of luxury and romance (or so it appears to her), shatters her married life for ever.

The three supporting images which reinforce La Vaubyessard are the wedding bouquet, the pet greyhound, and the statue of the *curé*. In view of what has been said about structure, it is interesting to notice that two of the images carry over from Part I to Part II, and that two reach out into Part III.

The first two images are simple, or at any rate simple by Flaubert's standards; the third is an excellent example of what might be called multiple reference. The burning of the wedding bouquet at the close of Part I is a sign that morally and psychologically Emma's marriage has come to an end, and points to the way in which her home will be "burnt up" by her financial and emotional extravagances. When the greyhound whose wild scurryings, as we are too pointedly told, reflect Emma's own unstable mood, jumps off the van during the move to Yonville, disappears into the open country and is never seen again, he clearly foreshadows the way in which Emma herself will "go off the rails."

The plaster statue of the *curé* reading his breviary, which stood in Emma's garden at Tostes, represents the piety and respectability of the first months of her married life. The plaster, however, is a symbol of the brittleness of both her religion and her virtue. When we learn towards the end of Part I that the *curé*'s face has become weather-stained and that he has lost a foot, we know that moral deterioration has set in. The announcement that the statue fell off the van on the way to Yonville and was smashed to pieces is another sign of Emma's impending fall. The plaster *curé* also points the way to the living but wooden Abbé Bournisien, who proves completely ineffectual when Emma appeals to him for help after the first temptation but before the first fall. The failure of religion is emphasized by the contrast between the statue of the *curé* falling and the statue of Cupid standing in the garden of the local solicitor at Yonville. The Christian religion sinks as the cult of Eros begins to rise. The Cupid suggests the secret propensities of the lawyer. It looks back to the innocent Cupid on Emma's wedding cake, and forward to the moment when we see the amorous lawyer at the feet of Emma, who has come to seek financial assistance. Religion and love are both caricatured in this book. One is reduced to a broken plaster statue, the other to an "old goat" grovelling on the floor. Nor should we overlook the *curé*'s foot. In an early chapter we are told that Charles's boot made him look as though he had a wooden foot. Charles's "wooden" foot is relayed by the *curé*'s missing foot and points to the amputation of the wretched Hippolyte's leg, and to the sound of the leg in real wood which will reverberate all through the rest of the novel.

The scene of the Comices is arranged in tiers recalling the tiers of Charles's hat. Emma and Rodolphe watch from a window on the first floor of the mayor's house, looking down on the guest of honor in the middle distance, the bourgeois on a lower plane, the peasants and the animals on the lowest plane of all. The platitudes about love coming down from the top layer echo and mingle with the platitudes about patriotism and agriculture which float upwards from the middle layer, and are punctuated by the sounds of the crowd and the animals on the two bottom layers.

The Comices, in which all the inhabitants of Yonville participate in some degree, is the epitome of the whole novel. It is a Fête de la Bêtise whose echoes are heard in the platitudes which pour out every time any of the characters open their mouths. Its intention is completely destructive. Everything—love, patriotism, agriculture —is reduced to a mindless babble. It is supported by the images of height and distance. Height stands for the exaltation of love and the fall which follows its satisfaction. Emma's first sight of Rodolphe is an ironical comment on the Romantic image of the Lady watching, from a tower or a balcony, the arrival of the Knight with the white plume riding the black steed—an image that haunts Emma's imagination. She first sees Rodolphe from her bedroom window, but he is on foot and prosaically bringing one of his farm hands to the doctor for bleeding. The declaration of love was made on the first floor of the mayor's house, but the lovers end up in the manner of the animals on the lowest plane rolling on the ground in the wood, which is the goal of their first ride together. The wood itself stands on high ground; Emma finds herself looking down on Yonville and trying to pick out her own house. She has the same impression when the diligence reaches the outskirts of Rouen where she has an assignation with Léon. It is matched by the reverse feeling—the sinking sensation—when the diligence plunges down into the valley on the return journey. The end of an affair is followed by the hallucinatory impression of the lover shrinking in size and vanishing into the distance: "And Léon suddenly appeared to her as far off as the others."

The Cathedral creates in the mind of the waiting Léon the image of a "gigantic boudoir." Emma arrives with the intention of breaking with him and hurries into the Lady Chapel to pray for strength. This produces not merely a conflict of mood, but a conflict of imagery. The chapel is pitted against the "boudoir," the image of Virtue Resisting against Léon's image of Virtue Succumbing. He is exasperated by the length of her orisons, but they are both exasperated by the intrusion on their privacy of the beadle who on week days acts as guide. His platitudes about the Cathedral correspond to the platitudes about agriculture at the Comices, but the reference to the tomb of Diane de Poitiers—the celebrated adulteress lying buried among the saintly and the worthy—is no more accidental than the guide's parting words: "At least leave by the north door . . . in order to see the Resurrection, the Last Judgment, Paradise, King David, and the damned in the fires of hell."

Rodolphe waits for several weeks before inviting Emma to go out riding: Léon bundles her into a cab and tells the driver to go where he likes so long as he keeps going. The cab with the drawn blinds not only repeats the image of the boudoir; it registers its triumph over the image of the chapel. The "naked" hand which emerges and throws away the pieces of the *lettre de rupture* is an ironical retort to the hands joined in prayer in the chapel. The fragments of the letter show that marriage vows have been torn up again; the "white butterflies" falling on the field of "scarlet" clover look back to the "black butterflies" formed by the charred remains of Emma's wedding bouquet flying up the chimney in Part I. The white fragments also seem to me to stand for clothes; they recall the strip-tease act with two people in a "boudoir," the door opening and closing as one garment after another comes flying out.

It will be apparent that each of these three main images represents not simply an attack on Emma's marriage, but a stage on her road to ruin. The first is the destruction of the *honnête femme;* the second the destruction of the Romantic idealist; the third the destruction of the woman herself.

The images of travel look at first like a borrowing from the Romantic stock-in-trade, but Flaubert gives them a personal interpretation. They form a chain which plays a larger part than any other set of images in welding the three parts into a whole, and we shall find that they have an unexpected connection with the images of destruction.

Flaubert's characters travel on horseback, in horse-drawn vehicles and on foot. This repeats the figures of "tiers" and "heights": their method of locomotion sometimes reflects the rise and fall of their fortunes. The first rides on horseback, as we have seen, take the unsuspecting Charles to the Bertaux where through misfortune and lack of insight he meets and marries the most unsuitable wife he could have chosen. These rides look forward to the tragic rides which are the result of the unheeded warning: the servants galloping frantically to fetch the specialists to the dying Emma, the doctors arriving too late, the father reaching Yonville to find his daughter's house draped in mourning. The rides of Charles and Emma cancel out. His are errands of mercy; hers, escapades which waste the money he has so laboriously earned on his rounds and bring them both to ruin.

The horse-drawn vehicles are a deliberately varied collection: the aristocratic tilbury, the post-chaise of Emma's daydream, Charles's unromantic *boc,* the strangely Freudian cab, the diligence. The last is the most important vehicle in the book. It is the vehicle which carries the Bovarys from Tostes to Yonville, and the reader out of Part I into Part II. It takes them to Rouen where they meet the returning Léon; Emma's overnight stay covers the transition from Part II to Part III which begins with the ride in the cab and the return journey to Yonville. Its shuttle service between Yonville and Rouen is a reflection of Emma's alternation between dream and reality. For most of her journeys, whether real or imaginary, are a search for the *pays bleu,* the land of Romantic love. It is characteristic of all of them that they end in disillusionment or disaster. The first carriage drive takes Emma to the disappointments of married life at Tostes. The second is the imaginary journey in the post-chaise whose "blue" blinds are recalled by the sight of Rodolphe's "blue" tilbury racing through Yonville as he flees from Emma after promising to elope with her. The move from Tostes takes her to the "bastard land"; the outings to Rouen lose their charm as her love for Léon turns to disgust.

The journeys on foot mingle with, repeat and sometimes mock the other journeys—the visits to Rodolphe's château early in the morning or the brief sorties to the arbor in the garden on a winter's night. In the closing pages there are journeys which cover the same ground, but which ironically have a different aim: the last journey to Rouen in the vain effort to raise money to save herself from being sold up, the last visit to Rodolphe's château in the hope of borrowing money, the desperate appeals to the solicitor, the tax-gatherer, the visit to Homais' shop where she steals the arsenic that kills her.

Although the immediate goal of the journeys may vary, the ultimate goal is either flight into an unreal world or flight from the very real world of menacing creditors. At this point the jig-saw begins to fit together. The central image in each part is, in reality, a double image of destruction and flight. La Vaubyessard leads to the flight to Yonville which is the scene of Emma's downfall; the Comices to the fatal ride with Rodolphe and to Rodolphe's flight from Emma; the meeting in the Cathedral to the ride in the cab; the ride in the cab to the journeys to Rouen and the last catastrophic round of visits. Destruction is inevitable, escape impossible; flight from destruction leads back to destruction.

Flaubert uses two other devices to heighten the sense of impending dissolution—the dissolution of all values whether spiritual or emotional—which is the heart of his experience. One is an ironical commentary which is employed on and through the characters. On the

night of the Bovarys' arrival at Yonville, Homais tells Charles in all
innocence that one of the advantages of the house he is to occupy is
the side door which enables a doctor to come and go without being
seen. It is the door that Emma will use for her clandestine meetings
with her lover. When Charles has bought his wife a riding outfit,
he writes to tell Rodolphe that his wife "is at his disposal" and that
"he counts on his good offices." As the pair set out on their first ride
they meet Homais who warns them, again in all innocence, to be
careful of "accidents." The intrinsic quality of this irony is open
to the same objections as the quality of some of Flaubert's images,
but it serves its purpose. It is the disruptive mutter which is over-
heard, unceasingly, in a world falling apart.

The other device is a variant of the recurring image. It is an
association of ideas which works destructively inside the minds of
the characters and helps to bring them down. La Vaubyessard is a
salient example. The thud of Hippolyte's wooden leg is a continual
reminder to Charles of his professional incompetence, and to Emma
of the humiliation of being married to such a man. Binet's lathe is
a much more arresting example. The tax-gatherer is the one man of
integrity at Yonville. He has been described as Emma's conscience.
He does "catch" her one morning when she is on her way back from
a visit to Rodolphe and he himself is engaged in some harmless
poaching expedition. His gun pointing in Emma's direction, before
he is able to see who she is, may well be a symbol of a finger pointing accusingly at the adulteress. Emma at once loses her head and
tells a wildly improbable story about visiting her daughter. When
it is first heard the sound of the lathe seems unimportant, but when
we come to the scene in which Emma is about to commit suicide
after Rodolphe's defection we see the reason for the careful preparation:

Beyond the roofs opposite spread the open country as far as eye
could reach. Below was the village square. There was not a soul
about. The pebbles of the footpath glittered: the weathercocks on the
houses were motionless. At the corner of the street a sort of moaning
sound, with occasional strident modulations, was coming from one of
the lower floors. It was Binet working at his lathe.

She leaned against the embrasure of the window and read the letter
with little harsh bursts of angry laughter. But the more she concentrated her attention on its contents, the more muddled her mind
became. She felt as though she could see his face, hear his voice, hold
him in her arms. The irregular beating of her heart, which was like
a battering-ram inside her chest, grew quicker. She stared about her

wishing that the earth would open. Why not have done with it all?
Who could stop her? She was free.

She went closer to the window and stared down at the paved road-
way.

"I'll do it!" she said to herself.

The light striking up at her from below seemed to draw the weight
of her body down into the great empty space. She felt as though the
surface of the square were spinning before her eyes, climbing up the
walls to meet her. The floor of the room was tilting like the deck of
a pitching ship. She stood there, almost hanging over its edge. All
round her was nothing but empty space. The blue of the sky enveloped her, the air eddied in her empty skull. She had only to let herself
go, only to let that nothingness receive her body. The whirring of
the lathe went on and on, like a furious voice calling to her:

"Emma!" cried Charles. "Emma!" She stopped.

"Where on earth are you? Come down!"

The thought that she had just escaped death made her almost faint
with terror. She closed her eyes. Then, at the touch of a hand on her
sleeve, she gave a start.

"Master's waiting for you, ma'am. The soup's on the table."

This scene is one of the most spectacularly impressive that Flaubert ever wrote. He succeeds marvellously in conveying an extraordinary sense of hallucination—the silent, deserted street, the remorse-
less sunlight striking up at Emma, the sudden sense that she has lost
her bearings, that reality is disintegrating, that street and room are
rocking like a pitching ship, the insistent whirring of the lathe
which in the midst of the unnatural silence seems to her disordered
imagination to be a furious voice bidding her throw herself down.
Then, very suddenly, the hallucination is dissipated and she is
brought back to reality with a shock by the sound of Charles's voice,
the hand laid on her shoulder, the matter-of-fact remark about the
soup.

This is not the last that we hear of Binet or his lathe. We hear
the lathe again when she goes to try to borrow some of the taxpayers'
money from him to keep her creditors at bay; we see him recoil as
though she were a "serpent" tempting him and catch his shocked:
"Madame, what on earth are you thinking of!" Then, when she
calls on her daughter's nurse, the sound of the spinning wheel not
only recalls Binet's lathe—it recreates horrifyingly in her mind the
scene of the attempted suicide and in a sense provokes the real one.

The two devices are combined in the figure of the hideously
mutilated Blindman, said to stand for Death or the Devil, to whom

Emma throws her last five-franc piece. His erotic song about little girls dreaming of love and their skirts being blown tantalizingly upwards by the wind is both a commentary on Emma's own behavior —being tipped up in wood and garden—and the signal to her that the terrifying apparition who haunts her mind is at hand.

Flaubert possessed many admirable qualities, but psychological insight was not among them. It was not so much a personal weakness as a failing which belonged to the age. The French novel produced no great psychologist between Stendhal and Proust. Flaubert's characters do not deepen our knowledge of human nature like those of the French classic novelists. The relations between them are not personal relations in the normal sense. They are figures in the pattern rather than people. The novelist manipulates them not merely with the same skill, but in the same way that he manipulates his images.

This is strikingly demonstrated as soon as we turn from the principal to the secondary characters. They not only have considerably less psychology than Emma; they are both simplified and stylized, and resemble the characters in primitive comedy or in allegory. They are sufficiently individualized for the novelist's purpose, but their individuality derives, as in primitive comedy, from repetition —from the constant repetition of the same foolish things in slightly different terms. The primitive-allegorical element is also apparent in Flaubert's choice of names. If Bovary fits Charles like a label, it is probably because it contains an allusion to the words *boeuf* or *bovin*. (This supposition is strengthened when we remember that after Emma's death Léon marries a Mlle Leboeuf.) The name of the Abbé Bournisien seems intended to suggest *borné*. Homais, as we know from Flaubert's notes, is a pejorative form of *homme*. Its owner is "the little man," the product of the brash enlightenment of the nineteenth century which was as abhorrent to Flaubert as to any *dévot*. Lheureux is the happy or fortunate man, and in this context the successful swindler.

It is not difficult to see how the characters fit into the allegorical framework. Charles is not merely the dumb ox; he is the stock figure of the dupe, the *cocu*, the *mari trompé*, who has been handed down from primitive comedy through the Molière of *George Dandin*. Bournisien is the Priest, Rodolphe and Léon the Faithless Swains, Lhereux the Usurer, Homais the Quack.

These are the people who form the society which is slowly choking

Emma and into whose hands she plays. She is tricked by her enemies and let down by her friends. Her husband fails her because he cannot understand her Romantic *élans*; the priest because her emotional religion is beyond his comprehension. Her lovers take fright and walk out on her. She plays Homais' game by egging her husband on to make the experiment on the club-foot because the quack can only rise if the qualified physician comes to grief. She plays into the hands of Lheureux by her extravagance; and her signature to his bills—that peculiarly nineteenth-century instrument of disaster which looms so large in Balzac—brings ruin to her husband and herself.

Although Emma's Romanticism is a species of *bêtise,* Flaubert felt a tenderness for her which he did not feel for any of his other characters. She may be foolish and deceitful, but she is more sympathetic and more sensitive than they, is in the last resort superior to them all. There were personal reasons for Flaubert's preference. Her predicament was his own. It was the predicament of the Romantic individualist trapped in a hostile civilization which provided no outlet for his natural aspirations. This brings us back to Charles's hat and the image of the circle. Emma is imprisoned in a double circle—a circle which is at once physical and psychological. It is the physical circle formed by the nondescript country, the "bastard land whose language is without accent as its landscape is without character"; and the psychological circle formed by the people with their maddeningly stupid remarks. In addition to everything else the journeys are attempts to break out of the double circle. One can go further still. Emma is not only imprisoned in a double circle; she is imprisoned in a shrinking circle. What makes the climax so dramatic is the spectacle of her going round and round in an ever-narrowing circle as Lheureux with his pack of bankers, bailiffs and process-servers close in on her. The victim's death does not put an end to the chase; it swells the pack which turns on the husband, recalling in an odd way the opening scene of the book. Once again poor foolish Charles finds himself the centre of a jeering hostile throng. The music mistress demands payment for lessons that Emma never had; the lending library for books she never borrowed. The trusted maid elopes with a lover and steals the remainder of her dead mistress's wardrobe. We are even told that Emma "corrupted" the widower from beyond the grave. It is, indeed, the discovery of her correspondence with her lovers which puts the finishing touch on the handiwork of Lheureux and the rest: the husband is hounded to death as surely as the wife.

"The world described in *Madame Bovary*," said Thibaudet, "is a world which is falling apart . . . But in every society when something is destroyed another thing takes its place." Homais and Lheureux do in fact triumph, and the novel closes with an ironical twist of the Quack receiving a medal for political services after getting rid of three more doctors, and having the unhappy Blindman shut up in the name of Progress because he cannot cure him with his dubious potions. We must, however, be clear about the meaning of these events. In Flaubert's Yonville, as surely as in Stendhal's Parma, we are watching a world in microcosm. However shabby its representatives, the world which is falling apart is the traditional world, the world of the liberal professions: the world which is taking its place, which is rising in the persons of Homais and Lheureux, is the world of "spivs." The exchanges between Bournisien and Homais are something more than comic relief, something more than the bickerings of the village priest and the village rationalist. They reflect the conflict between religion and science which rent France in the nineteenth century. There is, indeed, something prophetic about the pair Homais-Lheureux. It was the ascent of men like these which brought France to the brink of destruction. We cannot contemplate the activities of the small-time usurer without thinking of what was happening in Paris on a huge scale during the Second Empire, and was chronicled by Zola in a novel like *L'Argent*. We cannot forget that it was the triumph of the free-thinking lower-middle class, which emerged from the Revolution, that later produced the split between Right and Left in France—a split which completed in the moral sphere the damage done by speculation in the material sphere.

# *Madame Bovary* or the Book about Nothing

## *by Jean Rousset*

We speak today of *anti-novels.* Sartre contributed to putting
the term into fashion by his preface to Nathalie Sarraute's *Portrait
d'un inconnu:* "Anti-novels maintain the appearance and the contours of the novel . . . but that is to increase the deception: the
novel is being contested on its own grounds and being destroyed
before our eyes in the very time that it apparently is being con-
structed." In this there is a sign that "the novel is in the process of
reflecting upon itself."

If we extend the meaning of this a little, we may say that there
is an anti-novel when the novel has a bad conscience, when it turns
critical and autocritical and breaks with the existent novel. The
novel enters a crisis: today a crisis of character, of "psychology,"
finally of subject, which increasingly tends to be distinguished from
the work itself or to disappear purely and simply, if we call subject
the story, the plot, the web of events, what takes place. Robbe-Grillet
confessed recently: "In my first book, *Les Gommes,* there was a
conventional plot based on Oedipus Rex and having no importance
at all for me. It aimed neither at plausibility nor at authenticity.
The readers of *La Jalousie* also had no reason for wondering what
autobiographical content such a novel had; but that time it was for
an even more obvious reason: nothing, or almost nothing, happens
in it." [1]

But before Robbe-Grillet or Nathalie Sarraute, in other ways so
different from one another, there were the Gide of the *Faux-Mon-
nayeurs,* whose protagonist and double, Edouard, declared: "My

"*Madame Bovary* or the Book about Nothing." From *Forme et signification*
(Paris: José Corti, 1962), by Jean Rousset, pp. 109-133. Copyright © 1962 by
La Librairie José Corti. Reprinted by permission of Jean Rousset and La
Librairie José Corti. Translated by Raymond Giraud. This study first appeared
in *Saggi e ricerche di letteratura francese,* Vol. I (1960), pp. 185-208.

[1] *Prétexte,* Nouvelle série, no. I, January 1958, p. 100.

novel has no subject," and Virginia Woolf, whom George Moore warned: "Believe me, Mrs. Woolf, you will never succeed in writing a good novel without any subject at all." Such, however, was her dream, and who will say that she did not succeed?

May we go further back? The naturalists seem to parade analogous claims when Goncourt declares to Huret: "My thought is that in spite of the fact that more novels are being sold than ever, the novel is a worn-out, threadbare genre that has said everything it had to say, a genre in which I have done everything to kill *its novel-like quality* in order to turn it into autobiographies of sorts and memoirs of people without history." [2] But what is condemned here, and also in similar terms by Zola and Huysmans, is the plot and the fiction of previous literature rather than the subject, reference to the real world, the exclusion of which naturalist doctrine is very far from advocating. There were, however, some readers at the time who complained of the absence of a subject, just as the Impressionist painters were reproached for creating painting without any subject.

On the other hand, we have a right here to invoke Flaubert, a pure critical novelist, nourished from childhood by the great ancestor of all anti-novels, *Don Quixote*. We know the ambition he declared as early as the time when he was working on *Madame Bovary:* "What seems beautiful to me and what I should like to do is a book about nothing, a book with no exterior attachment . . . a book which would have almost no subject, or whose subject at least would be almost invisible, if that is possible." [3] And a bit later: "If this book that I am writing with so much trouble succeeds, I shall have established by the very fact of creating it these two truths which are axioms for me; to wit, first, that poetry is purely subjective, that there are no beautiful, artistic subjects in literature, and that Yvetot is therefore as good as Constantinople; and that consequently one can write anything at all as well as whatever you wish." [4]

That century-old declaration of war on the subject is enough evidence that the novel did not wait until 1950 to feel it was in a state of crisis and rupture. When the "new novel" of our time revolts against the "traditional novel," it is attacking a novel that had itself been in revolt. To be sure, differences exist, not only between the creations defended by these rejections—which is evident—but also

[2] Huret, *Enquête sur l'évolution littéraire,* 1891, p. 168.
[3] *Corr.,* II, p. 345.
[4] *Corr.,* III, p. 249.

between the condemned novels, and the non-subject of one often becomes the subject that will be rejected by those that come afterwards.

Nonetheless, Flaubert's search has become timely today. He is the first in date of the nonrepresentational modern novelists. Even if the subject—and the psychology—of *Madame Bovary* play their muted part in the concert of the novel and can no longer be detached from it, we have the right and perhaps the duty to put them between parentheses and to say, as Flaubert did to Goncourt: "The story, the adventure of a novel, doesn't matter to me." When one remembers that so modern profession of faith: "The works of art which I like above all others are those in which *art is in excess*. In painting, I like Painting; in verses, Verse" (8th September 1860), one is justified in completing the formula as follows: in the novel, the art of the novel, the style of the novel; and we feel invited by Flaubert himself to read *Madame Bovary* as a sonata. Perhaps we will then escape the reproach he had directed to the great critics of his time: "What shocks me in my friends Sainte-Beuve and Taine is that they do not take sufficient account of *Art,* of the work in itself, of composition and style, of what makes the Beautiful." [5]

There is a fact of composition of which Flaubert does not speak expressly, but which must have preoccupied him, though how consciously it would be difficult to evaluate. This is the point of view assumed by the writer toward the events and characters within the novel. Impartiality and panoramic view of the ideal witness? That would be the expected solution for those who recall the author's declared intention of making himself impersonal and objective in *Madame Bovary;* moreover, it was the normal mode of presentation in the Balzacian novel. But Flaubert does not believe in impersonal knowledge. There is no objective reality; every vision, every perception is an illusion proper to some person; all views are so many "colored glasses." Is not such an experience of a nature to put into question the privileged position of the omniscient author endowed with the absolute vision of God?

### An Introductory Character: Charles Bovary

We are at first astonished by the general arrangement of the book, which excludes the heroine from its overture and epilogue; that

[5] *Lettres à Tourguenieff,* February 1869, Monaco, ed. du Rocher, 1946, p. 15.

astonishment leads us directly to the problem of the point of view or points of view adopted by Flaubert.

The disposition that gives Charles Bovary a central piece at the beginning and at the end was foreseen in the very first preliminary sketches, the only modification having to deal with the increasing importance given to Homais in the last pages. Now these two characters, presented from a distance and from the outside—object-characters, opaque consciousnesses—assure the novel an entrance and an exit where reigns sovereignly the point of view of someone who installs himself at the edge of the spectacle, observes it from above and afar, and refuses to know anything of the secret motivations of the figures that he treats as puppets: Charles' entrance in the class, which is also his entrance into our field of vision (assimilated into that of the curious "we," summoned only to disappear immediately afterward); and at the other extremity, in a delicious symmetry that suffices to justify the initial plans of the book, the triumphantly comical exit of the apothecary. Flaubert has placed at the doors of the work, where he makes contact and takes leave, the maximum of irony and sad sarcasm, because it is there that he observes with the most estranged view. The novel is thus ordered in a movement which goes from the exterior to the interior, from the surface to the heart, from indifference to complicity, and then returns from the interior to the periphery. In Flaubert the first look at the world is borne from far away and only catches the outside, the crust, the mechanical, the "grotesque." [6]

But he is not long in penetrating beneath the outer shell. If Homais, from beginning to end, is always seen from the outside, which allows him to be used for the epilogue, it is not the same for Charles, starting with that preamble where the author, followed by the reader, begins the long road with him, getting progressively closer to the puppet as he becomes a man. A rapid flashback illuminates his origins, his childhood, and his adolescence; it is a way of getting into sympathetic relation with him. One is nonetheless a bit surprised to find oneself suddenly introduced into his intimate self and his dreams: "In the lovely summer evenings . . . he would open the window and watch. The stream . . . was flowing down below him. . . . Opposite, beyond the roofs, the great clear sky stretched away with the red sun setting. *How good it must be over there! How cool beneath the beeches. . . .*" [7]

[6] See, for example, the arrival in Egypt, *Corr.*, II, p. 119.

[7] *Madame Bovary*, I, p. 9. All references to the novel refer to the Dumesnil edition, Paris, Les Belles Lettres, 1945, 2 vol.

For a moment one might imagine some error: Flaubert normally attributes such aspirations before the window or such a reverie in open space to his heroine. He was not able to refrain from this tiny proof of complicity, this brief instant in which he assumes the point of view of his character, who provisionally resembles a protagonist and acquires some of the benefits thereof. In truth, this penetration is a furtive one. The author immediately separates himself. But Flaubert's drafts contain at this spot several pages of memories and dreams. Nearly all of this was cut out; it had the effect of bringing the character decidedly too close and into too intimate contact with the reader. But he did not succeed in treating him absolutely as an object. Perhaps he did not want to. Here appears Charles Bovary's function and the explanation of his dominant presence in the preamble.

In fact, it is in Charles' field of vision that Emma will rise into view. Charles will serve as a reflector until the moment when the heroine, progressively introduced and accepted, will come downstage and become the center and the subject. But she must begin, as her future husband did, in the subordinate role of an object-character known from the outside, with this difference: that she comes into view beneath a look that is not critical but dazzled, and in the mirror of a sensibility with which the reader has become familiar, into which he has even been sporadically allowed to penetrate, particularly at the time of the doctor's daydreams and his double perceptions when he rides in the early morning toward the Bertaux farm, just before Emma's first appearance. Thus Flaubert uses Charles to introduce Emma and to show her just as Charles sees her, closely adopting his perspective, his limited angle of vision, and his subjective vision, so that we go along step by step in his discovery of this unknown woman. Placing himself behind and sometimes within his character, Flaubert foreswears the privileged optic of the omniscient author, to give only a provisional, superficial, and changing image of his heroine.[8]

Charles arrives at the farm: "A young woman in a blue woolen dress trimmed with three flounces appeared on the threshold of the house." A blue dress: that is what he notices first; and it is also all that we are allowed to see. A page later he notices the whiteness

---

[8] It would be advantageous, however different and independent from one another are Flaubert's and Stendhal's methods, to read Georges Blin's admirable *Stendhal et les problèmes du roman*, Paris, Corti, 1954, the second part: "Les restrictions de champ."

of her fingernails, then her eyes. A bit further on, when he chats with her, it will be "her full lips." When she turns around, it is the hair gathered at the back of her neck, moving in a way "that the country doctor noticed for the first time in his life." Instead of a portrait in the manner of Balzac or, before him, of Marivaux, implying a global and atemporal view, expressing not the characters but the author's knowledge, Flaubert creates a fragmentary and progressive portrait or, rather, causes it to be created by the pointillist perceptions of his agitated character. Other glimpses will appear to add still more details, but still equally dispersed because they are always seen in the confused perspective of the suitor.

It happens that the early drafts allow us to catch Flaubert's efforts to penetrate this vision and respect its character. Thus he first writes: "She wore no neckerchief or collar, *her white shoulders were pink.*" [9] A lovely impressionistic notation of a light effect in a kitchen in summer, but too subtle for Charles Bovary. Flaubert, suppressing himself as author, sacrifices it and replaces it with an observation more in keeping with the character whose point of view he is using: "He could see little drops of sweat on her bare shoulders" (I, 23). It must be said, however, that this assumption of the limitations or myopias of a character is not rigorously carried out—we are still rather far off from a Faulkner shutting himself hermetically into the stream of consciousness of an idiot—and that Flaubert—whether through inconsistency or refusal to be systematic—does not fear enriching Charles' normal vision, just as he sometimes allows Emma reflections or an ironic nuance of which she would be incapable. The result is often a compromise in which contradictory views of the external observer and the inner subject are fused so that it is hard to distinguish between them. Flaubert does not even hesitate to commit the "fault" with which Sartre so bitterly reproaches Mauriac—as if he were the first one guilty of it—that of situating himself simultaneously within and outside of his character's consciousness: "As for Charles, he made no effort to wonder why it gave him pleasure to come to the Bertaux farm" (I, 17). Another example: "Was she speaking that way seriously? Emma probably had no idea herself" (II, 81).

What remains undeniable and visibly intentional is that throughout the preamble Charles is a central character, acting somewhat like a spotlight. We do not leave him one instant, and Emma is

[9] *Madame Bovary, Nouvelle version,* ed. Pommier-Leleu, Paris, Corti, 1949, p. 166.

seen only through him. We know of her only what he learns; the only words she pronounces are those she says to him, and we have not the slightest idea of what she really thinks or feels. Emma is systematically shown to us from the outside. This is required from Charles' point of view. On this point Flaubert proceeds with complete rigorousness. He even gives us an extreme indication. At the moment when the young girl takes the momentous decision to get married, which will set her pitiful destiny (and indeed the whole book that we are about to read) in motion, the novelist hides her from us; her dialogue with her father, her thoughts, her reply, all of this is indirectly presented to us and at a considerable distance— the distance at which Charles is located as he waits behind the hedge for the shutter of the window to be pushed against the wall. What she thinks of Charles and of the marriage, what she expects of it, what must have gone on within her during that half hour—we get a glimpse of all this only in a disconnected and refracted way later on, when Flaubert gets closer to her and opens up her inner thoughts to us. But for the moment she remains still the object-character contemplated from afar by Charles Bovary and of whom we, like him, know only a few facial features, a few gestures, a dress.

What there is behind this appearance, what this young woman is in reality, this we shall soon know, for there will be a change of focus. But Charles will never know any more than that. For him she will always be that indecipherable stranger that she will cease to be for us. He will continue to be unaware of what is hidden behind the veil that she appears to be for those who lack the novelist's power to identify himself with her. From the fifth chapter on the pivot turns slowly, what had been subject becomes object, the center of consciousness passes from Charles to Emma, and the reader enters that consciousness which until then had been closed to him, just as it still is for Charles.

That is probably the real reason why the doctor was given a central place in the first chapters, and also why his point of view is accorded constant respect, even including the most unexpected plumbings of his intimate thoughts. We thus not only see Emma through a sensibility that is immersed in the flux of time, but, even more, this disposition allows the reader to feel from within the quality of knowledge that Charles has and always will have of his wife. The memory that the reader, alerted this way, will keep once Emma has been moved up to the center of the stage will lend light and density to the fictional universe in which he is getting involved.

### The Art of Modulation

From chapter six on Emma slips toward the center and never leaves it again, except for brief interruptions. That is in no way exceptional. Balzac, a master of global and panoramic treatment, makes use of a central character, Rastignac for example, and develops his action around him. Flaubert's originality will be in combining the author's and heroine's points of view, in their alternation and interferences, and, above all, in the predominance granted the subjective vision of the character in perspective. From there on the problem is one of insuring that the displacements of point of view and the transitions from one perspective to another do not break the movement or the "web of style."

Witness the transition from Charles to Emma, the gradual introduction, by imperceptible stages, of the heroine's point of view. The beginning and end of this itinerary are indicated by the return of a single object that has been subjected to two different views: the garden of Tostes. "The garden, longer than it was wide, ran between two mud walls . . . to a hawthorn hedge that separated it from the field. In the middle was a slate sun dial . . . four flower beds. . . . At the far end, under the spruces, was a plaster curé reading his breviary" (I, 36). The simple state of the place, an objective observation of surfaces and materials, such as might emanate from an outside observer,[10] a vibrationless look—Robbe-Grillet would say: without anthropomorphic complicity with things. Emma has just entered her new home, and for us she is only a stranger to whom Flaubert has not yet given us access. But that access will have already been effected for some time when thirty pages further on he will give us an emotional vision that his disenchanted heroine has of that same little garden, sensitive now to everything that, even in objects themselves, betrays disgust, inertia, erosion, and decay. "The dew had left on the cabbages a silver lace with long bright threads spreading from one to another. No birds were to be heard, everything seemed to sleep; the espalier, covered with straw, and the vine, like a great sick snake under the coping of the wall, along which one saw, as one approached, woodlice crawling on their many feet. Amid the spruces near the hedge, the curé in his three-cornered hat reading

[10] "A third party who might have observed them face to face . . ." is what one reads in the rough draft at that point. Ed. Pommier-Leleu, p. 182.

his breviary had lost his right foot, and even the plaster scaling off
with the frost had left white scabs on his face" (I, 73).

In this interval all has changed. Not only the condition and mood
of the heroine, but the reader's position with respect to her. In an
artful pivoting movement the point of view has turned, and the
visual center has progressively fused with Emma's own: a first look
in her dreams, then analysis of her sentimental development with
a flashback into the past, but still not as she could have done it
herself; Flaubert's hand is always visible. A new and more studied
look into her dreams of a different honeymoon: "She would dream
at times," until the long reverie under the beeches (I, 49), which now
is totally subjective, with all the characteristics of Flaubertian
ecstasy.[11]

Apropos of one of his own novels, Henry James speaks of an
"artful rotation of aspects"; one might apply this expression to
Flaubert. This has to do with the art of modulation of points of
view, of which he is past master and of which he makes constant
use. Actually, although Emma always continues to occupy the focal
center of the novel, Flaubert does not abstain from occasionally
substituting, in brief intermissions, another character whose view
he adopts for an instant. Now these displacements of point of view
are not a simple matter for an author sensitive to the slightest
rupture of the rhythm and determined not to have recourse to a
novelist's staged tricks, such as those that abound in the first *Éducation*. That is why, when Flaubert momentarily abandons Emma's
point of view to take that of Charles or Rodolphe or simply to bring
into prominence some supernumerary or other, he manages to do
it without breaking the current by a system of transitions in closed
circuit. An example of this method is needed.

In the third chapter of the second part, after the arrival in Yonville, Emma enters her new house. The reader accompanies her, and
with her he feels "the cold of the plaster fall on her shoulders like
damp linen"; here the novelist has diverse information to offer about
the characters recently presented—Léon, Homais. To do this, he
has to disengage himself from his heroine, but how can he without
breaking the thread? By utilizing a glance of Emma's: "The next
day, when she awakened, *she saw the clerk* in the town square. . . .
Léon waited all day long," etc. In this way we have slid over to the
clerk, whom we accompany now for a moment. From the clerk,
whom M. Homais "respected for his education," we pass without a

[11] Which Georges Poulet has beautifully analyzed in "La Pensée circulaire de
Flaubert," *N.R.F.*, July 1955.

break to the pharmacist, his habits, and his behavior toward the new physician, and thus are able to get around to him as well: "Charles was sad; patients were not coming in," but on the other hand his wife's pregnancy made him happy. And so, with Charles' look at his pregnant wife, Flaubert, closing the circuit, returns to Emma and successfully completes his tour of these points of view: "He looked at her happily. . . . Emma at first felt a great astonishment." By juxtaposing the thoughts of the married couple Flaubert takes the opportunity to underline their divergence. He will be led to give up his method of imperceptible shifting from one point of view to another in order to show more clearly, through a sort of exceptional leap, the cross-eyed way they look at each other, the infinite distance that separates them, even though seated or lying side by side: "He saw himself dishonored. . . . Emma, opposite, was looking at him; she did not share his humiliation, but felt an entirely different one" (II, 11; *cf.* also II, 34-35). But as a general rule Flaubert concentrates on modulation. Thus, when Rodolphe and Emma end their last nightly dialogue, related entirely from the young woman's point of view:

> "Until tomorrow, then," said Emma in a last caress.
> And *she watched him* go away.
> He did not turn back. . . . He was already across the stream and was quickly walking through the pasture.
> At the end of a few minutes Rodolphe stopped (II, 39).

Carried again by Emma's look, the reader leaves her for the object of that look, and from then on accompanies Rodolphe, hears him think, watches him write the letter terminating their affair.

This art of modulation, this so manifest taste for imperceptible transitions and dissolutions represents in the particular context with which we are concerned in these pages Flaubert's general effort toward what he calls *style*. For style is for Flaubert an agglomerating principle, it is reduction to the homogeneous. What he seeks to obtain is a "web" as tight and as smooth as possible—it is continuity: "Continuity constitutes style, as constancy makes for virtue." [12] When he abuses one of Louise Colet's or Leconte de Lisle's poems, his criticism stresses the unevenness, the disparities of tone or of color. What constitutes in his eyes the quality of a work is not the pearls but the thread that holds them together; it is the uniform movement, the flow. Working on *Madame Bovary* and rereading

[12] *Corr.,* III, p. 401.

what he had done, he writes to Louise Colet: "I reread all that the day before yesterday and was frightened by how little it amounts to. . . . Every paragraph is good in itself, and there are, I am sure, some perfect pages. But precisely because of that, *it won't do.* It is a series of well-rounded paragraphs, each one complete, *but not flowing smoothly into the next.* I am going to have to pull them apart, loosen their joints." [13] The artist concentrates on these joints, which must be strong and supple, but invisible. Flaubert cements with infinite care and takes no less care to remove every trace of cement: "I have had to remove a great deal of cement which was oozing between the stones and have had to reassemble the stones so that the joints would not show." [14]

Big rocks, great stony masses were always seductive to Flaubert's imagination. At the end of his beautiful essay J.-P. Richard shows clearly that in response to the profound fluidity of the Flaubertian being there is in him, at the moment of creation, an effort toward sedimentation, toward petrification, successful insofar as it does not dry up the original humidity and plasma. Flaubert is faithful to himself when, in order to designate what constitutes in his eyes "beauty," he uses the image of the entirely smooth wall, the *bare wall.* We meet it in a letter of 1876, but it goes back to a youthful experience: "I remember the beating of my heart and a feeling of violent pleasure when I contemplated a wall of the Acropolis, a completely bare wall. . . . Well, I wonder whether a book, independently of what it says, cannot produce the same effect? In the precision of the joints, the economy of the elements, *the polish of the surface,* the harmony of the total effect, is there not an intrinsic virtue, a sort of divine force?" [15] And elsewhere: "Prose must hold itself erect from one end to another, like a wall." What fascinates Flaubert in the wall is the fissureless block, the immobile and compact mass, the "great smooth line" unbroken by any unevenness, that perfection of the continuous, which is assured, as we have just seen, by the unity of modulated passages.

This ideal of the "straight line" and massive masonry does not exclude, in the fabric of the novel, variations of tonality and motion, zones of more or less intense vibration which create the rhythm or palpitation of the book.

In this respect, and to keep strictly to the questions of optical focus and field of vision, we might take note of the role played by

[13] *Corr.,* III, p. 92.
[14] *Corr.,* III, p. 264.
[15] *Corr.,* VII, p. 294.

windows in *Madame Bovary*. The heroine's frequent presence before a window, to which Leon Bopp has rightly called attention, is responsible for some remarkable effects of distant perspective and views plunging downward which correspond to phases of maximum subjectivity and extreme intensity.

## Windows and the Plunging View

The Marie of *Novembre* already spent her days before her window, a spot for waiting, a vigil over the void from which a customer or an event might arise. The window is a privileged post for those Flaubertian characters who are both immobile and adrift, stuck in their inertia and given over to the vagabondage of their thoughts. In that closed place where the soul is moldering, here then is a rent through which one can be diffused in space without having to leave one's point of fixation. The window combines closing and opening, barrier and flight, confinement in the room and expansion outside, the unlimited in the circumscribed. Absent where he is, present where he is not, oscillating between contraction and dilation, as Georges Poulet has so clearly shown, the Flaubertian character was predisposed to fix his existence on this boundary point where one can both flee and stay, on this window which seems the ideal site of his reverie.

We read already in *Par les champs et par les grèves:* "Ah, air! Air! More space! Since *our constricted souls stifle and die on the window sill,* since our captive spirits, like the bear in his pit, always turn upon themselves and bump against their walls, at least grant my nostrils the perfume of all the winds of the earth, *let my eyes set off toward all the horizons."* [16]

Emma Bovary, herself a captive between the walls of her pit, finds before her window flight "toward every horizon": "she often placed herself there" (I, 145); at Tostes it is from her window that she watches the rain fall and the monotonously repeated days of village life; from her window at Yonville she watches the notary's clerk go by, sees Rodolphe for the first time; it is from the window overlooking the garden that she hears the ringing of the angelus that stirs up mystical notions in her, and there too her eyes wander amid the clouds or across the meanders of the stream. It is at the attic window that she has her first suicidal dizziness; and after her grave illness, when she resumes contact with life, "they would push her in

[16] *Par les champs et par les grèves,* ed. Conard, pp. 125-126.

her chair to the window, the one that overlooked the square" (II, 54).
Windows of boredom and reverie.

There are also closed windows and drawn curtains, reserved for
the rare moments when Emma, in harmony with herself and the
place of her existence, no longer needs to be diffused in the limitless-
ness of reverie, but is contained within herself in the initial and
happy phase of her passions: at Rouen with Léon in the "carriage
with drawn curtains . . . more tightly shut than the grave," then
in the hotel room where they live shut up all day long "with shutters
and doors closed"; "a hothouse atmosphere," says one of the preliminary sketches. It was the same with Rodolphe when Emma, at
the beginning of their affair, went to surprise him at La Huchette
in the penumbra that "the yellow curtains, hanging down the full
length of the windows" cast in his room. But that first passion is
habitually an open-air passion, for the forest or garden; here there
are no windows at all. In this way Flaubert contrasts the characters
of his two lovers while conforming to the significance of the windows
in his novel.

Together with its significance for the Flaubertian character, the
window offers the technician in novelistic setting and scenario structure interesting resources in perspectives, which Flaubert does not
fail to utilize to vary the perspectives of narration and to obtain
curious "optical effects." One thinks immediately of the brilliant
"symphonic" bit of the *Comices,* presented in the visual and auditory
perspective of the future lovers installed at the window of the town
hall on the second storey. The downward view has a double advantage: it serves first to reinforce the ironic distance from which the
author treats the agricultural gathering and, in counterpoint, the
idyll that is superimposed on it and blends with it; it also expresses
the movement of elevation that characterizes Emma's entrance into
the life of passion; we find that movement in the following phase of
the affair. In fact, the same aerial optic is used shortly afterwards,
at the time of the horseback ride during which the relationship that
began at the *Comices* is consummated. We arrive at the summit of
a slope; Flaubert arranges there a panoramic view of the landscape,
an image of the vision that Emma simultaneously has of her existence: "There was mist over the countryside. Vapors stretched out
at the horizon between the outlines of the hills; and others, moving
apart, rose and were dissipated. At times, *in a separation* of the
clouds beneath a ray of sunlight, *one could see far off* the roofs at
Yonville, with the gardens at the water's edge, the courtyards, the
walls and the church steeple. Emma half closed her eyelids to recog-

nize her house, *and that poor village where she lived had never seemed so small to her"* (I, 181). The entrance into passion is marked by an ascension above the habitual level of existence, the site of which is swallowed up and annulled beneath Emma's eyes. Yonville must diminish at a distance that the aerial perspective makes infinite, so that there can be substituted for it the imaginary space of love, depicted here as evaporating water: "From the heights where they were, the whole valley seemed an immense, pale lake, evaporating in the air." That is what becomes of the village and its houses at the moment when the author directs his exalted heroine's gaze to overlook the world beneath her: a mirage without contours or support.

When, a few pages later, Emma dreams that same evening of the new life which has just opened for her, it is still in terms in which height and the unlimited are associated in opposition to "ordinary existence," cast "beneath her," as if that afternoon's downward gaze had entered intact in the inner landscape of her mind: "She was moving into something marvelous, where all would be passion, ecstasy, delirium; a bluish vastness was all about her, the summits of sentiment sparkled beneath her thought, and ordinary existence appeared only as something far off, far beneath her, in the shadow between those heights" (I, 185).

For this summit point above the village Flaubert reserved another use toward the end of the novel, at a moment that is not less decisive but has an opposite meaning. Madame Bovary has seen Rodolphe for the last time, she is returning to Yonville, distracted, to put an end to her life; it is no longer the climb toward passionate ecstasy, but descent toward suicide; in the course of that hallucinatory walk at nightfall, she finds herself at the summit of a slope, perhaps the same one as before, above the village; she emerges abruptly from her dizzying ecstasy: "Everything disappeared. She recognized the lights of the houses, which shone from far away in the fog.

"And now her situation, like *an abyss,* became clear to her. . . . *She ran down* the hill" (II, 168). The return from the imaginary to the real means falling toward the village, which this time emerges from the fog instead of being reabsorbed into it; it is a descent into the abyss.

Thus, at the beginning and end of this amorous odyssey, on two pages far apart but symmetrically opposed, Flaubert places his heroine in the same dominant place where he reserves for her the same plunging perspective. It is up to the attentive reader to establish the connection and to perceive the wealth with which a book so ably composed is laden. He will compare this diptych with another in which the novelist combines use of the window and the vehicle (which will play so important a role in the *Éducation*): the double view of Rouen at the arrival and departure of the diligence at the time of the Thursday rendezvous with Léon. Once more a plunging view: "Thus seen from above, all the countryside seemed motionless like a painting." And this time too, in the distorting lens of an imagination agitated by passion, the countryside, motionless at first, stirs, palpitates, dilates.

But there is an important difference: Emma's look no longer moved downward toward Yonville and her "ordinary life" but, on the contrary, toward the place where she will live her passion; also, far from appearing to her at a distance that veils it and shrinks it to the point of annulment, the site of her desire, by an inverted mirage, emerges from the mist and is magnified into an "vast capital," measured only by the wide open space before her: "Before that space her love grew greater and was filled with confusion at the vague murmuring sounds which arose. She poured it out, on the squares, on the avenues, on the streets, and the old Norman city *stretched out before her eyes like an immense capital, like a Babylon that she was entering*" (II, 112).

Windows and plunging perspectives, openings into the distance and reveries in space, all are neuralgic points in the narration, knots at which the narrative stops; they correspond to very unusual angles of vision, when the novelist relinquishes his traditional divine rights, when the subjective vision begins to dominate and the author identifies himself most with his heroine, stands behind her, and sees things through her. Their distribution in the novel is significant. They are unequally distributed. Absent from the active phases, where passion is consummated, they multiply in periods of stagnation and waiting: at Tostes after the invitation to the chateau, when one first sees Emma, the ball over, open the window and lean out; [17]

---

[17] We know that Flaubert made some considerable cuts at this point: the young woman's stroll at dawn in the park and her long contemplation of the countryside through a window with colored panes (ed. Pommier-Leleu, pp. 216-217). This is a great shame. Flaubert still attached importance to these pages, and this we can understand. It is a perfect illustration of subjective vision; seen through panes of different colors, the same landscape does not change only in color, but also in form, dimensions, relationships between objects at different distances, and, finally, emotional tonality. In this way Emma will see the world through her own passion, through the diverse colors that it will assume.

it is a time of reverie that is beginning and that never ends, at Tostes as well as at Yonville, until the moment when she begins to live her great passion, returns to her husband, leaves him again after the episode of the clubfoot, prepares her flight, goes in for purchases and debts. After these chapters of action and accelerated movement the separation from Rodolphe introduces a new adagio, a new time of inertia and stagnation, announced again by a window opening before the heroine, but in a more tragic spirit, with vertigo and loss of consciousness anticipating the dénouement: the attic window where she reads the letter terminating their affair: "Opposite, over the roofs, the open countryside stretched out as far as the eye could see." She is about to go back to desiring and regretting, expanding beyond her limits, "floating" in an aerial environment which is that of her reverie and her plunging perspectives: "She stood at the very edge, almost suspended, surrounded by open space. The blue of the sky seemed to close in on her." [18]

But a relapse always follows those periodic flights constituted by the reveries before the window: " 'My wife! My wife!' Charles cried out. . . . And yet he had to go down! Dinner was waiting!" (II, 46-47). Flight and fall make the rhythmical movement of the work as well as the psychological life of the heroine. Thus, at the beginning of the sixth chapter of the second part, the open window and the tinkling of the angelus stimulate Emma to rove among her memories and to feel that weightless suspension that is expressed by images of flight and of a whirling feather: "She felt weak and totally abandoned, like a bird's downy feather whirled about in the storm." Then back from church, "she *dropped* into an armchair," caught up again in the heavy, closed world of the bedroom, in the monotonous fixedness of time and motionless objects, in the opaque presence of beings that "are there" like furniture. "The furniture in its place seemed to have become more immobile. . . . The clock was still ticking. . . . Between the window and the worktable little Berthe was there. . . . Charles appeared. It was dinner time." To rejoin existence after hours of flight toward the outer world of windows is always a matter of falling, falling back into reclusion.

This double movement dominates other essential pages, like the central phase of the *Comices* where Emma, disturbed by the smell of pomade and the "far-off" view of the diligence, confuses in a sort of ecstasy lovers and times, before turning down again toward the crowd in the square and the official orator's phrases. Or like that

[18] In the rough draft: "She was on the point of floating in emptiness to escape existence," ed. Pommier-Leleu, p. 444.

other ecstasy, of the same amorous nature, that opens her affair with Léon in the same way that the preceding one started her passion for Rodolphe: the performance of the opera in Rouen. The box from which Emma sees the house and then the stage "from above" is an avatar of the window, a new combination of the enclosure and the opening out on an expanse where an imaginary destiny is profiled. Here it is not she who is acting it out; it is being acted for her on the stage; but she loses no time in recognizing herself and in identifying herself with the young stage heroine, sharing her desire "*to fly* into an embrace" and seeing another Rodolphe in the singer: "A madness took possession of her; he was looking at her, she was sure of it! She wanted to throw herself into his arms . . . to cry out: 'Carry me away!' The curtain *fell* . . . and she fell back into her seat" (II, 69). After the flight the brutal breaking of the dream and the aerial perspective is accompanied by inevitable descent into confinement; on this occasion Flaubert insists on the heaviness of the air and the occlusion of space: "The smell of gas was mixed with people's breath; the waving of fans made the atmosphere more stifling. Emma suddenly wanted to leave; the crowd blocked the corridors, and she fell back into her seat with suffocating palpitations."

How can we fail to foresee in this scene the death agony of the young woman, panting and choking, asking for the last time: "Open the window. . . . I am stifling" (II, 170)? In this life, each ecstasy is followed by a little death; the ultimate death is harmoniously consonant with those that have preceded and prefigured it.

All these reveries of Emma, these descents into her intimate soul, which are the moments at which Flaubert most tightly mingles his point of view with his heroine's angle of vision, abound very logically in the phases of inertia and boredom which are also the novel's adagios, where time is emptied, repeats itself, and seems to become immobile. These are the most beautiful and most novel movements of the work, and they are at the same time the most Flaubertian; they are those where Flaubert to a large extent abandons the objective vision of the universal witness.

On the other hand, when the action must proceed and there is new action to deal with, the author resumes his sovereign rights and panoramic point of view, once more moves away from his heroine, can again present an exterior view of her. This is notably the case, as we have seen, at the beginning and end of the novel or in the first chapters of a new part. Each fresh beginning requires the presence of the stage manager who erects the setting while introducing the actors. Such is the great scene at the inn in Yonville at the beginning of the second part or, for opening the third part, Emma's and Léon's conversation in the hotel room in Rouen, the meeting at the cathedral, the long ride in the cab. Here Flaubert profits from the momentary remoteness of the heroine to increase the distance still more and obtain a surprising effect of perspective. The new lovers are in the cab with its drawn curtains, but the reader is not admitted into it with them. If the preceding pages denied him entrance into the protagonist's soul, he at least could see gestures and attitudes and hear words; here even that is refused him; he no longer sees anything at all and can only follow from a distance the carriage that rolls along ahead of him. During that decisive episode he is reduced to the most indifferent point of view, that of the townspeople for whom this woman is only a stranger, and it is in that light, to which he is all the more unaccustomed because he has been and will be admitted to the very depth of her soul, that he finally sees her leave the cab: "And *a woman* got out, walking with her veil lowered and without turning her head" (II, 91). An all the more striking effect because, with our prolonged intimacy, we are able to guess everything that is hidden behind that lowered veil.

The same sort of effect of distance is created a bit later by the point of view the author has us adopt to witness Emma's desperate visit to Binet from way up in an attic where two curious neighbors have climbed. We see from a distance, are barely able to hear, and are reduced to guessing and interpreting gestures and attitudes; it is a scene from the silent screen. We can suppose that Flaubert, who has had us accompany his character very closely in the preceding hours and live her drama with her, though we are outside, is so sure of our participation that he has allowed himself this brusque disconnection to tear us out of our complicity and for an instant to present us with the heroine as she appears to the foreign gaze of an outside witness and judge. Immediately afterward we even lose sight of her, just like the gossips who see her disappear at the far end of the street, going toward the cemetery, and who are lost in speculation. After that, with a new harsh stroke, the novelist brings us brutally back to Emma arriving at the nurse's and, so to speak, drops us back into her consciousness. These violent manipulations of the reader, in keeping with the pathetic quality of that phase of the narration, surprise him all the more because they are not Flaubert's habitual manner of proceeding most often throughout the novel by gradual changes and barely perceptible modulation.

The importance assumed in Flaubert's novel by the character's point of view and her subjective vision at the expense of action observed from outside her has the consequence of increasing considerably the proportion of slow movements while reducing the importance of the objective author, who gives up a varying proportion[19] of his rights as an impartial observer.

Probably slowness and the character's perspective are what is newest and profoundly original in Flaubert, novelist of interior vision and immobility. It is precisely these admirable virtues, so characteristic of him, that Flaubert discovers only by groping in a way that is more instinctive than voluntary, and not without some anxiety. No "action," no "movement," he states in his letters; "fifty uninterrupted pages in which there is not a single event." If he is troubled at first to see the shape his book is taking in spite of himself, it is because he is thinking of what the novel was before him, of Balzac especially, in whom everything was movement, action, and drama. Then he makes up his mind: "One must sing in his own voice; mine will never be dramatic or engaging. Besides, I am convinced that everything is a matter of style or, rather, of shape, of aspect." [20] He will try at least to balance action and inaction, event and dream: "I will have my hands full establishing an approximately equal proportion between adventures and thoughts." [21]

He never quite achieves this,[22] and it is just as well; the bent of his talent and his dreamy heroine's nature were opposed to it. It is part of the Flaubertian genius to prefer an event's reflection in consciousness to the event itself, to prefer the dream of passion to real passion, and to substitute for action the absence of action and for every presence a void. And that is where the art of Flaubert triumphs; what is most beautiful in his novel is what is not like usual fictional literature; it is these great empty spaces. It is not the

---

[19] As an indispensable complement to these reflections, one should read the excellent pages of Erich Auerbach in *Mimesis*, Bern, Francke, 1946, p. 428 ff., showing that it is at the same time Emma who sees and the writer who speaks.

[20] *Corr.*, III, p. 86.

[21] *Corr.*, III, p. 394.

[22] We note in comparing the rough draft and the text that, on the contrary, Flaubert, far from increasing the weight of the action in his novels, rather has the tendency to lighten it as he goes along; in the first drafts, Emma gave herself to Léon before her affair with Rodolphe; similarly, for the *Éducation* he had at first intended Madame Arnoux to become Frédéric's mistress (*cf.* M. J. Durry, *Flaubert et ses projets inédits*, Paris, Nizet, 1950, p. 137 *ff.*). He will abandon this. In the first *Éducation*, Henry and Madame Renaud flee and live far away the life that they had dreamed of; in *Madame Bovary*, Flaubert suppresses the voyage and allows only a plan for it to survive; Emma travels only in her imagination; the event is dropped in favor of a dream of the event.

event, which contracts under Flaubert's hands, but what is between the events, those stagnant expanses where all movement is immobilized. The miracle is that he succeeded in giving so much existence and density to those empty spaces, creating fullness out of hollowness.[23] But this reversal implies another subversion: one that in the objective, third-person narration permits expansion of the share given to the character's perspective and to the optic of his "thought," where the heart of the matter is.

Flaubert is the great novelist of inaction, of boredom and immobility. But he did not know it or did not yet know it clearly before writing *Madame Bovary;* he discovers it as he composes his novel, and not without some anguish. He thereby reveals to us or confirms what is perhaps a law of creation: we invent only in insecurity; the new is disquieting, and the first gesture of the discoverer is a gesture of rejection. But in this groping and disturbed quest he finds what is really his own. In the act of composing he recognizes himself. And this verifies another law of creation: even in as voluntaristic an artist as Flaubert, one as convinced as he is that everything is in the conception and the plan, invention is inseparable from execution; the conception of the work is completed in the operations that bring it into being.

[23] "Nothing happens, but that nothing has become a heavy, oppressive, threatening something." Auerbach, *op. cit.,* p. 434.

# Madame Bovary

## by Erich Auerbach

Mais c'était surtout aux heures des repas qu'elle n'en pouvait plus, dans cette petite salle au rez-de-chaussée, avec le poêle qui fumait, la porte qui criait, les murs qui suintaient, les pavés humides; toute l'amertume de l'existence lui semblait servie sur son assiette, et, à la fumée du bouilli, il montait du fond de son âme comme d'autres bouffées d'affadissement. Charles était long à manger; elle grignotait quelques noisettes, ou bien, appuyée du coude, s'amusait, avec la pointe de son couteau, de faire des raies sur la toile cirée.

(But it was above all at mealtimes that she could bear it no longer, in that little room on the ground floor, with the smoking stove, the creaking door, the oozing walls, the damp floor-tiles; all the bitterness of life seemed to be served to her on her plate, and, with the steam from the boiled beef, there rose from the depths of her soul other exhalations as it were of disgust. Charles was a slow eater; she would nibble a few hazel-nuts, or else, leaning on her elbow, would amuse herself making  marks on the oilcloth with the point of her table-knife.)

The paragraph forms the climax of a presentation whose subject is Emma Bovary's dissatisfaction with her life in Tostes. She has long hoped for a sudden event which would give a new turn to it —to her life without elegance, adventure, and love, in the depths of the provinces, beside a mediocre and boring husband; she has even made preparations for such an event, has lavished care on herself and her house, as if to earn that turn of fate, to be worthy of it; when it does not come, she is seized with unrest and despair. All this Flaubert describes in several pictures which portray Emma's world as it now appears to her; its cheerlessness, unvaryingness, grayness, staleness, airlessness, and inescapability now first become clearly apparent to her when she has no more hope of fleeing from it. Our paragraph is the climax of the portrayal of her despair. After it we are told how she lets everything in the house go, neglects herself, and begins to fall ill, so that her husband decides to leave Tostes, thinking that the climate does not agree with her.

The paragraph itself presents a picture—man and wife together at mealtime. But the picture is not presented in and for itself; it is subordinated to the dominant subject, Emma's despair. Hence it is not put before the reader directly: here the two sit at table—there the reader stands watching them. Instead, the reader first sees Emma, who has been much in evidence in the preceding pages, and he sees the picture first through her; directly, he sees only Emma's inner state; he sees what goes on at the meal indirectly, from within her state, in the light of her perception. The first words of the paragraph, "But it was above all at mealtimes that she could bear it no longer. . . ." state the theme, and all that follows is but a development of it. Not only are the phrases dependent upon "in" and "with," which define the physical scene, a commentary on "she could bear it no longer" in their piling up of the individual elements of discomfort, but the following clause too, which tells of the distaste aroused in her by the food, accords with the principal purpose both in sense and rhythm. When we read further, "Charles was a slow eater," this, though grammatically a new sentence and rhythmically a new movement, is still only a resumption, a variation, of the principal theme; not until we come to the contrast between his leisurely eating and her disgust and to the nervous gestures of her despair, which are described immediately afterward, does the sentence acquire its true significance. The husband, unconcernedly eating, becomes ludicrous and almost ghastly; when Emma looks at him and sees him sitting there eating, he becomes the actual cause of the "She could bear it no longer"; because everything else that arouses her desperation— the gloomy room, the commonplace food, the lack of a tablecloth, the hopelessness of it all—appears to her, and through her to the reader also, as something that is connected with him, that emanates from him, and that would be entirely different if he were different from what he is.

The situation, then, is not presented simply as a picture, but we are first given Emma and then the situation through her. It is not, however, a matter—as it is in many first-person novels and other later works of a similar type—of a simple representation of the content of Emma's consciousness, of *what* she feels *as* she feels it. Though the light which illuminates the picture proceeds from her, she is yet herself part of the picture, she is situated within it. . . . It is not Emma who speaks, but the writer. "The smoking stove, the creaking door, the oozing walls, the damp floor tiles"—all this, of course, Emma sees and feels, but she would not be able to sum it all up in this way. "All the bitterness of life seemed to be served to her on her plate"—she doubtless has such a feeling; but if she wanted to express it, it would not come out like that; she has neither the intelligence nor the cold candor of self-accounting necessary for such a formulation. To be sure, there is nothing of Flaubert's life in these words, but only Emma's; Flaubert does nothing but bestow the power of mature expression upon the material which she affords, in its complete subjectivity. If Emma could do this herself, she would no longer be what she is, she would have outgrown herself and thereby saved herself. So she does not simply see, but is herself seen as one seeing, and is thus judged, simply through a plain description of her subjective life, out of her own feelings. Reading in a later passage (part 2, chapter 12): "Never had Charles seemed to her so disagreeable, to have such square fingers, so dull a mind, ways so vulgar . . . ," the reader perhaps thinks for a moment that this strange series is an emotional piling up of the causes that time and again bring Emma's aversion to her husband to the boiling point, and that she herself is, as it were, inwardly speaking these words; that this, then, is an example of *erlebte Rede*. But this would be a mistake. We have here, to be sure, a number of paradigmatic causes of Emma's aversion, but they are put together deliberately by the writer, not emotionally by Emma. For Emma feels much more, and much more confusedly; she sees other things than these—in his body, his manners, his dress; memories mix in, meanwhile she perhaps hears him speak, perhaps feels his hand, his breath, sees him walk about, good-hearted, limited, unappetizing, and unaware; she has countless confused impressions. The only thing that is clearly defined is the result of all this, her aversion to him, which she must hide. Flaubert transfers the clearness to the impressions; he selects three, apparently quite at random, but which are paradigmatically taken from Bovary's physique, his mentality, and his behavior; and he arranges them as if they were three shocks which Emma felt one after the other. This is not at all a naturalistic representation of consciousness. Natural shocks occur quite differently. The ordering hand of the writer is present here, deliberately summing up the confusion of the psychological situation in the direction toward which it tends of itself—the direction of "aversion to Charles Bovary." This ordering of psychological situation does not, to be sure, derive its stand-

ards from without, but from the material of the situation itself. It is
the type of ordering which must be employed if the situation itself
is to be translated into language without admixture.

In a comparison of this type of presentation with those of Stendhal
and Balzac, it is to be observed by way of introduction that here too
the two distinguishing characteristics of modern realism are to be
found; here too real everyday occurrences in a low social stratum,
the provincial petty bourgeoisie, are taken very seriously (we shall
discuss the particular character of this seriousness later); here too
everyday occurrences are accurately and profoundly set in a definite
period of contemporary history (the period of the bourgeois monarchy)—less obviously than in Stendhal or Balzac, but unmistakably.
In these two basic characteristics the three writers are at one, in
contradistinction to all earlier realism; but Flaubert's attitude toward his subject is entirely different. In Stendhal and Balzac we
frequently and indeed almost constantly hear what the writer thinks
of his characters and events; sometimes Balzac accompanies his narrative with a running commentary—emotional or ironic or ethical
or historical or economic. We also very frequently hear what the
characters themselves think and feel, and often in such a manner
that, in the passage concerned, the writer identifies himself with the
character. Both these things are almost wholly absent from Flaubert's work. His opinion of his characters and events remains un-
spoken; and when the characters express themselves it is never in
such a manner that the writer identifies himself with their opinion,
or seeks to make the reader identify himself with it. We hear the
writer speak; but he expresses no opinion and makes no comment.
His role is limited to selecting the events and translating them into
language; and this is done in the conviction that every event, if one
is able to express it purely and completely, interprets itself and the
persons involved in it far better and more completely than any
opinion or judgment appended to it could do. Upon this conviction
—that is, upon a profound faith in the truth of language responsibly,
candidly, and carefully employed—Flaubert's artistic practice rests.

This is a very old, classic French tradition. There is already something of it in Boileau's line concerning the power of the rightly used
word (on Malherbe: *D'un mot mis en sa place enseigna le pouvoir*);
there are similar statements in La Bruyère. Vauvenargues said:
"There are no errors that would not vanish by themselves, if clearly
expressed." Flaubert's faith in language goes further than Vauvenargues's: he believes that the truth of the phenomenal world is
also revealed in linguistic expression. Flaubert is a man who works

extremely consciously and possesses a critical comprehension of art
to a degree uncommon even in France; hence there occur in his
letters, particularly of the years 1852-1854 during which he was writing *Madame Bovary* (*Troisième Série* in the *Nouvelle édition aug-
mentée* of the *Correspondance*, 1927), many highly informative statements on the subject of his aim in art. They lead to a theory—
mystical in the last analysis, but in practice, like all true mysticism,
based upon reason, experience, and discipline—of a self-forgetful
absorption in the subjects of reality which transforms them (*par une
chimie merveilleuse*) and permits them to develop to mature expression. In this fashion subjects completely fill the writer; he forgets
himself, his heart no longer serves him save to feel the hearts of
others, and when, by fanatical patience, this condition is achieved,
the perfect expression, which at once entirely comprehends the
momentary subject and impartially judges it, comes of itself; subjects
are seen as God sees them, in their true essence. With all this there
goes a view of the mixture of styles which proceeds from the same
mystical-realistic insight: there are no high and low subjects; the
universe is a work of art produced without any taking of sides, the
realistic artist must imitate the procedures of Creation, and every
subject in its essence contains, before God's eyes, both the serious
and the comic, both dignity and vulgarity; if it is rightly and surely
reproduced, the level of style which is proper to it will be rightly and
surely found; there is no need either for a general theory of levels,
in which subjects are arranged according to their dignity, or for
any analyses by the writer commenting upon the subject, after
its presentation, with a view to better comprehension and more
accurate classification; all this must result from the presentation of
the subject itself.

It is illuminating to note the contrast between such a view and
the grandiloquent and ostentatious parading of the writer's own
feelings, and of the standards derived from them, of the type inaugu-
rated by Rousseau and continued after him; a comparative interpretation of Flaubert's "Our hearts should only serve to give us insight
into those of others," and Rousseau's statement at the beginning of
the *Confessions*, "I feel my own heart and understand all men,"
could effectually represent the change in attitude which had taken
place. But it also becomes clear from Flaubert's letters how laboriously and with what tensity of application he had attained to his
convictions. Great subjects, and the free, irresponsible rule of the
creative imagination, still have a great attraction for him; from this
point of view he sees Shakespeare, Cervantes, and even Hugo wholly

through the eyes of a romanticist, and he sometimes curses his own narrow petty-bourgeois subject which constrains him to tiresome stylistic meticulousness (*dire à la fois simplement et proprement des choses vulgaires*); this sometimes goes so far that he says things which contradict his basic views: "and the distressing thing is to think that even if it is perfectly successful, it [*Madame Bovary*] can be no more than adequate and because of its very essence will never be beautiful." Withal, like so many important nineteenth-century artists, he hates his period; he sees its problems and the coming crises with great clarity; he sees the inner anarchy, the "lack of theological foundation," the beginning menace of the mob, the lazy eclectic Historism, the domination of phrases, but he sees no solution and no issue; his fanatical mysticism of art is almost like a substitute religion, to which he clings convulsively, and his candor very often becomes sullen, petty, choleric, and neurotic. But this sometimes perturbs his impartiality and that love of his subjects which is comparable to the Creator's love. The paragraph which we have analyzed, however, is untouched by such deficiencies and weaknesses in his nature; it permits us to observe the working of his artistic purpose in its purity.

The scene shows man and wife at table, the most everyday situation imaginable. Before Flaubert, it would have been conceivable as literature only as part of a comic tale, an idyl, or a satire. Here it is a picture of discomfort, and not a momentary and passing one, but a chronic discomfort, which completely rules an entire life, Emma Bovary's. To be sure, various things come later, among them love episodes; but no one could see the scene at table as part of the exposition for a love episode, just as no one would call *Madame Bovary* a love story in general. The novel is the representation of an entire human existence which has no issue; and our passage is a part of it, which, however, contains the whole. Nothing particular happens in the scene, nothing particular has happened just before it. It is a random moment from the regularly recurring hours at which the husband and wife eat together. They are not quarreling, there is no sort of tangible conflict. Emma is in complete despair, but her despair is not occasioned by any definite catastrophe; there is nothing purely concrete which she has lost or for which she has wished. Certainly she has many wishes, but they are entirely vague—elegance, love, a varied life; there must always have been such unconcrete despair, but no one ever thought of taking it seriously in literary works before; such formless tragedy, if it may be called tragedy, which is set in motion by the general situation itself, was first made conceivable as literature by romanticism; probably Flaubert was the first to have

represented it in people of slight intellectual culture and fairly low
social station; certainly he is the first who directly captures the
chronic character of this psychological situation. Nothing happens,
but that nothing has become a heavy, oppressive, threatening something. How he accomplishes this we have already seen; he organizes
into compact and unequivocal discourse the confused impressions
of discomfort which arise in Emma at the sight of the room, the
meal, her husband. Elsewhere too he seldom narrates events which
carry the action quickly forward; in a series of pure pictures—pictures transforming the nothingness of listless and uniform days into
an oppressive condition of repugnance, boredom, false hopes, para-
lyzing disappointments, and piteous fears—a gray and random human destiny moves toward its end.

The interpretation of the situation is contained in its description.
The two are sitting at table together; the husband divines nothing
of his wife's inner state; they have so little communion that things
never even come to a quarrel, an argument, an open conflict. Each
of them is so immersed in his own world—she in despair and vague
wish-dreams, he in his stupid philistine self-complacency—that they
are both entirely alone; they have nothing in common, and yet they
have nothing of their own, for the sake of which it would be worthwhile to be lonely. For, privately, each of them has a silly, false
world, which cannot be reconciled with the reality of his situation,
and so they both miss the possibilities life offers them. What is true
of these two, applies to almost all the other characters in the novel;
each of the many mediocre people who act in it has his own world
of mediocre and silly stupidity, a world of illusions, habits, instincts,
and slogans; each is alone, none can understand another, or help
another to insight; there is no common world of men, because it
could only come into existence if many should find their way to their
own proper reality, the reality which is given to the individual—
which then would be also the true common reality. Though men
come together for business and pleasure, their coming together has
no note of united activity; it becomes one-sided, ridiculous, painful,
and it is charged with misunderstanding, vanity, futility, falsehood,
and stupid hatred. But what the world would really be, the world of
the "intelligent," Flaubert never tells us; in his book the world
consists of pure stupidity, which completely misses true reality, so
that the latter should properly not be discoverable in it at all; yet it
is there; it is in the writer's language, which unmasks the stupidity
by pure statement; language, then, has criteria for stupidity and thus

also has a part in that reality of the "intelligent" which otherwise never appears in the book.

Emma Bovary, too, the principal personage of the novel, is completely submerged in that false reality, in *la bêtise humaine,* as is the "hero" of Flaubert's other realistic novel, Frédéric Moreau in the *Éducation sentimentale.* How does Flaubert's manner of representing such personages fit into the traditional categories "tragic" and "comic"? Certainly Emma's existence is apprehended to its depths, certainly the earlier intermediate categories, such as the "sentimental" or the "satiric" or the "didactic," are inapplicable, and very often the reader is moved by her fate in a way that appears very like tragic pity. But a real tragic heroine she is not. The way in which language here lays bare the silliness, immaturity, and disorder of her life, the very wretchedness of that life, in which she remains immersed ("All the bitterness of life seemed to be served to her on her plate"), excludes the idea of true tragedy, and the author and the reader can never feel as at one with her as must be the case with the tragic hero; she is always being tried, judged, and, together with the entire world in which she is caught, condemned. But neither is she comic; surely not; for that, she is understood far too deeply from within her fateful entanglement—though Flaubert never practices any "psychological understanding" but simply lets the state of the facts speak for itself. He has found an attitude toward the reality of contemporary life which is entirely different from earlier attitudes and stylistic levels, including—and especially—Balzac's and Stendhal's. It could be called, quite simply, "objective seriousness." This sounds strange as a designation of the style of a literary work. Objective seriousness, which seeks to penetrate to the depths of the passions and entanglements of a human life, but without itself becoming moved, or at least without betraying that it is moved—this is an attitude which one expects from a priest, a teacher, or a psychologist rather than from an artist. But priest, teacher, and psychologist wish to accomplish something direct and practical—which is far from Flaubert's mind. He wishes, by his attitude—"no shrieks, no convulsion, nothing but a steady thoughtful gaze"—to force language to render the truth concerning the subjects of his observation: "style itself and in its own right being an absolute manner of viewing things" (*Corr.* II, 346). Yet this leads in the end to a didactic purpose: criticism of the contemporary world; and we must not hesitate to say so, much as Flaubert may insist that he is an artist and nothing but an artist. The more one studies Flaubert, the clearer it becomes how much insight into the problematic nature and the hollowness of nineteenth-century bourgeois culture is contained in his realistic works; and many important passages from his letters confirm this. The demonification of everyday social intercourse which is to be found in Balzac is certainly entirely lacking in Flaubert; life no longer surges and foams, it flows viscously and sluggishly. The essence of the happenings of ordinary contemporary life seemed to Flaubert to consist not in tempestuous actions and passions, not in demonic men and forces, but in the prolonged chronic state whose surface movement is mere empty bustle, while underneath it there is another movement, almost imperceptible but universal and unceasing, so that the political, economic, and social subsoil appears comparatively stable and at the same time intolerably charged with tension. Events seem to him hardly to change; but in the concretion of duration, which Flaubert is able to suggest both in the individual occurrence (as in our example) and in his total picture of the times, there appears something like a concealed threat: the period is charged with its stupid issuelessness as with an explosive.

Through his level of style, a systematic and objective seriousness, from which things themselves speak and, according to their value, classify themselves before the reader as tragic or comic, or in most cases quite unobtrusively as both, Flaubert overcame the romantic vehemence and uncertainty in the treatment of contemporary subjects; there is clearly something of the earlier positivism in his idea of art, although he sometimes speaks very derogatorily of Comte. On the basis of this objectivity, further developments became possible. . . . However, few of his successors conceived the task of representing contemporary reality with the same clarity and responsibility as he; though among them there were certainly freer, more spontaneous, and more richly endowed minds than his.

# Salammbô

## by Georg Lukács

Flaubert's *Salammbô* is the great representative work of [a] phase of development in the historical novel. It combines all the high artistic qualities of Flaubert's style. Stylistically, it is the paradigm of Flaubert's artistic aims; which is why it shows so much more clearly than the writings of the mediocre and untalented writers of this period the unresolved contradictions, the irremovable inner "problematic" of the new historical novel.

Flaubert formulated his aims programmatically. He says that he wished to apply the procedure and method of the modern novel to antiquity. And this programme was fully acknowledged by the important representatives of the new trend of naturalism. Zola's criticism of *Salammbô* is essentially a realization of this statement by Flaubert. Zola admittedly finds fault with a number of details, but accepts that Flaubert has applied the methods of the new realism correctly to historical material.

Outwardly *Salammbô* has not had the outstanding success of *Madame Bovary*. Nevertheless its echo has been quite strong. The leading French critic of the period, Sainte-Beuve, devoted a whole series of articles to it. Flaubert himself considered this critique so important that in a letter to Sainte-Beuve, published later, he took up all his critic's points in detail. This controversy illuminates so sharply the new problems which had arisen in this new phase of the historical novel that we must deal at length with the main arguments of the polemic.

Sainte-Beuve's basic critical position is deprecatory, despite his respect for Flaubert's literary personality. What makes this deprecation so interesting for us is that the critic himself takes up a philosophical and literary position similar in many respects to the Flau-

"*Salammbô.*" From *The Historical Novel* (London: Merlin Press, Ltd., 1962), by Georg Lukács, pp. 184-195. Translated by Hannah and Stanley Mitchell. Copyright © 1962 by Merlin Press, Ltd. Reprinted by permission of Merlin Press, Ltd.

bert he criticizes. The difference is that the older Sainte–Beuve is still somewhat bound to the traditions of the earlier period; he is more flexible and willing to compromise than Flaubert, particularly in artistic questions. Flaubert pursued his path to its logical conclusion with the radical disregard of a deeply convinced and important writer. Sainte-Beuve's criticism, therefore, of Flaubert's creative method is certainly not that of the Scott-Balzac period, as we shall see. Indeed in this period Sainte-Beuve proposed and even realized artistic views which in many respects approached those of Flaubert and sharply contrasted with those of Balzac.

Flaubert keenly felt this affinity between his own basic position and that of his critic. Thus, in his letter to Sainte-Beuve, the author of *Port Royal,* he presents his critic with the following *argumentum ad hominem:* "One last question, master, an improper question: why do you find Schahabarim almost comic and your good fellows of Port Royal so serious? For me M. Singlin is funereal beside my elephants. . . . And it is precisely because they [the characters of Port Royal] are very distant from me that I admire your talent in trying to make them intelligible to me. For I believe and wish to live in Port Royal even less than I do in Carthage. Port Royal, too, was exclusive, unnatural, forced, all of a piece and yet true. Why do you not want two truths to exist, two contrary excesses, two different monstrosities?"

It is interesting to compare Flaubert's praise for Sainte-Beuve here with Balzac's entirely negative judgment on *Port Royal.* Balzac and Flaubert are fairly close to one another in their judgment of the world which Sainte-Beuve, as an historian with artistic pretentions, presents. Both see the fragmented, eccentric, bagatelle nature of Sainte-Beuve's picture of history. But while Balzac passionately rejects such a conception of history, Flaubert regards it with an interested and sceptical curiosity. And there is no question here of simple politeness on the part of Flaubert towards the famous critic. His discussion in his correspondence of the Goncourts' historical pictures of the eighteenth century, for example, clearly proves the sincerity of these remarks, for there these Sainte-Beuve tendencies are pushed to the extreme. What comes out in all these cases is the new feeling of the leading ideologists towards history.

Of course, Flaubert's position in this process is not an average one. His literary greatness is expressed in the fact that the general tendency of the time appears in his work with an honest, passionate consistency. While in most other writers of the time, a negative attitude towards the contemporary prose of bourgeois life was simply a matter of aesthetic amusement or, frequently, of reactionary feeling, in Flaubert it is an intense disgust, a vehement hatred.

This disgust and hatred are behind Flaubert's interest in history: "I am weary of ugly things and sordid surroundings. Bovary has disgusted me with bourgeois morals for some time to come. I am going to live, for several years perhaps, inside a subject of splendour, far from the modern world of which I am heartily sick." And in another letter, also written while he was at work on *Salammbô*: "When one reads *Salammbô*, one will not, I hope, think of the Author. Few will guess how sad one had to be in order to resuscitate Carthage! There's a Thebaid to which disgust with modern life has driven me."

Thus Flaubert set himself a consistent programme: to reawaken a vanished world of no concern to us. It was precisely because of his deep hatred for modern society that he sought, passionately and paradoxically, a world which would in no way resemble it, which would have no connection with it, direct or indirect. Of course, this lack of connection—or rather the illusion of such—is at the same time the subjective factor which connects Flaubert's exotic historical subject matter with the everyday life of the present. For one must not forget that he tried to plan and execute his social novels, too, as a bystander, a non-participant. The letters he wrote while working on them testify to this again and again. And similarly one has to see that in both cases the programmatic non-partisanship, the famous "impassibilité" turns out to be an illusion: Flaubert reveals his attitude to both Emma Bovary and Salammbô through the atmosphere he creates. The only difference one can really discover in the treatment of the two themes is that the author is not in fact very emotionally involved with the masses of protectors and enemies of Carthage, while the everyday world of the contemporary novels kindles unceasing hatred and love in him. (It would be too superficial altogether to overlook this factor; it is enough to think of Dussardier in *L'Education Sentimentale*.) This all explains why Flaubert could think it possible to use the same artistic means for both *Salammbô* and *Madame Bovary*. At the same time, however, it also explains the completely different artistic results: the artistic fruitfulness of genuine hatred and love, however hidden and suppressed in the one case, the transformation of disinterestedness into sterile exoticism in the other.

In the attempt to solve this task artistically, the contradictions in Flaubert's position come out very plainly. Flaubert wishes to portray this world realistically, using the artistic means which he himself had discovered a few years earlier for *Madame Bovary* and there brought to perfection. But now it is not the grey everyday reality of French provincial life to which this realism of minutely observed and exactly described detail is to be applied; instead it is the alien and distant, incomprehensible but picturesque, decorative, grandiose, gorgeous, cruel and exotic world of Carthage which is to arise before us. This explains Flaubert's desperate struggle to evoke a graphic picture of old Carthage by means of exact study and exact production of archaeological detail.

Sainte-Beuve has a strong sense of the artistic discrepancy which results from this aim. He is always pointing out how the description of objects in Flaubert, the dead environment of men, overwhelms the portrayal of the men themselves: he criticizes the fact that, though all these details are correctly and brilliantly described in Flaubert, they do not add up to a whole, not even in relation to the dead objects. Flaubert describes doors, locks etc., all the components of a house, but the architect who builds the whole is nowhere to be seen. Sainte-Beuve sums up this criticism as follows: "the political side, the character of the persons, the genius of the people, the aspects whereby the particular history of this seafaring and, in its own way, civilizing people is of concern to history in general and of interest to the great current of civilization, are sacrificed here or subordinated to the exorbitant, descriptive side, to a dilettantism which, unable to apply itself to anything but rare ruins, is compelled to exaggerate them."

That these remarks hit a central defect in *Salammbô* is shown by Flaubert's despairing letters written while at work on the book. Thus he writes to a friend: "I am now full of doubts about the whole, about the general plan; I think there are too many soldiers. That is History, I know quite well. But if a novel is as tedious as a scientific potboiler, then Good Night, there's an end to Art. . . . I am beginning the siege of Carthage now. I am lost among the machines of war, the balista and the scorpions, and I understand nothing of it, neither I nor anyone else."

But what can a world thus re-awakened mean to us? Granted that Flaubert successfully solved all the problems which he raised artistically—has a world so represented any real living significance for us? Flaubert's paradoxes with regard to subjects which do not concern us, and which are artistic because they do not concern us, are very characteristic of the author's moods, but they also have their objective aesthetic consequences which are already known to us. Sainte-Beuve denies that the world of *Salammbô* has this significance for us. He uses an interesting argument, which shows that something of the old tradition of the historical novel is still alive in him. He doubts whether one can treat antiquity artistically, whether it can be made the theme of a really living historical novel. "One can reconstruct antiquity, but one cannot bring it back to life." And he refers specifically to the living, continuous relation between Scott's themes and the present, to the many living links which make it possible for us to experience even the distant Middle Ages.

But his chief objection to the theme of *Salammbô* is not confined to this general doubt. Flaubert's subject, he says, occupies a special, remote, unrelated position even among the themes of antiquity. "What do I care about the duel between Tunis and Carthage? Speak to me of the duel between Carthage and Rome, that's a different matter! There I am attentive, there I am involved. In the bitter struggle between Rome and Carthage the whole of future civilization is at stake; our own depends on it. . . ."

To this decisive objection Flaubert has no concrete answer. "Perhaps you are right in your considerations of the historical novel as applied to antiquity, and it is very possible that I have failed."

But he has nothing more concrete to say about this question and, while rejecting the artistic significance of archaeological authenticity, simply speaks of the immanent connections within the historical world he has so selected and portrayed. And he maintains that he is right or wrong according to whether he has been successful or not with regard to this immanent harmony.

Apart from which he defends his subject-matter and portrayal in a more lyrical and biographical vein. "I believe even," he says, "that I have been less hard on humanity in *Salammbô* than in *Madame Bovary*. The curiosity, the love which made me seek out vanished religions and peoples has something moral and sympathetic about it, so it seems to me."

The comparison between *Salammbô* and *Madame Bovary* does not derive from Flaubert himself; it occurs already in Sainte-Beuve's critique. Sainte-Beuve analyses the figure of *Salammbô*: "She talks to her nurse, confides to her her vague anxieties, her stifled sense of unease, her listlessness. . . . She looks for, dreams of, calls to something unknown. It is the situation of more than one daughter of Eve, Carthaginian or otherwise; to some extent it is that of *Madame Bovary* at the beginning, when life has become too tedious for her and she goes off on her own to the beech-grove of Banneville. . . . Well, poor Salammbô experiences in her own way the same feeling of vague yearning and oppressive desire. The author has only transposed, with great art, and *mythologised* this muffled lament of the heart and the senses." In another connection he compares Flaubert's general attitude to his historical characters with Chateaubriand's manner of portrayal. He says that Flaubert's Salammbô is less a sister of Hannibal than of Chateaubriand's Gallic maiden, Velléda.

The reproach of *modernization* is clearly contained in these comparisons, although Sainte-Beuve does not make an issue out of this question and often shows a great deal of tolerance toward modernization. Nor has Flaubert's protest anything to do with the general methodological problem of modernization. This he takes to be self-evident. His disagreement is only with the concrete comparisons which Sainte-Beuve makes. "As for my heroine, I do not defend her. According to you she resembles . . . Velléda, Mme. Bovary. Not at all! Velléda is active, intelligent, European, Mme. Bovary is stirred by multiple passions; Salammbô, on the contrary, is rooted in a fixed idea. She is a maniac, a kind of Saint Theresa. What does it matter? I am not sure of her reality, for neither I, you, nor anyone, neither ancient nor modern can know the oriental woman, because it is impossible to associate with her."

Thus Flaubert is protesting only against the concrete form of modernization which Sainte-Beuve has attributed to the figure of Salammbô. The modernization itself he grants as self-evident; for it is really quite immaterial whether one attributes to Hannibal's sister the psychology of a French *petite bourgeoise* of the nineteenth century or of a Spanish nun of the seventeenth. To which must be added that Flaubert is, of course, also modernizing the psychology of Saint Theresa.

This is not a minor aspect of the work and influence of Flaubert. He chooses an historical subject whose inner social-historical nature is of no concern to him and to which he can only lend the appearance of reality in an external, decorative, picturesque manner by means of the conscientious application of archaeology. But at some point he is forced to established a contact with both himself and the reader, and this he does by modernizing the psychology of his characters. The proud and bitter paradox which contends that the novel has nothing at all to do with the present, is simply a defensive paradox contending against the trivialities of his age. We see from Flaubert's explanations which we have already quoted that *Salammbô* was more than just an artistic experiment. It is for this reason that the modernization of the characters acquires central importance; it is the only source of movement and life in this frozen, lunar landscape of archaeological precision.

Naturally it is a ghostly illusion of life. And an illusion which dissolves the hyper-objective reality of the objects. In describing the individual objects of an historical *milieu* Flaubert is much more exact and plastic than any other writer before him. But these objects have nothing to do with the inner life of the characters. When Scott describes a medieval town or the habitat of a Scottish clan, these material things are part and parcel of the lives and fortunes of people whose whole psychology belongs to the same level of historical development and is a product of the same social-historical ensemble as these material things. This is how the older epic writers produced their "totality of objects." In Flaubert there is no such connection between the outside world and the psychology of the principal characters. And the effect of this lack of connection is to degrade the archaeological exactness of the outer world: it becomes a world of historically exact *costumes and decorations,* no more than a pictorial frame within which a purely modern story is unfolded.

The actual influence of Salammbô is in fact also connected with this modernization. Artists have admired the accomplishment of Flaubert's descriptions. But the effect of Salammbô herself was to provide a heightened image, a decorative symbol, of the hysterical longings and torments of middle-class girls in large cities. History simply provided a decorative, monumental setting for this hysteria, which in the present spends itself in petty and ugly scenes, and which thus acquired a tragic aura quite out of keeping with its real character. The effect is powerful but it shows that Flaubert, because of his embitterment with the shallow prose of his time, had become objectively untruthful and distorted the real proportions of life. The artistic superiority of his bourgeois novels lies precisely in the fact that in them the proportions between emotion and event, between desire and its translation into deeds, correspond to the real, social-historical character of emotion and desire. In *Salammbô* the emotions, in themselves quite unmonumental, are falsely and distortedly monumentalized and hence inwardly unequal to such artistic heightening. The way in which the figure of Salammbô was regarded as a symbol during the obvious decline of Royalism and the psychological reaction which set in against Zola's naturalism, is best shown by the analysis which Paul Bourget gives of her: "It is a constant law in his [Flaubert's] eyes that human effort must end abortively, first of all because external circumstances run counter to one's dreams, secondly because even favourable circumstances cannot prevent the soul from devouring itself in the gratification of its chimera. Our desire floats before us like the veil of Tanit, the embroidered

*Zaïmph*, before Salammbô. While she cannot seize it, the girl languishes in despair. As soon as she touches it, she must die."

This modernizing determines the structure of the plot. It basis is formed by two motifs which are only very externally connected: a "crown and state" conflict between Carthage and the rebellious mercenaries, and the love episode of Salammbô herself. Their involvement with one another is quite external and inevitably remains so. Salammbô is as much a stranger to the interests of her homeland, to the life-and-death struggle of her native city, as Madame Bovary is to the medical practice of her husband. But while in the bourgeois novel this indifference can be made the vehicle of a plot with Emma Bovary at the centre precisely because she is a stranger to provincial daily life, here instead we have a "crown and state" story, outwardly grandiose and requiring therefore extensive preparation, with which Salammbô's destiny has no organic connection. The links are all either pure accidents or external pretexts. But in the presentation of the story the external pretext must inevitably suppress and stifle the main theme. External occasions take up the major part of the novel; the main theme is reduced to a small episode.

This lack of relation between the human tragedy, which is what kindles the reader's interest, and the political action clearly shows the change already undergone by historical feeling in this age. The political plot is not only lifeless because it is cluttered up with descriptions of inessential objects, but because it has no discernible connection with any concrete form of popular life that we may experience. The mercenaries in this novel are the same kind of wild, irrational, chaotic mass as the inhabitants of Carthage. True, we are told in exhaustive detail how the quarrel arises, namely the fact that the mercenaries have not been paid, and by what circumstances this quarrel grows into a war; yet we have not the least idea of the real social-historical and human driving force which causes these clashes to take place in the way they do. These remain an irrational, historical fact despite Flaubert's detailed portrayal. And since the human motives do not spring organically out of a concrete social-historical basis, but are given to isolated figures in a modernized form, they only confuse the total picture still further, reduce still further the social reality of the entire story.

This comes out at its crudest in the love episode of Mâtho. Sainte-Beuve, in his analysis of this love-maddened mercenary, rightly recalls the so-called historical novels of the seventeenth century, in which Alexander the Great, Cyrus or Genserich appeared as love-stricken heroes. "But Mâtho in love, this African Goliath, who behaves so wildly and childishly in sight of Salammbô, seems just as false to me; he is as outside nature as he is outside history."

And Sainte-Beuve rightly remarks on the feature peculiar to Flaubert here, what is new in this distortion of history as compared with the seventeenth century: whereas the lovers of the old novels had been sweet and sentimental, Mâtho has a bestially savage character. In short, those brutal and animal features are emphasized and placed at the centre, which occur later in Zola as characteristics of the life of modern workers and peasants. Thus Flaubert's portrayal is "prophetic." Not, however, in the sense in which Balzac's works were prophetic, anticipating the actual, future development of social types, but merely in a literary-historical sense, anticipating the later distortion of modern life in the works of the Naturalists.

Flaubert's defence against this criticism of Sainte-Beuve is extremely interesting, illuminating yet another aspect of his method of approach to history. This is how he defends himself against the charge of modernization in the figure of Mâtho: "Mâtho *prowls like a madman* round Carthage. Madness is the right word. Wasn't love, as conceived by the ancients, a madness, a curse, an illness sent by the gods?"

This defence bases itself apparently on historical evidence. But only apparently; for Flaubert never examines the real nature of love within the social life of antiquity, the connection of its different psychological forms with other forms of ancient life. His starting point is an analysis of the isolated *idea* of love, as we find it in certain ancient tragedies. Flaubert is right when he says for instance that the love of Phaedra in Euripides' *Hippolytus* is presented as a sudden passion, innocently visited upon her by the Gods. But it is an entirely unhistorical modernization of ancient life to take merely the subjective side of such tragic conflicts and then to blow this up into a "psychological peculiarity" of the whole of antiquity. Obviously, in certain cases individual love and passion did irrupt "suddenly" into people's lives and cause great tragic collisions. It is also true that these collisions were far more unusual in ancient life than in the period of development from the Middle Ages until modern times, when similar problems occurred, though in a different form in keeping with the changed social circumstances. The special manifestation of passion in the portrayals of the ancients is connected in the closest possible way with the special forms of the break-up of gentile society in antiquity. But this is the final ideological result of a particular development. If this result is then torn out of its social-historical context, if its subjective-psychological side is isolated from

the causes which produce it, if therefore the artist's point of departure is not existence but an isolated idea, then whatever one's apparent historical evidence one's only approach to this idea is via
modernization. Only in Flaubert's imagination does Mâtho embody
ancient love. In reality, he is a prophetic model of the decadent
drunkards and madmen of Zola.

This connection between approaching history from the standpoint
of an idea and portraying it as a compound of outward exoticism
and inner modernity is so important for the whole artistic development of the second half of the nineteenth century that we may be
allowed to illustrate it by a further example. Richard Wagner, whose
points of similarity with Flaubert Nietzsche disclosed with spiteful
shrewdness, discovers the brother-and-sister love of Siegmund and
Sieglinde in the Edda. This is an unusually interesting, exotic phenomenon, and is made "intelligible" by a lavish display of decorative pomp and modern psychology. Marx in few words revealed
Wagner's falsification of the social-historical connections. Engels, in
his *Origin of the Family*, quotes this letter of Marx: "Was it ever
possible that brother embraced sister as a bride?" To these "lewd
gods" of Wagner who, quite in the modern manner, spice their love
intrigues with a little incest, Marx replied: "In primitive times the
sister *was* the wife, and that was moral." Wagner's example shows
even more clearly than Flaubert's how, by starting from an isolated
idea rather than from actual existence, one inevitably ends up by
misrepresenting and distorting history. What remains are the outward, soulless facts of history (here love between brother and sister)
which are injected with an entirely modern sensibility, and the old
story, the old occurrence serves only to give picturesqueness to this
modern sensibility, to add to it a decorative grandeur which, as we
have seen, it does not deserve.

This question has, however, still another side which is of exceptional importance for modern developments. As we have seen, the
inner emptiness of social-historical events, left by the rift between
the outward happenings and the modernized psychology of the characters, give rise to the exotic historical *milieu*. The historical event,
emptied in this subjectivist manner of its inner greatness has to
acquire a pseudo-monumentality by other means. For it is precisely
the longing to escape from the triviality of modern bourgeois life
which produces these historical themes.

One of the most important means of producing this pseudo-monumentality is the emphasis on brutality. We have already seen how
the most significant and influential critics of the period, Taine and

Brandes, lament the absence of such brutality in Scott. Sainte-Beuve, belonging to an older generation, notes its presence and predominance in *Salammbô* with great unease: "he cultivates atrocity. The man is good, excellent, the book is cruel. He believes that it is a proof of strength to appear inhuman in his books."

For anyone who knows *Salammbô* it is hardly necessary to quote examples. I shall simply mention the great contrast during the siege of Carthage: while Carthage's supply of water is cut off and the whole city is dying of thirst, the most terrible hunger rages in the camp of the mercenaries. Flaubert takes delight in giving detailed and cruel pictures of the sufferings of the masses in and around Carthage. There is never any humanity in this suffering; it is simply horrible, senseless torment. No single member of the masses is individually characterized, the suffering yields no single conflict or action which might humanly interest or grip us.

Here we may see the sharp opposition between the old and the new representation of history. The writers of the classical period of the historical novel were only interested in the cruel and terrible happenings of previous history insofar as they were necessary expressions of definite forms of class struggle (e.g. the cruelty of the Chouans in Balzac) and also because they gave birth of a similar necessity to great human passions and conflicts, etc. (the heroism of the Republican officers during the Chouans' massacre of them in the same novel). The placing of the cruel processes of social development in a necessary and intelligible connection and the relationship between these and the human greatness of the combatants take from the events their cruelty and brutality. Which does not mean that the cruelty and brutality are in any way ironed out or mitigated—the reproach which Taine and Brandes levelled at Scott; they are simply given their rightful place inside the total context.

Flaubert begins a development where the inhumanity of subject-matter and presentation, where atrocity and brutality become ends in themselves. These features acquire their central position owing to the weak presentation of what is the chief issue—the social development of man; indeed for the same reason they assume even more importance than even this position warrants. Since real greatness is everywhere replaced by extensiveness—the decorative splendour of the contrasts replaces the social-human connections—inhumanity, cruelty, atrocity and brutality become substitutes for the lost greatness of real history. At the same time they spring from the morbid longing of modern man to escape from the suffocating narrowness of everyday life, a longing which he projects into this pseudo-

monumentality. Disgust with small and petty office intrigues produces the ideal image of the mass poisoner, Cesare Borgia.

Flaubert felt deeply hurt by Sainte-Beuve's accusation. But his
objections to the critic do not exceed a feeling of injury. And this is
not accidental. For the extraordinarily sensitive and highly moral
Flaubert has against his will become the initiator of the inhuman in
modern literature. The development of capitalism not only levels
and trivializes, it also brutalizes.

This brutalization of feeling manifests itself in literature to an
ever increasing extent, most clearly of all in the description and
portrayal of love, where the physical-sexual side gains growing as-
cendancy over the passion itself. Think how the greatest portrayers
of love—Shakespeare, Goethe and Balzac—confined themselves to
the merest intimations in their description of the physical act itself.
The interest shown by modern literature in this aspect of love on the
one hand derives from the increasing brutalization of the real emotions of love, which occurs in life itself, and on the other has the
consequence that writers are forced to search for more and more
exquisite, abnormal, perverse, etc. themes in order to escape monotony.

Flaubert himself, in this respect, stands at the beginning of this
development. And it is very characteristic both for him as well as
for the entire development of the historical novel during the crisis
of decline of bourgeois realism that these tendencies are much more
pronounced in his historical novels than in his pictures of modern
society. In both, hatred and disgust for the pettiness, triviality and
meanness of modern bourgeois life are expressed with equal force,
yet very differently in keeping with the difference of subject-matter.
In his contemporary novels Flaubert concentrates his ironic attack
on the portrayal of everyday bourgeois life and average bourgeois
man. As an outstanding realist artist he thus achieves an infinitely
nuanced picture of that dismal greyness which is a real aspect of
this everyday life. Precisely his naturalist tendencies restrain Flaubert from any eccentricity in his treatment of the inhuman forms of
capitalist life. But his historical novel, as we have seen, he considered a liberation from the fetters of this monotonous flatness. All
that his naturalist conscience had forced him to renounce in his picture of contemporary reality found a place here. In terms of form—
the colourfulness, the decorative monumentality of an exotic *milieu;*
in terms of content—eccentric passions in their fullest extent and
uniqueness. And it is here that we clearly see the social, moral and
ideological limitations of this great and sincere artist: while he

sincerely hates the capitalist present, his hatred has no roots in the great popular and democratic traditions either of the past or present and therefore has no future perspective. His hatred does not historically transcend its object. Thus if, in the historical novels the suppressed passions break open their fetters, it is the eccentric-individualist side of capitalist man which comes to the fore, that inhumanity which everyday life hypocritically seeks to conceal and subdue. The later decadents already portray this side of capitalist inhumanity with boastful cynicism. In Flaubert it appears in the Bengal illumination of a romantic-historical monumentality. Thus the sides which Flaubert here reveals of the new manner of portraying life do not become widespread until later and he himself was not yet aware of them as such general tendencies.

But the contradiction between Flaubert's ascetic disgust with modern life and these inhuman excesses of a riotous and demented imagination does not alter the fact that he appears here as one of the most important precursors of dehumanization in modern literature. This inhumanity is not, of course, in every instance a simple and straightforward capitulation to the dehumanizing tendencies of capitalism, which is the simple and most general case, in literature as in life. The important personalities of this crisis of decline, Flaubert, Baudelaire, Zola and even Nietzsche, suffer from this development and savagely oppose it; yet the manner of their opposition leads to an intensification in literature of capitalist dehumanization in life.

# L'Éducation sentimentale: Profanation and the Permanence of Dreams

## by Victor Brombert

### I. *The Bordello: In the End Is the Beginning*

Ten years after the publication of *L'Éducation sentimentale,* Flaubert was still pained by the critics' hostile reaction. To his friend Turgenev, he wrote in 1879: "Without being a monster of pride, I consider that this book has been unfairly judged, especially the end. On this score I feel bitter toward the public." [1] Few endings of novels have indeed baffled, even outraged more readers. The hero's flat assertion that an adolescent excursion to a brothel has been the most precious experience of a lifetime confirmed suspicions that Flaubert was an incurable cynic. It was bad enough that the "hero," Frédéric Moreau, after a life distinguished by failure, returns to the somnolence of a provincial existence, a death-in-life which corresponds to a total abdication and to a permanent vocation for nothing. But did the author have to bring Frédéric and Deslauriers together in this scene, pointing up the weakness and bad faith inherent in their reconciliation? Did he have to indulge in an inventory of decay? And does the exalted expedition to the provincial bawdy-house not cheapen whatever might have been salvaged (the very memory of Madame Arnoux!) by stressing venal love and by linking almost perversely the prurient excitement of early adolescence with the impotence of precocious senility?

Yet Flaubert felt surer of the validity of this scene than of almost any other scene in the novel. Endings were for him a matter of utmost concern even when, as in *Madame Bovary* or *L'Éducation*

"*L'Éducation sentimentale:* Profanation and the Permanence of Dreams," by Victor Brombert. From the Christian Gauss seminar on criticism, presented at Princeton University in April 1964 by Victor Brombert. Reproduced by permission of Victor Brombert. These pages are only a part of the chapter on *L'Éducation sentimentale* in a book to be published in the near future.

[1] *Lettres inédites à Tourgeneff*, p. 206.

*sentimentale,* they may at first appear like an unfunctional appendix. But the anticlimactic last three chapters in *Madame Bovary* are far from gratuitous. In *L'Éducation sentimentale,* the ending is even more intimately bound up with the very structure and meaning of the book. Paradoxically, it almost engenders the very beginning. It is an epilogue, no doubt: but this epilogue echoes and parallels one of the earliest passages in the book. I refer to the second chapter, which is partly a flashback to Frédéric's and Deslauriers' childhood, and partly an early conversation between the two friends as they look forward to the future, but already have a past to talk about. Thus the book can be said to begin and to close with a conversation between Frédéric and Deslauriers in which projects or reminiscences take priority over action. The immediate effect of this extension in time (the prologue carries us back to 1833, the epilogue forward to the winter of 1867) is a feeling of temporal circularity and erosion. All the dreams have come to nought. And already during the first conversation, the light the two friends can see shining from the small window of the *maison basse,* the house of ill repute, seems like a shimmering symbol of unattainable desire. "I am of the race of the disinherited," says Frédéric, convinced before the event that no worthwhile woman will ever love him. In the meantime, they do not have enough money to respond to the blinking light. But they do remember a common adventure of some years back, the same adventure that, twenty-seven years later, they will tell each other, agreeing that it had been the best moment in their lives. *"C'est là ce que nous avons eu de meilleur."*

If, however, we look at this last scene more closely, we must notice that the bordello motif is not exploited for its sheer anecdotal value, nor even primarily to allow for the devastating final comment. The episode, as remembered by the two friends—though it occurred some time before the events of the novel itself—does in fact sum up, in miniature fashion, a whole pattern of events and meanings. What happened is banal enough: on a late Sunday afternoon, the two boys plucked some flowers, gathered them into bouquets and proceeded furtively to the house of "La Turque."

> Frédéric presented his bouquet, as a young man might to his fiancée. But the heat of the day, the fear of the unknown, a kind of remorse, and even the excitement of seeing at a glance so many women at his disposal, affected him so much that he grew very pale and could neither move nor speak. They all laughed, amused at his embarrassment. Thinking that he was being made fun of, he ran away; and since he had the money, Deslauriers was forced to follow him.

Several aspects of this passage deserve analysis. To begin with, the author provides here a subtly nuanced sketch of Frédéric's character. The naïve gesture of appearing with flowers at a brothel points up a latent and ineffectual idealism. The comparison with the boy-friend and his fiancée is touching enough, but suggests a tendency to see reality through a deforming imagination. The heat which paralyzes him reminds us of many other states of dreamy indolence in Frédéric's life. The vague sense of guilt, which here, one must assume, is related to a mother-image, is elsewhere associated with the pure and "maternal" image of Marie Arnoux. The multiplicity of women making the choice impossible corresponds not only to the constant and inconclusive wavering, within the novel, from one woman to another, but to Frédéric's basic inability to focus on anything and impose a single direction on his life. The immobility, the speechlessness and the ultimate flight underline a chronic timid-ity, the fear of judgment and humiliation. Thus he also tears up his first letter to Madame Arnoux: "he did nothing, attempted nothing —paralyzed by the fear of failure." And the flight itself corresponds, of course, to a flight from the realities of the capital and a return to the sheltered life of the province.

But there is more to this passage. The naïve arrival in the whore-house, the flustered departure, the very fiasco of the expedition symbolize the poetic illusion that clings tenaciously to unfulfilled love. It symbolizes the orgyless orgy, the love-dream remaining pure because it was unrealized. After all, Frédéric leaves "La Turque" chaste! The debauches have been of the imagination: mere velleities. So that the final comment (*"C'est là ce que nous avons eu de meil-leur"*), far from being exclusively a cynical remark, or a symptom of arrested development, must also be interpreted as a lasting nostalgia for innocence.[2] This preference for the past conceals another form of idealism. Memory illumines. And although both friends seem to have lost everything, this final dialogue between the man who sought Love and the man who sought Power reveals that it is the search for Love (no matter how clumsy and frustrating) which retrospec-tively bestows the only meaning. The episode thus combines in the most ambiguous manner touching illusion and adult disillusion-ment, flights of fancy and retreat into the self, attraction to the multiform manifestations of life and paralysis caused by the very proliferation of forms and possibilities, eternally youthful memory

---

[2] A nostalgia for innocence which, as Harry Levin suggests, goes hand in hand with the need to be "sheltered from the contingencies of adult experience" (*The Gates of Horn*, p. 229).

and the pathos of aging. In other words, it is a retrospective prolepsis of the very essence of the novel. Even the relationship of Frédéric and his friend is prefigured in the terse remark that since the one had the money, the other was obliged to follow him!

The Bordello motif, or in a more general sense the image of the Prostitute and the theme of Prostitution, is at the core of *L'Éducation sentimentale*. Frédéric's erotic sensibility and erotic dreams as a boy crystallize around visions of satin-covered boudoirs where he and his friend will experience "fulgurant orgies with illustrious courtesans." Such exotic passions are inevitably linked to dreams of success. He and Deslauriers spend so many hours constructing and peopling their harems that they are exhausted as though they had indulged in real debauches. Later, when Frédéric actually penetrates into the world of Parisian women, he is almost overcome by the luxurious *odor di femmina*. There is, to be sure, a certain literary tradition behind this particular mystique of the senses. Romanticism had cast the eternal *hetaera*, whether simple *fille de joie* or high-class courtesan in the role of initiator to the deep mysteries of life. Even social, artistic and political success—in nineteenth century literature —is often seen related to one form or another of prostitution. Such literary expressions no doubt correspond to certain social and psychological patterns: the bourgeois adolescent looked at the prostitute with mixed feelings of admiration, contempt, desire to redeem, and even a yearning for profanation. There is for instance a curious letter of Le Poittevin to Flaubert which tells of the young man's desire to desecrate in the company of a whore places where he has been "young and credulous." [3] As for Flaubert himself, it is clear that he is haunted by the image of the prostitute whom he associates, in an almost Baudelairean manner, with equally complex monastic and ascetic urges.

In the novel, the Bordello motif and the theme of prostitution assume in part a satiric function. The world of the *lorettes* into which Frédéric is ironically introduced by Madame Arnoux's husband, appears to him at first in the guise of a masked ball, where the most tempting display of flesh, costumes and poses inevitably brings to mind the variegated offerings of an elegant house of prostitution providing "specialties" for every whim. Frédéric is so dazzled that, during the first moments, he can distinguish only silk, velvet and naked shoulders. Then, gradually, he takes stock of the contents of this Parisian seraglio: the languorous Polish beauty, the placid and falsely modest Swiss siren, the provocative Fishwife, the Primi-

[3] *Une Promenade de Bélial et œuvres inédites*, pp. 194-195.

tive with peacock feathers, the avid Bacchante, the carnival Work-
woman—all the "refinements of modern love"—dance before him,
and the beads of perspiration on their foreheads further suggest a
hot-house atmosphere. This scene, ending in a collective hangover
the following morning, recalls the famous Taillefer orgy in Balzac's
*La Peau de chagrin:* the same display of available carnality, the
same specter of disease and death, the same garish coupling of the
lascivious and the macabre. Only Flaubert is not concerned with
sheer pyrotechnics. He is not out to rival Petronius' description of
decadence in the *Satyricon*. His aim is neither sensational nor allegorical. He works and weaves his images patiently and deliberately
into the general pattern of the novel. But there are some immediate
effects, and the most noteworthy is a vertiginous proliferation of
forms and gestures which ultimately transforms human beings into
mechanized objects. In her drunken stupor, one of the women imi-
tates "the oscillation of a launch."

The easy-virtued world of Rosanette is not the only one to be
described in terms of lupanar images. Frédéric's suggestive vision
imposes these very same images onto the assembly of elegant feminine guests in the salon of Madame Dambreuse. The upper-class
ladies all sit in a row, "offering" their bosoms to the eye; the rustling
of their gowns suggests that dresses are about to slip down. The lack
of expression on their faces is in perverse contrast to their "provocative garments." The animal-like placidity of these ladies in décolleté
evokes the "interior of a harem." Flaubert's intention becomes quite
explicit, for he adds: "A more vulgar comparison came to the young
man's mind." Here too, the salon provides a sampling of physical
and regional types to satisfy every possible taste: English beauties
with keepsake profiles, Italians with ardent eyes, three Norman sisters "fresh like apple trees in April"—an alluring and appetizing
display of sophisticated impudicity. The total effect is once again
dehumanization: the crescendo of feminine chatter sounds like the
cackle of birds.

Even public locales (cafés, restaurants, *bals publics*) are seen as
places of prostitution, for instance the Alhambra where, according
to Deslauriers, one can easily get to know "women." The exotic
name corresponds to fake exotic architecture, or rather to jarring
elements of architecture: Moorish galleries, the restaurant side in
the form of a Gothic cloister, Venetian lanterns, a Chinese roofing
over the orchestra, neo-classical painted Cupids. This shocking combination is not merely a sign of vulgarity. It represents the particular
attempt at facile poetry or rather at facile estrangement, which is

the special function of all purveyors of bought pleasures. In this light, the Bordello becomes the convenient metaphor for any catering to the thirst for illusion. The Alhambra provides sensual pleasures for the public. The reader witnesses a collective debauchery: the last firecracker of the evening provokes an orgastic sigh. But in reality, nothing really happens. The policemen who wake up Frédéric on the boulevard bench where he has fallen asleep, and who are convinced that he has *"fait la noce,"* are as wrong as his own mother concerning his visit to "La Turque." For Frédéric, it has been an innocent orgy, combining in characteristic fashion exposure to depravity with an exacerbated yearning for ideal love. Frédéric's only activity right after the Alhambra is to stare at Madame Arnoux's window.

This aspect of the metaphorical unity of *L'Éducation sentimentale* is further strengthened by the presence of key characters who, in one form or another, are for sale. The most important of these is Rosanette Bron, "La Maréchale." That Rosanette is a kept woman, and most often kept by several men at the same time, is of course no secret. Her true calling is perhaps never more graphically suggested than by her portrait, commissioned by M. Arnoux, eventually purchased by Frédéric, but which in the meantime stands exposed in the window of a gallery with the following words written in black letters underneath: "Mme Rose-Annette Bron, property of M. Frédéric Moreau de Nogent." True to her vocation, she specializes, one might say, in sexual provocation. Innumerable passages in the novel stress this talent. Her laughter has a whip-like effect on Frédéric's nerves. At times, she assumes the poses of a "provocative slave." Most often, her sex-appeal is less indolent: her way of pulling up her stockings, her movements, her very chignon are "like a challenge." When she eats, and the redness of the fruit mixes with the purple of her lips, the insolence of her look fills Frédéric with mad desires. As for her innumerable caprices, her disconnected desires, they correspond to the usual versatility associated with the prostitution metaphor, only here the multiplicity of forms and possibilities is internalized. The capricious, unpredictable nature of Rosanette also corresponds to her treachery—and in a broader sense, to the theme of treason so important in this novel. Hers is partially an irresponsible type of cruelty best exemplified by her coldly abandoning Frédéric at the Café Anglais after accepting from de Cisy a bracelet with three opals.

A far more cold-blooded selfishness is the main feature of the *"grande dame,"* the regal prostitute Madame Dambreuse. Frédéric finds that she has something "languorous" and "dry." Her sterile cupidity appears in full light when, after the death of her husband, and in the presence of her lover, she stares, disconsolate, into the empty strongbox! As for the perfidious Vatnaz, the eternal procuress, she provokes only disgust. The mere touch of her "thin, soft hand" sends shivers down Frédéric's spine. The world of Paris thus insistently proposes to Frédéric images of prostitution: *lorettes* at the hippodrome; streetwalkers under the gaslight; scenes of slave markets with lewd sultans and cheap puns in boulevard plays. At the horse races, he glimpses an obscenely made-up queen of the burlesque theater known as the "Louis XI of prostitution." Everywhere he turns, it would seem that, as in Baudelaire's "Tableaux Parisiens," "*La Prostitution s'allume dans les rues.*"

But actual prostitution is of course not the only form of prostitution. There are less literal manifestations, all pointing to some manner of depravity. For the Bordello motif is closely bound up with Frédéric's apprenticeship of life. His "education" in Paris— the subject as well as the title of the novel place it squarely in the tradition of the *Bildungsroman*—is to begin with the discovery of one type or other of pandering, cheapening or desecration. One could almost take one by one every character and every activity. The very name of Arnoux' hybrid establishment, *L'Art industriel,* is like a profanation of art. And his career sadly illustrates this profanation: an amateur painter, he is in turn director of an art magazine, an art dealer, the owner of a pottery factory manufacturing "artistic" soup plates and mythological decorations for bathrooms. With every chapter he takes a step down. After designing letters for signboards and wine labels, and going bankrupt through shady deals, he has the idea of a *café chantant* and of a military hat-making business, and he finally winds up dealing in beads and cheap "religious art." The very word "decadence" aptly sums up his career. There is the same brutal devaluation in the life of Pellerin, the painter who wanted to rival Veronese, then places his art in the service of politics, and ends up being a professional photographer. The actor Delmar, a coarse histrion, similarly illustrates the prostitution of art: he sells out his vulgar talent to political parties, and gives public recitals of humanitarian poetry on . . . prostitution. This propensity for selling out is most strikingly symbolized by the epitaph-like résumé of the life of the financier Dambreuse who "had acclaimed Napoleon, the Cossacks, Louis eighteenth, 1830, the working-man, every régime, adoring Power with such intensity that he would have paid in order to have the opportunity of selling himself."

As for Frédéric himself, much could be said. In a letter to Amélie Bosquet, written some ten years before the publication of *L'Éducation sentimentale,* Flaubert makes this revealing confession: "One has spoken endlessly about the prostitution of women, but not a word has been said about that of men. I have known the tortures of prostitutes, and any man who has loved for a long time has experienced them." Unquestionably Frédéric's ambiguous situation vis-à-vis the Arnoux household, combining the duplicity of an adulterer, the frustrations of an unsuccessful suitor and the embarrassment of being Arnoux' rival not only with his wife, but with his mistress, exposes him to complex compromises and turpitudes. His dilettantish vacillations and reliance on others are almost those of a "kept" person. Frédéric is not only weak (Flaubert often depicts strong women and weak, virginal men), but passive and "feminine." He holds, for his friend Deslauriers *"un charme presque féminin."* The projected marriage to Mme Dambreuse, for money and social prestige, shows us Frédéric morally at his most depraved.

Finally, the prostitution motif provides a link between individual and collective attitudes. Society itself, as represented by various groups, corporations or institutions, is the great whore who always embraces the winner. Like Rosanette, who after despising the revolutionaries now declares herself in favor of the Republic, so do all the representative authorities—"as his lordship the Archbishop had already done, and as the magistracy, the Conseil d'Etat, the Institut, the marshals of France, Changarnier, M. de Falloux, all the Bonapartists, all the Legitimists, and a considerable number of Orleanists were about to do with a swiftness displaying marvelous zeal." Politics in particular, which held a somewhat perverse fascination for the apolitical Flaubert, is viewed as a slattern. During the obscenely violent and profanatory sack of the Tuileries palace, a slut is seen, on a heap of garments, assuming the motionless, allegorical pose of the Statue of Liberty.

The bitterness of an image such as this stresses the coarseness and the fickleness of political allegiances. But it is part of a more general theme of betrayed ideals. *L'Éducation sentimentale* is a novel of bankruptcy and of pathological erosion. Certain chapters accumulate one form of betrayal on top of another, until the feeling is that of an immense desertion. Friendship, ambition, politics, love—nothing seems immune from this chronic deterioration and devaluation.[4] The most brutal manifestation of this aspect of the novel is the

[4] For instance, in chapter 2, part II, Rosanette betrays both Arnoux and Frédéric, Arnoux betrays his wife, and Frédéric betrays the confidence of Arnoux.

double betrayal of the political turncoat Sénécal, the former Socialist now turned police agent, who during the coup d'état of 1851, cold-bloodedly kills the sentimental revolutionary Dussardier. This stunning act which leaves Frédéric agape is like an allegory of treason destroying idealism.

And it is no gratuitous coincidence that makes Frédéric the witness to this despicable deed. The images of prostitution and degradation exist primarily in relation to Frédéric's personal vision, to his longings, his sadness, his disappointments and his defeats. The Bordello motif may permeate the novel as a whole and may have a universal significance within its context. It represents ersatz, on all levels, transmuting almost every gesture into parody: the duel with de Cisy is no real duel; the props Pellerin uses for his "Venetian" portrait are fake props; all creative efforts are derivative. But it is in relation to Frédéric's "sentimental education" that all this counterfeit acquires dramatic meaning. No matter how obviously depraved the objective world may be, it is his sentimental life which, subjectively, is most affected by the principle of degrading vicariousness. Thus Frédéric bounces from one woman to another, permanently oscillating between contradictory desires and contradictory experiences, always driven to seek a poor substitute for the *authentic* experience he dreams of, and which, in the process, he steadily defiles. One desire awakens a contradictory desire, suggesting a repetitive discontinuity. "The frequentation of the two women provided, as it were, two strains of music in his life, the one playful, passionate, amusing; and the other almost religious. . . ." And there are not two women in his life, but four—if one includes the young girl, Louise Roque. This oscillation at times obliges Flaubert to resort to devices which appear extraneous: chance encounters, unexpected letters, coincidences which further underline the passivity of the hero and his easy surrender to the easiest path. Almost symbolically, at one point, the "strumpet" Rosanette (Flaubert actually uses the word *"catin"*) interrupts a love scene in progress, thus making the ideal "irrevocably impossible."

What is worse, Frédéric *uses* the image of one woman in his relationship with another. It is bad enough that he has learned to make one sentiment serve multiple purposes: in his courtship of Mme Dambreuse, he "makes use of his old passion" for Mme Arnoux; he repeats to Mme Dambreuse the very oath he just uttered to Rosanette, sends them both identical bouquets and writes them love letters simultaneously. Even more sadly, he has to rely on substitute images to stimulate himself sexually. "He found it necessary to evoke the image of Rosanette or of Mme Arnoux." (Thus Flaubert himself once told the Goncourts that "all the women he ever possessed were no more than the mattress for another woman he dreamed of." [5]) In the novel, this sexual substitution takes place quite literally when Frédéric, desperate because Mme Arnoux did not show up at their rendezvous, makes love to Rosanette on the very bed he so devoutly prepared for Mme Arnoux.

Such a pattern of substitution and profanation—underlined by the permanent prostitution motif—leads to contradictory results. On the one hand, we witness a strange paralysis, reminiscent of the scene in the brothel when Frédéric could not make his "choice." Life is a planned orgy which never quite amounts to one. As boys, Frédéric and Deslauriers had such extravagant dreams that they were "sad as after a great debauch." Frédéric feels destined to accept defeat before even attempting a victory. He has a keen sense of loss before even having possessed. His imagination builds and furnishes Moorish palaces (always the exotic yearning!); he sees himself lounging on cashmere divans listening to the murmur of a fountain —and these sensuous dreams become so precise "that they saddened him as though he had lost them." Make-believes and mental aphrodisiacs turn out to be manifestations of impotence.

The other result appears as a complete contrast to this atony: a vertiginous proliferation. But this proliferation, much like the dizzying display of women at "La Turque" only leads to another form of futility. Innumerable examples in *L'Éducation sentimentale* illustrate this coupling of diversity with sterility: the different esthetic "theories," the contradictory literary projects, the cacophony of political ideas, the jarring clash of opinions and inept clichés. Polymorphism, in the Flaubertian context, is nearly always a sure sign of an almost hypnotic attraction to nothingness, a suicidal yearning for annihilation. "Exhausted, filled with contradictory desires, no longer even conscious of what he wanted, he felt an extraordinary sadness, the desire to die."

It is significant that this allurement to nothingness, so explicitly stated, should be experienced by Frédéric while in the company of a high-class prostitute. For somehow, in Flaubert's own imagination, prostitution and an almost ascetic staring into the emptiness of existence are closely related.[6] To Louise Colet he writes that the

---

[5] Goncourt, *Journal*, VI, p. 172.

[6] As a young man, Flaubert was wont to greet each new year in a brothel— a gesture which, he felt, expressed cynicism and an almost metaphysical contempt.

sight of streetwalkers and of monks "tickles" his soul in its deepest recesses, that prostitution evokes simultaneously "lewdness, bitterness, the nothingness of human relations. . . ." The theme of sterility and even abortion in *L'Éducation sentimentale* is illumined by a comment such as this. Flaubert's admiration for the Marquis de Sade, which he shares with Baudelaire, makes him suspect Nature and explains in part why he views the Prostitute both as an antiphysis and the very incarnation of sterility. With bitter irony, Flaubert describes the *"maison de santé et d'accouchement,"* where Rosanette gives birth to a sickly offspring, in terms that are most equivocal: the chambermaid looks like a "soubrette," the director of the establishment is called "Madame," the establishment itself (with its closed shutters and continuous sounds of piano-playing) is called a *"maison discrète"*—leaving little doubt as to the analogy the author had in mind. Originally, Flaubert had even planned to have the "Madame" explain to Frédéric how to dispose of the newborn baby! And when the sickly child soon after dies, Rosanette's grief coincides with the grief of Madame Dambreuse as she realizes that her husband has left all his wealth to someone else. "A mother grieving beside an empty cradle was not more pitiful than Mme Dambreuse at the sight of the open strongboxes." The theme of sterility could not possibly be pushed much further.

Profanation, betrayal, sterility . . . and yet. And yet the reader is never permitted to forget the ideally pure figure of Mme Arnoux. Frédéric may use other women, and forget himself with them; they are nothing but substitutes for an ideal. One might even say, paradoxically, that profanation is here in the service of purity. Ever since *Mémoires d'un fou,* written at the age of seventeen, Flaubert was haunted by the contrasts between idealized woman (*le ciel*) and cheap love (*la boue*). The narrator of *Mémoires d'un fou,* still writing under the recent impact of his meeting with Mme Schlésinger, the model for Mme Arnoux, feels guilt and shame because he has lost his virginity with a promiscuous creature, "as though my love for Maria were a religion that I had profaned." In *Novembre,* written at the age of twenty, he attempted to synthesize in one figure the dual visage of woman. *L'Éducation sentimentale* again insists on a polarity. It is clear that the very concept of immaculate beauty required, in Flaubert's imagination, the drama of inaccessibility, as well as the antithesis of corruption.[7]

[7] From the notebooks published by Marie-Jeanne Durry, it is obvious that these two elements are associated in the earliest stages of the novel's genesis.

This persistent idealism, strengthened by profanation as though made holier by it, is implicit in the Bordello exploit, the subject of the last scene of the book. Just as the narrator of *Mémoires d'un fou* was haunted by the loss of virginity, so here Frédéric is filled with nostalgia for a lost innocence. For the memory is altogether a chaste one, and even on the level of sheer venery, the incident is marked by a sort of poetry of unrealized love. The memory, however, coming as it does at the end of the book (and especially after the ultimate, deeply moving encounter with Mme Arnoux), acquires an additional aura. And it is significant that Frédéric says not a word of this unforgettable last meeting to Deslauriers. For this is a private realm, a regal chamber open to no one. All throughout the novel it is Mme Arnoux's image that shines forth from behind the Parisian fog, keeping alive an "invincible hope." The very name Marie (same name in *Mémoires d'un fou* and in *Novembre*) suggests purity. And in the service of this "image," despite all his weaknesses and abdications, Frédéric acquires nobility. For the sake of this "image," he has in the long run given up everything.

In fact, Marie Arnoux is more than an image, she is a *vision*. But this carries us from the last scene back to the very first scene of the novel.

## II. *The River and the Boat: In the Beginning Is the End*

On the 15th of September, 1840, Frédéric—a young man about to begin the study of law—is traveling on a river-boat. *L'Éducation sentimentale* begins among the whirlwinds of smoke, on a vessel which is about to steam away. The destination is Nogent, where Frédéric is to remain with his mother until the fall term begins.

Flaubert was evidently in no way compelled to begin his novel with a river journey. Yet the earliest, very sketchy outline of the novel—not even twenty lines in length—already envisions this as a key scene: "—*traversée sur le bateau de Montereau. un collégien.*" [8] The special care with which the scene was eventually written is revealed by the number of drafts—at least seven, it would seem. But

---

Frédéric is attracted simultaneously to "Prostitution" and to "ideal exaltation." Flaubert explains to himself that "cynicism hides timidity." As for Mme Arnoux, the notebooks reveal a compelling need to *purify* her. In some of the earliest scenarios she actually does show up at the rendezvous. The author's yearning for purity, visible in the very act of creation, is at the heart of the novel. (*Flaubert et ses projets inédits*, pp. 137-138, 150, 163).

[8] *Flaubert et ses projets inédits*, p. 137.

such statistics are hardly needed to communicate the importance and suggestive power of these opening pages. Not only does the river journey establish the geographic poles of the novel (the capital and the provincial home), but it provides an ideal setting for the fleeting encounter with Mme Arnoux. Flaubert knew only too well the hopeless dreams that can crystallize around a figure met under ephemeral circumstances: his first meeting with Elisa Schlésinger took place on the beach in Trouville. The ship provided an even more dramatic setting.[9]

The symbolic potential of the scene is more significant still. For this is not an exotic sea voyage, with the excitement of hoped-for discoveries and possible adventures. Although there is the hustle and bustle of a real departure, nothing could be more prosaic, more commonplace, than the itinerary of the *Ville de Montereau* and the bourgeois vulgarity of its human cargo. It is a departure which fails to bring about an authentic voyage. So too, the movement of the boat is only another form of immobility. A passenger is not an active agent. But here the passivity is double: the boat itself merely follows the inevitable course of the river. Submissiveness to an ineluctable flow, the monotony of the landscape as it slowly glides by, the ability to see its details and yet the inability to hold on to impressions as they merge and fade away—these characteristics of the river navigation are exploited here as an almost prophetic symbol of Destiny and Time, and anticipate the drifting, languid and perpetually dreamy quality of Frédéric's life.

For passiveness and the propensity to dream are closely bound up. The vibrations of the ship are conducive to drowsy well-being. The two banks "unroll" like "two large ribbons": the image almost suggests a film in slow-motion. And there is a curious harmony between the outer landscape, slowly gliding by, and the inner landscape with its permanent mutations. To these evanescent forms the mind of Frédéric easily surrenders. Motion, real or imagined, will in fact always be for him an invitation to dream, a liberation from reality. Gaston Bachelard's observations about the excitement of railway travel could easily apply to Frédéric's experience on the boat: "The trip unfolds a film of dream houses . . . with the salutary prohibition of ever *verifying*." [10] As the ship passes by a hill, a vineyard, a windmill—Frédéric's imagination sketches out entire novels of his many impossible lives. His mind is filled with *projects*.

---

[9] Elsewhere Flaubert himself associates travel, especially ship travel, with the *"amertume des sympathies interrompues"* (III, chapter 6).

[10] *La Poétique de l'Espace*, p. 69.

And this tendency, which the distance between the boat and the land brings out literally and symbolically, will remain a constant trait of his character. Frédéric "dreams his life" (as opposed to Mme Bovary, who dreams about life), explains Albert Thibaudet.[11] But at the origin of this trance-like state there is the habit of projecting himself into time and space: "he saw Mme Arnoux, ruined, crying, selling all her furniture"; "he glimpsed, as though in a lightning, an immense fortune . . ."; "already he saw himself in a waistcoat with lapels and a tricolored sash." Often the very "projection" is closely bound up with an image of motion or travel (thus dreams engender dreams!): "They would travel, they would go to Italy, to the East!" "He saw her standing on a little hill, gazing at a landscape"; "He saw himself with her at night in a post-chaise; then on a river's bank on a summer evening. . . ." The result is an almost self-hypnotizing, almost hallucinated state. The word hallucination actually occurs on several occasions. ("His daydream became so intense that he had a kind of hallucination." [12]) The river boat, in the first scene of the book, provides an initial setting in which the capacity to dream is closely linked with the attraction to the impossible: movement and distance are inseparable.

But there is also irony in the fact that dreams take shape in the midst of the floating mediocrity of public transportation. The passengers are not exactly models of refinement. Except for a few "bourgeois" in first-class, they are representative of humanity at its shabbiest. Flaubert goes to great length in describing a repulsive assembly: sordid clothes, worn-out hats, dirty shirts, torn ties. People eat and sleep pell-mell. The deck is soiled with nut shells, cigar butts and garbage. A sordid "reality" thus seems to engender the very dream-world. But does the presence of this "reality" not also soil the dream? Or does it heighten its beauty?

The fact is that Flaubert very deliberately placed this scene of grotesque filth and crudeness immediately before the dazzling first encounter with Mme Arnoux. *"Ce fut comme une apparition."* The word "apparition" must be taken here in its strongest sense: the earthly manifestation of an unworldly being. Mme Arnoux is like a vision—a vision made concrete, and yet so resplendent that it imme-

[11] *Gustave Flaubert*, p. 145.
[12] D. L. Demorest, with the support of striking quotations, has shown that the tendency to exaltation at times leads to states akin to "somnambulism" (*L'Expression figurée et symbolique dans l'œuvre de Gustave Flaubert*, pp. 531-532). Flaubert himself seems to associate such states with movement. See the comparison, in *L'Éducation sentimentale* (II, chapter 1): "He felt somewhat stunned, like a man who gets off a ship."

diately obliterates all that which surrounds it. She sits alone, or so it seems, for Frédéric suffers from a momentary blindness (*"éblouisse-ment"*) caused by too great a splendor. Everything in this passage suggests the vision of an angelic creature. The rays which emanate from her eyes, the spiritualized oval contours of the face, the features that stand out against a blue sky which here is like a background in a religious painting, the *"splendeur"* of her brown skin, her deli-cate, almost immaterial hands through which light flows—all this, as seen through Frédéric's eyes, and Flaubert's art, transmutes a woman into an apparition, and makes of her, in the midst of a nineteenth century scene of everyday life, a sister to Beatrice.

> e par che sia una cosa venuta
> da cielo in terra a miracol mostrare.

Frédéric might have recited to himself these lines from Dante's *Vita Nuova*. He, too, feels a "deeper yearning," a curiosity that knows no limits. The mystical overtones of these pages are further stressed by Frédéric's giving "alms" to the harpist, a gesture which vaguely corresponds, in his own mind, to an idea of blessing and to an almost religious impulse.

These images of spirituality are of the utmost thematic impor-tance. One of the earliest sketches indeed sums up this initial meet-ing with the single word: *éblouissement* (dazzlement).[13] Throughout the novel, Mme Arnoux repeatedly "appears" as a vision (". . . *Ma-dame Arnoux parut"*). Her role as Madonna is brought out by a number of scenes in which she is shown together with her children in the "tranquil majesty" of a maternal pose.[14] Her hands seem for-ever to be ready to spread alms and wipe away tears. Frédéric fre-quently sits and merely "contemplates" her. Most often, however, her figure is associated with a particular quality of light. "Madame Arnoux was sitting on a big rock with this incandescent light at her back"—the image here is one of a halo. Her glances penetrate his soul "like those great rays of sunlight which descend to the bottom of the water." When Frédéric meets her in the street, "the sunlight surrounded her" and her entire person seems invested with an "extraordinary splendor": an "infinite suavity" emanates from her eyes. At times Frédéric uses nothing but the capitalized personal pronoun *Elle* when he thinks of her. Her entire person is not only

---

[13] *Flaubert et ses projets inédits*, p. 163.
[14] One of Flaubert's most striking early impressions of Elisa Schlésinger was the sight of her nursing her baby.

extraordinarily radiant (light pours from her as from a glory), but even the tiniest part of her body is infinitely precious. "Each of her fingers was for him more than a thing, almost a person." [15] In short, Frédéric places her "outside the human condition." She fills him alternately with religious awe and with an "undefinable beatitude." Nothing better illustrates Flaubert's skill at objectively presenting a subjectivity—and of simultaneously stressing the drama of this subjectivity—than the manner in which he idealizes Mme Arnoux through the eyes of Frédéric. One wonders how Henry James could have reproached Flaubert for what is precisely one of the main achievements of this novel: the fact that Mme Arnoux is offered us preponderantly through Frédéric's vision. Henry James obviously missed the point.[16] What matters is not whether Frédéric is a worthy medium through which to view so noble a soul, nor even whether the lady really is so sublime a creature (a futile question!)—but the tragic urge to create such a figure, to believe in her, and to cling stubbornly to the beauty of a vision engendered, as it were, by the very banality of existence.

The thematic importance of the first scene is further brought out by the fact that the image of Mme Arnoux is very frequently associated with the idea of travel. In part this corresponds to a characteristic Flaubertian yearning for the exotic. Thus already in the first scene, on the ship, exotic elements are introduced and amplified by the hero's imagination. He attributes Mme Arnoux's complexion to an Andalusian origin: when he sees her Negro servant, he imagines that she has brought her from the West Indies, and that she herself is a Creole. The harpist on the boat plays an "Oriental ballad" all about daggers, flowers and stars. And later in the novel when Frédéric dreams of Mme Arnoux, he sees himself traveling with her to distant lands, on dromedaries, elephants or elegant yachts. Such images are to some extent ironic, but not altogether. They also represent a genuine lyricism.[17] For Frédéric, just as for Flaubert, the ideas of love and passion are commonly associated with ideas of motion and travel to distant lands. Frédéric frequently fancies him-

[15] Is it not likely that this remark concerning Madame Arnoux's fingers corresponds to the curious notation in Flaubert's notebooks which baffled Marie-Jeanne Durry: *"toutes les dents sont des personnes"* ["all teeth are persons"]? *(Flaubert et ses projets inédits*, pp. 192-193).

[16] *Notes on a Novelist*, p. 86. On James's curious antagonism to Flaubert, see Edmund Wilson, "The Ambiguity of Henry James" in *The Triple Thinkers*, pp. 141-142.

[17] On the non-ironic qualities of exoticism in *L'Éducation sentimentale*, see Raymond Giraud's *The Unheroic Hero*, pp. 159-160.

self *in movement* with "Her." (It is in a carriage that he almost dares touch her hand!) But movement can also mean separation; travel can mean remoteness, estrangement, inaccessibility. It can mean that the loved one is elsewhere. Thus, already on the boat, Frédéric's destination and Mme Arnoux's destination are not the same: he will get off in Nogent, while she will proceed with her husband to Montereau, and from there to Switzerland. As his mother talks to him, his mind tries to follow the image of Mme Arnoux: he pictures her sitting in a diligence, wrapped up in her shawl, her head leaning against the cloth of the coupé. There is a similar image of departure and separation almost at the end of the book: he conjures up a vision of her, sitting in a railway carriage or on the deck of a steamship "like the first time he met her." The very reference to the first scene of the novel testifies to the permanence of the dual themes of encounter and separation. The very symbol of an exalted meeting thus tragically turns out to be a symbol of an irretrievable loss.

The travel motif is thus, broadly speaking, charged with a sense of poetic bitterness. Frédéric perpetually dreams of "distant countries and long voyages"—yet the only long voyage takes place during the hiatus which precedes the epilogue. He travels to forget, and appropriately the trip itself is barely mentioned: it is forgotten, swallowed by Time and meaninglessness. It is a *blank,* a void, a vacancy—almost an initiation to death.[18] As for his other trips, they are all derisory. His second arrival in Paris, at the beginning of Part II, is by coach. The trip begins in exhilaration, but as the heavy carriage, slowed down by rain, moves through the outskirts of the capital, the prevailing mood becomes one of ugliness and sterility, as Frédéric glimpses empty lots, branchless trees, chemical works, puddles of dirty water, sordid courtyards littered with refuse, midwives' signboards. Similar effects of disenchantment are achieved through other scenes of locomotion. The excursion to Creil to see Mme Arnoux in her husband's factory ends in discomfiture. The hedonistic journey to Fontainebleau with Rosanette (the lovers are constantly on the move) is made trivial by Rosanette's inept comments during the visit to the chateau. The impetuous trip to Nogent after the double rupture with Rosanette and Mme Dambreuse only leads to another "defeat": Frédéric arrives just in time to witness the marriage of Louise Roque to Deslauriers. And even in town,

---

[18] It is significant that Marcel Proust should have prized above all in *L'Éducation sentimentale* this "blank" (the expression is his) which communicates, by means of a stupendous "change of gears," the poetical qualities in the rhythmical fluctuations of time (*Chroniques*, p. 205).

vehicles and motion most often communicate a feeling of interrupted flow, for instance during the traffic jam, after the races. The entire book seems to be conceived under the ambiguous sign of continual motion and stasis, which correspond to Frédéric's contradictory need to escape outside his solipsistic self and yet to seek refuge, to *dissolve* within it.

Images of dissolution, of liquefaction, are indeed extremely important in the metaphorical texture of the novel. *L'Éducation sentimentale* begins with a scene of travel, but it is travel by water. The Seine is where the destinies of Mme Arnoux and Frédéric meet, and it is also where, in the very first pages, they prophetically separate. The Seine is part of the Parisian landscape—and it occupied an even greater portion of the landscape Flaubert himself had constantly before his eyes from his room in Croisset. But although Flaubert was far from insensitive to its beauty, it is, in *L'Éducation sentimentale,* a river of sadness and of cruel indifference. Frédéric, in his despondent moments, watches the river flow between the somber quays blackened by the seams of the sewers. (How different from the graceful, carefree Seine of Hugo, the melodramatic Seine of Balzac, the picturesque Seine of Zola!) Flaubert's Seine has no definite color (it is *"jaunâtre"*—vaguely yellow). It is a river associated with loss and tragic unconcern. An old man cries; his son was probably killed during the uprising: "The Seine flowed calmly." Tears and dirty water—they are part of the same scenery.

Albert Thibaudet has admirably shown the omnipresence of the river image in Flaubert's description of Parisian traffic and in the "liquid continuity" of the imperfect tense.[19] In fact, at one point the Champs-Elysées are quite explicitly likened to a river. But the Parisian crowds also—whether peaceful strollers on the Boulevards or riotous mobs—are compared to liquid masses in motion. What Frédéric surveys near the Madeleine is an *"immense flot ondulant";* the revolutionary mobs, later in the novel, are seen as *"flots vertigineux":* images which appropriately suggest ineluctable forces, as well as an energy that eventually flows away or evaporates.

For images of liquid in *L'Éducation sentimentale* are intimately related to images of vapor. At the beginning of the novel, a wandering haze covers the surface of the water. As the novel progresses, the poetic mist (still associated with hope in the scene where Deslauriers and Frédéric contemplate the delicate haziness in the direction of the river) becomes a tenacious fog. The characteristic weather in Flaubert's Paris is a steady drizzle and a depressing fog. At times rain

[19] *Gustave Flaubert,* p. 144.

becomes torrential: streets are transformed into waterways. But most often an almost anesthetizing fog seems to settle. Frédéric feels himself surrounded by "damp air"; a "humid gloom" descends into the depths of his heart. But it is also a strangely luminous fog: from behind it shines the invisible, but effulgent figure of Mme Arnoux. This opaque luminosity is one of Flaubert's most notable achievements in *L'Éducation sentimentale*. It makes of him not only one of the outstanding poets of Paris (together with Hugo and Baudelaire), but also a brother to the impressionist painters.[20]

This vaporous liquefaction admirably conveys states of passiveness and expectancy, and a strange mixture of stubborn hope and inherent defeatism. Thus while waiting interminably in a café, Frédéric (though not in the least bit thirsty) absorbs one "liquid" after another: a glass of rum, then a glass of kirsch, followed by a glass of curaçao, then various hot and cold grogs. Variety once more betrays futility. Drinking becomes almost literally a manner of "killing time." And repeatedly liquids and liquefaction evoke the erosive quality of Time, as well as a sense of dissolution and loss. Sitting near the river with Louise Roque, Frédéric plays with sand, letting it slip through his fingers, while close by the sound of a cascade and the bubbling whirlpools can be heard. The sand, trickling through his fingers as though liquefied, no doubt signifies Time slipping away. And this dissolving quality of Time, so central to the meaning of *L'Éducation sentimentale*, is almost redundantly imparted by means of "liquid" associations. Thus while the rain pours outside, Frédéric, sitting in the café and still waiting, looks at the clock in such a manner that, if objects could be worn out by looking at them, "Frédéric would have dissolved the clock." The same image of dissolution recurs as Frédéric waits for Mme Arnoux who does not show up at their rendezvous: "He felt himself dissolve from utter dejection." Even the political disintegration of Louis-Philippe's regime is expressed in terms of a liquefaction (which is of course also a liquidation): "the Monarchy was melting away in rapid dissolution."

*L'Éducation sentimentale*, viewed in this light, appears as a novel of steady flow and indefinite expectation. No final catastrophe ever interrupts the fluidity of existence. Tragedy here stems not from the brutal interruption of life, but from its hopeless and self-destructive continuity. The gradual bankruptcy of an entire generation is experienced, often circuitously, through the consciousness of an

[20] Harry Levin, in a perceptive discussion of this city-poetry, links Flaubert's art with that of Monet, Degas, Renoir and Pissaro (*The Gates of Horn*, p. 230).

individual who himself is the victim of slow disintegration. The auction sale of Mme Arnoux's private belongings, toward the end of the novel, admirably symbolizes this impression of a whole life being liquidated. As Frédéric witnesses the profanation of her most intimate objects—her hats, her shoes, her lingerie—he experiences a sense of "dissolution," a mournful torpor akin to spiritual death. This feeling of slow disintegration, this wearing down by life itself, is perhaps one of the reasons why young readers are so often impatient with this book. But the theme of progressive deterioration is only one of the strands in *L'Éducation sentimentale*. The poetic power of the novel is largely to be attributed to its inner contradictions reflected in the enigmatic double ending of the epilogue which juxtaposes a scene of transcending love and one which almost smugly surveys a life of defeats. And there is a double irony here. For just as the dreams associated with lovely images of travel and water are doomed to a fiasco, so the apparently cynical memories of the brothel in the final scene mask a never-defeated and never-satisfied craving for innocence and beauty.

# Chronology of Important Dates

1821      (December 12) Birth of Gustave Flaubert in Rouen.

1832-1840    Studies at Collège de Rouen.

1836      First meeting with Elisa Schlésinger at Trouville.

1838      Writes *Mémoires d'un fou* (published posthumously).

1840      Baccalaureate at Rouen and travels in Pyrenees and Corsica.

1841      Enrolls at Law Faculty in Paris.

1843      Fails examination in law, writes *Novembre*.

1844      "Nervous crisis," abandons studies, family moves to Croisset.

1845      Marriage of sister Caroline, Flaubert family accompanies newly-weds on honeymoon, Flaubert sees Breughel's painting of Saint Anthony in Genoa, writes first version of *L'Éducation sentimentale*.

1846      Death of Flaubert's father and sister Caroline. Meets Louise Colet.

1847      Trip with Maxime Du Camp in Brittany (described in *Par les champs et par les grèves*).

1848      Death of Alfred Le Poittevin. Flaubert witnesses Revolution in Paris.

1849      Reads *La Tentation de Saint Antoine* to Bouilhet and Du Camp; departs for Orient with Du Camp.

1851      Return from Orient. Work on *Madame Bovary*.

1856      Definitive break with Louise Colet. Du Camp begins publication of *Madame Bovary* in *Le Revue de Paris*.

1857      Trial and acquittal; *Madame Bovary* appears as a book.

1858      Flaubert travels to Tunisia.

1862      *Salammbô* published.

1869      Death of Louis Bouilhet. Flaubert completes and publishes second version of *L'Éducation sentimentale* (begun in 1863).

1872      Death of Flaubert's mother. Third version of *La Tentation de Saint Antoine* completed.

1874     *La Tentation de Saint Antoine published.* Production of play, *Le Candidat.*

1877     *Trois Contes* published.

1880     (May 8) Death of Flaubert.

1881     *Bouvard et Pécuchet* published.

1884-1892  First publication of Flaubert's correspondence.

1885     *Par les Champs et par les grèves* published.

# Notes on the Editor and Authors

RAYMOND GIRAUD, the editor of this volume, is the author of *The Unheroic Hero in the Novels of Stendhal, Balzac and Flaubert* and other studies of French literature. He is Professor of French Literature at Stanford.

ERICH AUERBACH, the author of *Mimesis, Dante als Dichter der Irdischen Welt,* and numerous other philological and literary works, was one of the great romance scholars of this century. At the time of his death in 1957, he was Sterling Professor of Romance Philology at Yale.

CHARLES BAUDELAIRE, the poet of *Les Fleurs du mal,* was also one of the most penetrating critics of literature and art in the nineteenth century. His review of *Madame Bovary* is included in these pages because of its striking modernity.

VICTOR BROMBERT, author of *Stendhal et la voie oblique* and *The Intellectual Hero: Studies in the French Novel, 1880-1955,* has also written on T. S. Eliot and has published many articles on French, Italian, and English literature. He is Professor of French Literature at Yale.

JOHN C. LAPP, author of *Aspects of Racinian Tragedy, The Universe of Pontus de Tyard,* and *Zola before the Rougon—Macquart,* has also published numerous articles on every period of French literature. He is Professor of French Literature at Stanford.

HARRY LEVIN, author of *The Gates of Horn,* is well known for his work on Joyce, Shakespeare, Poe, Marlowe, Hawthorne, and Ben Jonson. He is Irving Babbitt Professor of Comparative Literature at Harvard.

GEORG LUKÁCS was Minister of Culture in Hungary in 1919 and again in 1956. From 1945 to 1956 he held the chair of Aesthetics at the University of Budapest. Probably the most brilliant of Marxist literary critics, he has won respect for his studies of Goethe, Hegel, Balzac, and Stendhal, among others, and is well known in France for his *Existentialisme ou Marxisme?* The English translation of his *Historical Novel* (first published in Moscow in 1937) appeared in 1962.

GEORGES POULET has achieved international reknown for his *Studies in Human Time* and *Métamorphoses du cercle.* He has taught in Scotland and America and now holds a chair in French Literature at the University of Zürich.

JEAN-PIERRE RICHARD is the author of two important collections of critical studies: *Littérature et sensation* and *Poésie et profondeur.* He has also published a rich and penetrating book on Mallarmé, *L'Univers imaginaire de Mallarmé*. He is presently at the Institut Français of Madrid.

JEAN ROUSSET has recently published a collection of critical studies, *Forme et signification*. He holds a chair at the University of Geneva.

JEAN-PAUL SARTRE, the founder of *Les Temps Modernes* and leader of the "Paris school" of existentialism, has distinguished himself as philosopher, novelist, playwright, and literary critic. His most recent important works are *Search for a Method, Critique de la Raison dialectique,* and the autobiographical volume, *Les Mots.* He is the subject of another volume of critical essays in this series.

MARTIN TURNELL is the author of *The Art of French Fiction, The Novel in France,* and *The Classical Moment,* as well as studies on Baudelaire and Jacques Rivière.

# Selected Bibliography

## FLAUBERT'S WORKS

The standard edition of Flaubert is the 20-volume Conard edition published in Paris in 1910, including unpublished juvenilia and the correspondence, the latter superceded by a nine-volume edition of the correspondence (Conard, 1926-1933), and four supplementary volumes edited by Jean Pommier, René Dumesnil, and Claude Digeon (Conard, 1954). The fictional works are also available in two volumes of the Bibliothèque de la Pléiade, edited by Albert Thibaudet and René Dumesnil (Gallimard, 1951-1952) and in individual volumes of the Classiques Garnier, edited by Edouard Maynial. Also of note is the edition of the *Œuvres complètes* edited by René Dumesnil for the Collection des Textes Français (Société des Belles-Lettres, 1945-1948) in 10 volumes.

Additional drafts, fragments, and variants are contained in the following: *Œuvres posthumes, Madame Bovary, ébauches et fragments inédits,* ed. Gabrielle Leleu 2 vols. (Paris: Conard, 1936); *Madame Bovary, Nouvelle version, précédée de scénarios inédits,* ed. Jean Pommier and Gabrielle Leleu (Paris: Corti, 1949); and Marie-Jeanne Durry, *Flaubert et ses projets inédits* (Paris: Nizet, 1950).

## BOOKS ON FLAUBERT

Bopp, Léon. *Commentaire sur Madame Bovary* (Neuchâtel: La Baconnière, 1951).

Bruneau, Jean. *Les Débuts littéraires de Gustave Flaubert 1831-1845* (Paris: Armand Colin, 1962).

Demorest, D. L. *L'Expression figurée et symbolique dans l'œuvre de Gustave Flaubert* (Paris: Conard, 1931).

Descharmes, René and Dumesnil, René. *Autour de Flaubert* (Paris: Mercure de France, 1912).

Dumesnil, René. *Gustave Flaubert, l'homme et l'œuvre,* 3rd ed. (Paris: Desclée de Brouwer, 1947).

———. *La Vocation de Gustave Flaubert* (Paris: Gallimard, 1961).

Dumesnil, René, and Demorest, D. L. *Bibliographie de Gustave Flaubert* (Paris: Giraud-Badin, 1939).

Gaultier, Jules de. *Le Bovarysme* (Paris: Mercure de France, 1902).

Gérard-Gailly. *Flaubert et les fantômes de Trouville* (Paris: La Renaissance du Livre, 1930).

La Varende. *Flaubert par lui-même* (Paris: Éditions du Seuil, 1951).

Spencer, Philip. *Flaubert, A Biography* (New York: Grove Press, 1952).

Steegmuller, Francis. *Flaubert and Madame Bovary* (New York: Farrar, Strauss & Co., 1950).

Thibaudet, Albert. *Gustave Flaubert, sa vie, ses œuvres, son style,* 11th ed. (Paris: Gallimard, 1935).

Thorlby, Anthony. *Gustave Flaubert and the Art of Realism* (London: Bowes and Bowes, 1956).

# TWENTIETH CENTURY VIEWS

242

S-TC-37 MALRAUX, edited by R. W. B. Lewis
S-TC-38 AUDEN, edited by Monroe K. Spears
S-TC-39 O'NEILL, edited by John Gassner
S-TC-40 SHAKESPEARE: THE TRAGEDIES, edited by
Alfred Harbage
S-TC-41 MOLIÈRE, edited by Jacques Guicharnaud
S-TC-42 FLAUBERT, edited by Raymond Giraud
S-TC-43 KEATS, edited by Walter Jackson Bate
S-TC-44 MARLOWE, edited by Clifford Leech

# Forthcoming Titles

BECKETT, edited by Martin Esslin
BLAKE, edited by Northrop Frye
CERVANTES, edited by Lowry Nelson
CHEKHOV, edited by Robert Jackson
COLERIDGE, edited by Kathleen Coburn
DANTE, edited by John Freccero
FAULKNER, edited by Robert Penn Warren
HAWTHORNE, edited by Norman Pearson
HOPKINS, edited by John Hollander
IBSEN, edited by Rolf Fjeld
SAMUEL JOHNSON, edited by Donald J. Greene
JOYCE, edited by Cleanth Brooks
MILTON, edited by Louis Martz
POE, edited by Harrison Hayford
SHAKESPEARE: THE HISTORIES, edited by Eugene M. Waith
SHAKESPEARE: THE COMEDIES, edited by Kenneth Muir
G. B. SHAW, edited by R. J. Kaufman
SHELLEY, edited by George Ridenour
SOPHOCLES, edited by Bernard Knox
TOLSTOY, edited by Ralph E. Matlaw
VIRGIL, edited by Steele Commager
WORDSWORTH, edited by M. H. Abrams